CAST OF CHARACTERS

Takeaki Aoyagi—victim
Kyoichiro Kaga—detective, Nihonbashi Precinct

Shuhei Matsumiya—detective, Homicide Division, Tokyo
    Metropolitan Police
Sakagami—detective, Homicide Division, Tokyo Metropoli-
    tan Police
Kobayashi—squad leader, Homicide Division, Tokyo Metro-
    politan Police
Ishigaki—unit chief, Homicide Division, Tokyo Metropoli-
    tan Police

Fumiko Aoyagi—wife of the victim
Haruka Aoyagi—teenage daughter of the victim
Yuto Aoyagi—teenage son of the victim

Yoshinobu Kotake—factory manager, Kaneseki Metals, direct subordinate of the victim

Fuyuki Yashima—prime suspect, former employee of Kaneseki Metals
Kaori Nakahara—girlfriend of the suspect

Itokawa—teacher and swim team coach at Shubunkan Junior High School

Tatsuya Sugino—friend and former teammate of Yuto Aoyagi
Shota Kurosawa—friend and former teammate of Yuto Aoyagi
Tomoyuki Yoshinaga—former teammate of Yuto Aoyagi

A
DEATH
IN
TOKYO

1

It must have been just before nine o'clock in the evening that the man made his way past the Nihonbashi Bridge police station. The duty officer, who had stepped outside a little earlier to survey the street, saw him from behind.

Rather early to be quite so drunk, the officer thought. The man was visibly unsteady on his feet. Since the officer couldn't see his face, it was hard to guess how old he was, but his hairstyle and other indicators suggested late middle age. Neither fat nor thin, tall nor short, he was dressed very respectably. Even from a distance, you could tell that his dark brown suit was of high quality. In the end, the officer decided that there was no need to bother him.

The man was walking toward the bridge, lurching from side to side as he did so. The bridge was Nihonbashi Bridge, a historic landmark dating from 1907. The man started to make his way across the bridge and appeared to be heading for the Mitsukoshi department store on the far side.

The officer looked away and took stock of his immediate environs. He got the impression that while there were slightly fewer pedestrians around than before, the number of cars crisscrossing the tangle of roads in front of him was the same as ever. Even though there was a recession—no, probably *because* there was a recession—people still had to work. Despite the late hour, there were plenty of trucks and other commercial vehicles out on the road. The only change from the boom times was that the goods they were transporting were probably worth less. And this place was ground zero, the place from which all the hardworking merchants and businesspeople set off for the rest of Japan.

A group of around fifteen Chinese tourists were wandering across Nihonbashi Bridge, looking up at the expressway that ran at a right angle directly above it. It wasn't difficult for the officer to imagine the conversations they were having. They were most likely asking why on earth someone had gone and dumped something so brutish and ugly right on top of such a beautiful structure. Coming from such a vast country themselves, how could they possibly understand how, when Japan needed the expressways as part of hosting the 1964 Tokyo Olympics, it had built them above the capital's old canals and rivers because there was no spare land available?

The officer once again let his eyes wander. They came to a stop and focused on something. It was that man again. In the middle of Nihonbashi Bridge, there is an ornamental column with a pair of *kirin*, mythical Chinese beasts, on either side. The man was leaning against the parapet near the base of the column.

The officer watched him for a while. He didn't look as if he was planning to go anywhere. He was completely immobile.

"Oh, please! You're not seriously going to fall asleep there at this time of night—"

With a disapproving click of his tongue, the officer marched onto the bridge.

There was the usual stream of people crossing the bridge, none of whom paid the man any attention. Whether homeless or simply drunk, a person lying or sitting at the side of the road wasn't an unusual sight in central Tokyo.

The officer approached him. The man was immediately beneath one of the *kirin* statues, which, unlike the typical *kirin*, resemble dragons. His back was rounded as if bent forward in prayer.

"Excuse me, sir. What seems to be the problem?" The officer placed a hand on the man's shoulder. He didn't react. "Come on, rise and shine." The officer gave him a shake.

The man began to slither down the stone base. The officer grabbed hold of him and held him upright. *What's with this guy? He must be smashed out of his mind.* Then the officer sensed that something wasn't quite right. *I can't smell any alcohol on him. He isn't drunk. Is he sick? No, that's not it either—*

Struggling to hold him up, he looked at the man's chest.

There was something sticking out of it. And there was a blackish red stain on his shirtfront.

Oh no! I've got to call the station. He let the body drop and reached for his radio.

2

She opened the calendar on her phone and placed it on the table so her companion could also see the screen.

"The anniversary of his death falls on the third Wednesday of next month. What would you say to the Saturday or the Sunday before that? Timing-wise, that would work for me," Tokiko said, pointing to the relevant days on the screen. She got no reply. Glancing up, she realized that the attention of the other person was focused somewhere else entirely; somewhere behind her.

"Mr. Kaga?" Tokiko said his name. Kaga lifted his hand, in a gesture telling her to stop. He maintained his focus behind her, his eyes glinting keenly.

Tokiko took a discreet look over her shoulder. Seated a couple of tables away was an old woman wearing glasses, busy fiddling with her phone. They looked like reading glasses.

Kyoichiro Kaga got to his feet and strode over to her. He said hello and the two of them chatted briefly in low voices. Kaga then returned to Tokiko's table.

"What's the problem?"

"Nothing major." Kaga took a sip of his coffee. "I noticed her borrowing a pen from the waitress earlier."

"So?"

"She was in the middle of a conversation on her cell phone when she borrowed the pen and jotted something down on her paper napkin. After she finished the call, I saw her looking at whatever she'd written down and doing something on her phone. I thought, 'Uh-oh, is this what I think it is?'"

"Which is what?"

"That someone had called to tell her their new phone number. I asked and, sure enough, that was the case. It was her grandson, a university student. I told her to try the old number before replacing it with the new one."

"Because you think . . . ?"

"That's right," Kaga said. "I thought it might be a scam. It's a common enough technique. The scammers start off by getting you to change one of the numbers in your contact list and then call you back the next day. Since it's the grandson's name that pops up on the screen, the recipient is primed to think that that is who's really calling."

The old woman came bustling over.

"That was a close call. You were right. When I called the old number, my grandson picked up. He hasn't lost his phone and he hasn't changed his number either. And his voice was quite different too. I so nearly got taken in."

"That's good to hear. Why don't you register that new number under the name *scam*. If it rings again, whatever you do, don't pick up. Go as quick as you can to the nearest police station and file a report."

"I'll do that. You're a lifesaver. Thank you." The old woman bobbed her head up and down in gratitude, before making for the cash register by the door.

Kaga grinned as he sipped his coffee. The stern gleam had gone from his eyes.

"You've got a real nose for crime," Tokiko commented.

"What, like a dog?"

"That's not what I said. But it must be exhausting to keep an eye out all the time like that."

"It's what they call *professional deformation*—a condition for which, sadly, there is no cure." Kaga put his coffee cup down and looked at the phone on the table. "Sorry about that. Shall we pick up where we left off?"

Tokiko repeated her suggestion about the dates. Kaga looked uncomfortable.

"I've a hunch I'm going to be busy next month. I'd prefer another day."

"How about the Saturday of the week before, then? I can probably work something out."

"No," Kaga said baldly. "This month and next, we've a lot going on at the station. The middle of the month after next would be best for me."

Startled, Tokiko scrutinized his well-chiseled face.

"No way. No way we can hold the memorial service *after* the actual anniversary."

7

"I really don't think I can make the time for it, though. The police station I work at covers a wide area and we're short-staffed. The cases are piling up."

"Why not have a word with your boss and get transferred back to Nerima Police Station?"

"Well," Kaga said, scratching his eyebrow distractedly. "It's hardly like I was at loose ends at Nerima either."

Tokiko sighed.

"Look, I know you're busy. I know cases come in suddenly. That's not going to change just because we wait another month. You're just procrastinating—and you know you are."

"No, I'm not."

"Yes, you are. I'm doing my best to be constructive here, so just do what I tell you to. We'll have the memorial service for your father on the second Saturday of next month, starting at eleven in the morning. You're happy with that, right? You'll let me arrange everything?"

Kaga furrowed his brow and sank into thought.

Tokiko smacked the tabletop. "Mr. Kaga!"

He jerked upright with a start. "Calm down."

"I need a clear answer from you. You're okay with my plan?"

Kaga was in the process of agreeing—albeit with every sign of reluctance—when something started buzzing in the inside pocket of his jacket. "Sorry," he said, pulling out his cell phone and walking off.

Resisting the urge to cluck her tongue disapprovingly, Tokiko reached for her cup of tea. She glanced at her watch as she did so. It was already after nine p.m. She had made her way to this café after having finished her shift at the hospital and having dinner at a restaurant she liked. Kaga, who worked out of the nearby Nihonbashi Precinct, had told her he wouldn't be available until late.

He was pale when he came back to the table.

"Sorry. Something urgent's come up," Kaga said, rather shamefacedly.

"You're going back to work now? That's got to be against the Labor Standards Act!"

She meant it as a joke, but Kaga didn't smile.

"An emergency. There's been an incident very near here. I've got to get going."

Seeing the serious look in his eyes, Tokiko realized that now wasn't the moment for levity.

"Okay, then, what shall we do about this?" Tokiko pointed at the calendar on her cell phone.

For a second or two Kaga looked unsure, then he nodded his head.

"Let's go with the day you just suggested. You can take care of everything. But—" Kaga fixed his eyes on Tokiko and ran his tongue over his lips. "I can't promise that I'll be able to make it."

Tokiko bristled and glared up at him.

"Sorry, but I need you to promise you'll be there. No ifs or buts."

Kaga grimaced. Tokiko's face softened when she noticed his discomfiture.

"Oh, I give up. Your dead father would probably urge you to put your work first too."

Kaga scratched his head in embarrassment. "I'll try my best," he said.

On the sidewalk outside the café, Kaga raised his arm and hailed a taxi. "You take this one," he said, gesturing to Tokiko. She shook her head.

"The train's fine for me. You take it, Mr. Kaga."

"Sure? All right. Have a safe trip home."

"Don't overdo it."

Kaga nodded, smiling as he sprang into the back of the cab. His face reverted to that of a detective when he gave the driver his desired destination. The taxi moved off. As it drove past, Kaga smiled at Tokiko again. His smile was different this time; it felt forced.

Watching the taxi drive off, Tokiko thought about the day, two years ago, that Takamasa Kaga, Kaga's father, had died. As the nurse in charge, she had been at his bedside.

Kaga, who was the only child, showed up only after Takamasa had breathed his last. Takamasa's sister and nephew were the sole members of the family there when the old man died. And it wasn't that Kaga couldn't get there in time; he made a deliberate choice to stay away. It wasn't just that one occasion either; Kaga had barely visited his father the whole time he was in the hospital. Even if you weren't family, it was hard not to see him as callous, uncaring, and unfilial. His cousin and his aunt were very displeased.

Tokiko, however, knew that Kaga was far from unfeeling. In his heart, he was more upset than anyone at his father's approaching end and hoped that the old man would be able to leave life with as much dignity as possible. At the same time, he was not someone who expressed his feelings openly. Only in the emails he sent Tokiko from time to time could one get a glimpse of what he really felt.

Tokiko made up her mind to attend Takamasa's funeral, which was held three days after his death. Most of the mourners seemed to be colleagues from the police force. Seeing the reverence with which they contemplated the photograph of the dead man, she got a sense of how highly his colleagues regarded him.

Kaga did a good job of representing the mourning family. Standing off to the side with his cousins, he watched attentively as the participants filed up to offer incense to the deceased. When Tokiko walked past the family, she saw his lips form the words, "Thank you."

A year after Takamasa's death, she sent Kaga an email inquiring about the one-year anniversary. His reply was almost instantaneous. He said something to the effect that he had no time and had done nothing to mark the anniversary. His tone gave her the impression that he hadn't even been to visit his father's grave.

Tokiko sent a follow-up email. This time she suggested that they pay a visit to the grave together. She even proposed some specific dates.

As she read his reply, Tokiko pictured Kaga with an expression of mild bewilderment. He was at least making some effort to respond. Tokiko promptly decided on a schedule, which she sent back to him.

He must think that I'm a complete busybody. Tokiko didn't really know why this whole thing was weighing so heavily on her. As a nurse, she'd watched patients die before. There were people she'd looked after for years and with whom she'd developed an almost familial bond, but she always made a point of trying not to get too emotionally involved when they died. With this particular father-and-son pair, however, she found herself unable to forget about them. She felt a duty to do something.

She and Kaga visited Takamasa's grave on the agreed day. This was indeed the first time Kaga had been there since the interment, and Tokiko was shocked that Kaga's cousins were more frequent visitors than he was.

"I just don't think it's what my dad would want. He's more like, 'Here I am in this nice quiet place, so why won't you just leave me alone?'" Kaga said in a flat voice as he looked at the gravestone. Shooting him a sideways glance, Tokiko felt she should say something to him, she just didn't know quite what—it was frustrating.

After that, they continued to exchange emails on other subjects, and Tokiko always signed off with the same question: "Have you visited your father's grave?" Although Kaga was quite good about replying, he never answered that particular question.

Now another anniversary was fast approaching. Tokiko mailed Kaga to ask what his plans were this time around. True to form, he said that he had yet to plan anything.

He absolutely must observe the second-year anniversary, she replied. She would be happy to help out if he was busy. "As the son, it's your duty to provide an opportunity for people to remember your father," she wrote. Her tone was quite sharp.

Kaga had called her a couple of days ago. His aunt and cousins were also making a fuss, so he had decided to mark the second anniversary after all. Would she really help out with it?

Of course she would, Tokiko immediately replied. Something that had stalled for two years finally seemed to be moving forward.

3

When Shuhei Matsumiya reached the crime scene, one side of Nihonbashi Bridge was closed to traffic. The one-way street that runs parallel to the river had been blocked off completely and a uniformed policeman was directing the traffic. On the far side of the street, there was a line of TV camera crews.

There weren't many bystanders about. The victim had been rushed to the hospital and there were no visible traces of the crime, so there was nothing to stare at even if you happened to be walking in the neighborhood. Matsumiya had a sense of something like anticlimax. He'd been expecting to have to push his way through crowds of gawkers.

He was putting on gloves and an armband when someone slapped him on the right shoulder. It was Kobayashi, the squad leader. His eyes were narrow and his chin came to a sharp point.

"Oh! Evening, sir."

"Poor Matsumiya, always the unlucky one! Bet you were out on a date?"

"What makes you think so?"

"You were in high spirits when quitting time came around. It was written all over your face: 'Thank God I didn't get picked for extra duty.'"

"I'm sure you're happy enough too, sir, when you're on call and nothing comes in. You get to spend some time with your family."

Kobayashi snorted derisively.

"You should have seen my daughter's face when the call came in. She was thrilled at the idea of not having to see her dad's miserable mug for an evening! My wife was there and she had the exact same expression on her face. Believe me, Matsumiya, if you get married and you have a kid and that kid's a girl, the moment she goes to junior high school she's lost to you forever."

Matsumiya grimaced. "I'll bear that in mind," he said.

They nodded to the officer responsible for guarding the crime scene and entered the area that was off-limits to the public. No one from the Forensics team was there. Dispatch had made it clear that the actual crime had taken place elsewhere.

Matsumiya, who was in the Homicide Division of the Tokyo Metropolitan Police Department, had been relaxing at home when he'd gotten the call. Most of the other officers there must have been ordered out long before he arrived. After all, a man had been stabbed in the center of Tokyo and the attacker was still unknown. The emergency deployment order had been issued not only to everyone in the local precinct but to all the neighboring precincts as well. Matsumiya assumed that checkpoints would have been set up on all the main roads connected to the bridge.

Matsumiya and Kobayashi looked over at the neighborhood police station at the far end of the bridge. The duty officer there, a man called Yasuda, had discovered the victim.

Officer Yasuda looked around thirty years old. He had a strained expression on his face and, moving rather stiffly, he came over to greet the men from TMPD Homicide. The hand with which he saluted them was trembling slightly.

"Our unit chief will be along in a moment. You can give us a full account then. For now, I'd like just a simple overview." Despite this, Kobayashi got Officer Yasuda to provide a very detailed account of what had happened. Matsumiya stood off to one side and took notes.

That's odd, Matsumiya thought as he listened to Yasuda's account. He didn't have any problem with the fact that the victim had kept moving even after being stabbed in the chest. Various possibilities suggested themselves: maybe he was trying to flee from his attacker, or perhaps he was looking for help. In that case, though, why had he staggered past the police station?

That was the first question that Kobayashi, who must have had the same doubts, put to Officer Yasuda. The officer tilted his head to one side.

"I have no idea. He went right past it without so much as a glance. At the time, I just assumed he was weaving around because he was drunk."

If the victim had come up from behind before walking past him, then all Yasuda would have seen of him was his back. It was reasonable enough for him not to have realized that something was wrong.

"Perhaps he'd lost so much blood that he was barely conscious. He may not even have noticed that there was a police station," Kobayashi ventured.

Unit Chief Ishigaki and the other members of his team arrived soon after. Before getting Officer Yasuda to talk him through the events, Ishigaki got everyone together. "I've been told the victim didn't make it," he said. "That means that this is now a murder inquiry. The deputy commissioner and the director are now over at the Nihonbashi Precinct station. If the current deployment doesn't result in the quick capture of a suspect, I expect them to activate the mobile unit. I hope you all understand that."

After they had all listened to Officer Yasuda's account for a second time, Fujie, the unit chief of the Nihonbashi precinct, came over to greet them. He was a thin man, somewhere north of forty.

"We've located what appears to be the actual crime scene. It's just one block that way. I'll show you."

Fujie started walking down the blocked-off road that ran parallel to the river, and Ishigaki and his team, along with Matsumiya, followed. The guys from Forensics were spread out along the sidewalk to their left, hard at work.

"They found blood dotted along the sidewalk. Not very large quantities. The victim must have been bleeding as he was walking," Fujie explained.

Right up against the narrow sidewalk stood the headquarters of a well-known investment bank. You could feel the history emanating from the façade of the building even in the darkness. What was the victim thinking as he made his way along this street with a knife stuck in his chest?

"Not a lot of foot traffic here?" asked Ishigaki.

Fujie nodded in acknowledgment of Ishigaki's question.

"I'm not sure about the daytime, but at night, no, not much. There's nothing here except that investment bank."

"So no surprise that no one noticed our critically injured victim."

"Precisely."

"You managed to ID the victim, didn't you? Have you notified the family?"

"That's been taken care of. They should be en route to the hospital right now."

The place Fujie led them to was just in front of an on-ramp for the expressway. A footpath went down from the sidewalk and into an underground passageway. The area had been cordoned off with crime scene tape. The technicians from Forensics were bustling about energetically.

"As you're probably aware, this underground passage takes you to the foot of Edobashi Bridge." Fujie was pointing downstream at the Edobashi Bridge, the next bridge over. "The passage is short—just over ten meters. We found bloodstains halfway along. And no further bloodstains have been found beyond that point."

"Making the midpoint of this underground passage the crime scene?" asked Ishigaki.

"We think so," said Fujie.

Matsumiya, after slipping on a set of shoe covers, went into the passage with Kobayashi. Tape had been stuck to the ground to indicate the area they could walk on, so they were careful not to stray onto the other side.

At three meters wide, the passage was narrower than Matsumiya had expected. It was also on the low side; a little jump was enough for a tall man to touch the ceiling. It was ten meters long, as Fujie had said, and there were traces of blood on the ground about halfway in. There wasn't much blood: just a blackish stain about five centimeters in diameter.

There was no other visible evidence of the crime. Matsumiya and his companions went on to the far end of the passage, where Ishigaki and his men were waiting. They found themselves on the sidewalk of Edobashi Bridge.

Fujie consulted his notebook.

"As I think you're all aware, Patrolman Yasuda of the Nihonbashi Bridge police station called this in at precisely nine p.m. About four minutes later, we activated an emergency deployment for the entire district. We haven't yet found anyone who reports seeing a suspicious person."

Nodding his acknowledgment, Ishigaki scrutinized the area. "Wonder what foot traffic on this bridge is like?" he asked under his breath.

"There aren't many pedestrians at nine in the evening. And I don't think many people use the underground passageway either. As you can see, though, there's a high volume of vehicle traffic," said Fujie.

There was an incessant stream of cars and trucks coming and going over Edobashi Bridge.

"The victim managed to make it all the way to Nihonbashi Bridge after being stabbed. What sort of time . . . do you think that would take?" Ishigaki asked Matsumiya.

"Three, possibly four minutes under normal conditions. Given that he'd been stabbed in the chest, I'd say it probably took about twice that long," he answered. He spoke circumspectly as he tried to picture the scene in his head.

"Sounds about right to me. Let's say it was roughly ten minutes . . . With that much time, the attacker's options for fleeing the scene are almost limitless."

"We've already contacted all the taxi companies," Fujie said. "No drivers report picking up anyone suspicious in this area."

"He didn't need to catch a cab," said Kobayashi quietly, pointing to the opposite bank. "If the attacker got to the other side of the river, it would have been easy for him to escape."

Matsumiya looked to where Kobayashi was pointing. There was a pedestrian crossing just beyond the far end of the bridge. Even at this hour of night, many people were still using it.

Kobayashi's right, thought Matsumiya. If the attacker had managed to blend in with the crowd, then they were really in trouble.

4

They were almost at the hospital when Fumiko, who was in the backseat of the cab, started rummaging around noisily. She had to be looking for something in her bag. Her agitation communicated itself to Yuto, who was in the front seat next to the driver.

"What's the problem?" Haruka asked.

"Think I left it at home," Fumiko replied in a small voice.

"What is it? Your wallet?"

"Yes."

Haruka gasped. Yuto couldn't stop himself clicking his tongue. "What's wrong with you?"

"It's not my fault. I was in a hurry."

Yes, but even so, Yuto wanted to say—but he stopped himself. This wasn't the first time for his mother to make a mess of things in an emergency.

The driver must have overheard their discussion. "Did you leave something at home?"

"I'm afraid I did," Fumiko answered. She sounded embarrassed.

"Should we turn around?"

"No need. I've got cash on me." Yuto glanced at the taxi's meter. Yuto pulled out his wallet and checked his money. "We should be fine."

"Oh, thank goodness," said Fumiko, her voice a feeble murmur. She wasn't really concerned about her wallet.

They had driven at high speed all the way from their home in Meguro. Although it was almost eleven o'clock at night, the roads were still busy. There seemed to be a particularly large number of police cars. "I wonder if something's going on," the cab driver said. Feeling he couldn't just ignore him, Yuto gave a noncommittal reply. "Yeah, I wonder."

They finally reached the hospital. They got out of the taxi at the main entrance, but the lobby was pitch-black and the automatic glass doors refused to open.

"That's odd. Wonder how we're meant to get in?" Fumiko peered around nervously.

"When they called you, didn't they say something about the nighttime entrance, Mom?"

Fumiko clapped her hand to her mouth when Haruka pointed this out.

"Yes, you're right. The man from the police did say that."

Yuto clicked his tongue again. "What's wrong with you? Get a grip."

The three of them went around to the side of the building to look for the nighttime entrance. As soon as they turned the corner, they were confronted by a stocky man with a flashlight. "Are you the Aoyagis?"

"Yes, we are," Fumiko replied.

The man switched off his flashlight, walked up to them, and showed them a Tokyo Metropolitan Police badge. "I've been expecting you."

He was a detective from the Nihonbashi precinct.

"So, my husband . . . ," Fumiko asked. "How's he doing?"

The detective looked uncomfortable. He was evidently shocked to discover that they were still in the dark. It was at that moment that Yuto intuited what had happened.

"I'm truly sorry," said the detective. "Uhm . . . I'm truly sorry, but your husband was declared dead shortly after he got to the hospital."

Yuto listened with a sense of detachment as the detective stumbled over his words. There was a confused tangle of emotions in his mind: a refusal to accept the reality along with the sense that he'd been expecting this all along.

Haruka clapped both her hands over her mouth. Her eyes were open wide and she stood rooted to the spot.

"No, I can't believe it!" shrieked Fumiko. "It's simply not true. Why? Why? Why should anyone want to kill him?"

Yuto grabbed his mother by the arm as she flung herself, shouting, at the detective. Fumiko's legs gave way and she crumpled to the ground, where she started wailing.

Haruka stood there and began to sob. The cries of the two women echoed around the place.

"Dad's . . . my father's body . . . where is it?" Yuto asked the detective.

"It's this way. I'll take you to him."

"Come on, Mom. Haruka. There's no point crying out here." Yuto helped Fumiko back to her feet and herded them both inside.

Takeaki's face looked much better than Yuto had imagined it would. The suntan he'd had from playing golf was still intact, and—aside from the fact that he wasn't breathing—his face looked more or less the same as it did when he was asleep. If anything, his expression was untypically serene.

"Oh, my darling!" said Fumiko, kneeling and touching her dead husband's face. "Why? Why?" she repeated. Haruka buried her face in the side of the mattress. Her back shook, and now and then you could hear the sound of a sob.

The detective had been tactful enough to leave the three of them alone in the room. Confronted with his father's dead body, Yuto had no idea how to behave. On a rational level, he knew that he was supposed to grieve, but he didn't feel the slightest trace of sadness. As he looked at his sniveling mother and sister, he was thinking coldly to himself, *When all you two ever did was bitch about him behind his back!*

There was the sound of a knock and the door opened. The detective peered in.

"May I come in? I'd like to ask you a couple of questions, if you don't mind."

Yuto glanced down at his mother. "What do you want to do?"

Fumiko nodded, wiped away her tears with a handkerchief, and pulled herself to her feet.

"It's okay. I've got a lot of questions myself."

"I'm sure you do," the detective said. "Please follow me."

The three of them trooped after the detective to a room on the same floor marked "Lounge".

"You all know Nihonbashi?" the detective asked. "I'm not talking about the whole Nihonbashi area, I mean the actual Nihonbashi Bridge itself."

"The one near the Mitsukoshi department store?"

"That's right." The detective nodded.

"Your husband was found on the bridge at around nine o'clock this evening. He'd been stabbed. The person who found him was the officer stationed at one end of the bridge.

"He was stabbed, however, at another location and Mr. Aoyagi managed to drag himself to Nihonbashi Bridge. As soon as we found him, he was brought in here by ambulance."

"Was my husband still alive?"

"We think so. But his condition was already extremely serious. We won't know more until we get the results of the autopsy."

The word *autopsy* made Yuto acutely aware that this was a serious crime and that he and his family were directly involved.

"Uh . . . but who stabbed my husband?" Fumiko asked. "Did you catch the person who did it?"

"No, the perpetrator is still at large. And we currently have no clue as to their identity. Since we can't locate your husband's wallet, it's possible that this was a random attack by someone who was after his money. Everyone—not just the local Nihonbashi police but the officers from all the nearby precincts—has been mobilized and is combing the area, hunting for the attacker. The Tokyo Metropolitan Police's mobile unit has also been sent in. I imagine you saw quite a few police cars and motorbikes on your way here?"

We certainly did. Yuto nodded, but said nothing.

"The attacker can't have got far. We'll find him soon enough."

The detective sounded very confident. Yuto managed to stop himself asking, "And then what?" His father was dead. Even if they caught and executed the killer, that wouldn't bring his father back to life. From tomorrow on, Yuto's existence was going to become a nightmare, physically and emotionally. The darkness of the future he saw stretching before him almost made him dizzy with despair.

The dizziness was suddenly replaced with fury. What right did a complete stranger have to so totally screw up his life?

The detective started asking them basic questions about Takeaki: his date and place of birth, his job and his career, as well as his everyday routine. He also threw in some questions about who he socialized with, whether he had quarreled with anybody, and whether he had been experiencing any problems at work or in his private life. None of the three could provide a decent answer to any but the simplest questions.

The truth was, Takeaki almost never discussed his work at home and, if they were honest, none of them were really all that interested.

The detective looked a little put out as he reviewed his notebook. He had been jotting down all their replies, but Yuto got the impression that nothing they'd said was likely to be much help in the investigation. He wondered if the detective was getting irritated with them for being so useless.

A buzzing noise came from the detective's chest pocket. "Excuse me a moment," he said and left the room.

Fumiko gave a deep sigh. She pressed her fingers to her temples as if to quell a headache.

"Why, though? Why did this have to happen to us?"

"Can you think of a reason, Mom?"

"No, not a one. Who says there even has to be a reason? Ah . . . how are we going to get by? Will your father's company look after us?"

Fumiko seemed to be worried about the financial side of things. She may have only just lost her husband, but Yuto didn't feel he had the right to criticize her. In one corner of his mind, he was worrying about exactly the same thing. How would their lives be affected? Would he be able to go to college?

The detective came back into the room. He looked tenser, more animated.

"I just got an important update. We've found a suspicious person."

Yuto swallowed.

"Is it the killer?" Fumiko asked.

"We don't yet know. It's a young man, I'm told. There are some things we need to discuss with you in connection with him. Do you feel up to accompanying me to Nihonbashi Precinct?"

"What, will we get to see him?" Fumiko replied. There was a hint of desperation in her voice. "The man who killed my husband?"

The detective waved away the idea.

"No, definitely not. There are some things we need you to verify. Besides, we don't know for sure that the young man really is the culprit. Can you come with me?"

Fumiko turned to look at Yuto. He couldn't think of any reason not to go. "We're happy to," he said.

Around half an hour later, the police car containing Yuto, his mother, and his sister arrived at Nihonbashi Police Station. There was a cluster of what looked like TV trucks parked outside. Yuto was worried they would get bombarded with questions, but no one came running over when the three of them got out of the car. Perhaps the media didn't yet know who they were.

On the outside, the police station looked as sleek and featureless as any ordinary office building, but the atmosphere changed completely the moment you stepped inside. The first thing that struck Yuto was the grand staircase in the front lobby, with its massive, ponderous, and elaborately carved handrail. The old-fashioned reception counter was made of marble, and the light fixtures hanging from the ceiling were clearly vintage. The detective explained that the plan to demolish the original, beautiful old police station had provoked such an outcry that parts of the original structure had been incorporated into the new building.

He took the three of them into a small meeting room. When he asked them if they wanted anything to drink, they all said no. Nonetheless, a policewoman came in with some green tea a few minutes later.

Fumiko took a sip. "So it was a young man . . . ," she murmured.

"Any idea who it could be?" Yuto asked.

"I don't know." Fumiko gave a feeble shake of the head. "I suppose there are loads of young men working in your father's company."

Yuto had even less interest in Takeaki's job than Fumiko. All he knew was that his dad worked for a firm that made building components and that he was in quite a senior position.

The detective finally reappeared after a little under an hour.

"Very sorry to have kept you waiting. Could you come with me?"

The detective took them to still another meeting room. Several men were standing around a very large table. Some wore suits and others were in uniform. Their faces were so stern and the mood so tense that Yuto couldn't bring himself to make eye contact with any of them.

The detective introduced the three of them to the group. The men said nothing and nodded in their general direction. *That's their idea of offering condolences,* Yuto thought to himself.

"I am going to get the family members of the deceased to identify the articles in question," the detective announced in a loud voice, before gesturing for them to approach the table.

A number of transparent plastic pouches with objects inside were arranged on the tabletop. Yuto squinted at them. He had a pretty good idea what they were.

"Earlier this evening, I informed you that we had located a suspicious person," the detective said. "That person had a wallet in his possession. Since the wallet contained a driver's license and other similar items, all belonging to Takeaki Aoyagi, we concluded that the wallet was Mr. Aoyagi's property and confiscated it. We also found Mr. Aoyagi's briefcase in the place where the suspicious person had been hiding. What you can see here on the table are the wallet, the briefcase, and their respective contents. Could you start by examining the wallet? You can handle the articles through the plastic. Feel free to pick them up and have a good look at them."

Fumiko picked up the wallet while Yuto and Haruka watched her. The wallet was made of black leather and long and slim in shape. It was old, and the part where the owner's thumb rubbed up against it was quite heavily worn.

"That's Dad's," Haruka said in a murmur.

Yuto found himself picturing the way that Takeaki would pluck the wallet from inside his suit and whip out a ten-thousand-yen note like a magician when the time came to pay the check at a restaurant. Recently, though, they'd stopped eating out as a family.

"This is definitely my husband's," Fumiko said.

The detective nodded curtly and pointed at another cluster of plastic pouches.

"What about the contents of the wallet? I'd like you to tell us if anything that should be there is missing, or if there's anything in there that strikes you as suspicious."

There was cash, a driver's license, a variety of credit cards, an insurance card, and some receipts. The individual items had been put into separate plastic pouches. The money, which had been divided into notes and coins, came to a total of 114,850 yen. Someone had jotted the number down on a piece of paper and stuck it to the pouch.

"What do you think? Is this the sort of sum your husband would normally have on him? Or did he normally carry more cash?"

Fumiko responded to the detective's question by tilting her head to one side. "I think this is about normal for him," she answered. "I leave money matters completely in his hands, so I can't really say . . ."

"What about the other items? Is anything missing?"

When the detective pressed her further, Fumiko said nothing. She had probably never seen the contents of her husband's wallet before. The same was true for Yuto. While he knew what his father's wallet looked like on the outside, he had no idea what he'd kept inside it. Nor did he care.

Among all the different cards, only one caught his attention. It was a membership card for an internet café. His father had a computer at home and he would definitely have one at his office, so why would he need to sign up at a place like that? Yuto didn't, however, put his concern into words.

"I'll take that to mean that nothing strikes you as out of the ordinary, then," said the detective, as if making doubly sure. "Shall we now turn our attention to the briefcase?"

Fumiko picked up the large plastic pouch containing the briefcase. It was dark brown with a zip along the top that was protected by a flap. It had buckles at either end, but the shoulder strap that went with them had been removed.

"This is my husband's," Fumiko said. "I'm sure of that. He had me buy it for him."

The detective nodded and pointed to another set of plastic pouches. "What about the briefcase contents?"

Yuto shifted his gaze. The next set of plastic pouches, which were arranged in a neat row, contained some documents, a notebook, an eyeglasses case, a business card case, a few pens and pencils, and a paperback, among other things. Yuto, who was seeing all these items for the first time, had nothing to say about them.

There was one item that caught his eye. A digital camera. Fumiko must have felt the same way, as she reached out and picked it up.

"Is there something unusual about it?" the detective asked.

Cocking her head to one side, Fumiko showed the camera to Yuto and Haruka. "Have either of you seen this before?"

"No," Yuto replied. Haruka shook her head.

"Your husband didn't use a camera at work or as a hobby?"

"I don't know. I don't think he was interested in photography . . ." Fumiko put the camera back down on the table.

That was when it happened. "May I?" a voice said. The speaker was a tall man in a dark gray suit. He had strong features and intelligent-looking eyes. He stretched out one long arm and picked up one of the plastic pouches. It contained a pair of eyeglasses and a case for them. "Are you sure this belongs to your husband?" he asked. He was looking fixedly into Fumiko's face as if he wanted to peer into her mind.

"I know for a fact the glasses are his."

"What about the case? Did you buy it, Mrs. Aoyagi?"

"No. I've never seen it before. My husband must have bought it for himself."

The case was decorated with a traditional Japanese motif. Yuto hadn't seen it before either.

"I see," said the tall detective as he replaced the pouch on the table.

"Is there something special about that case?" Fumiko asked. The detective shook his head. "No, nothing special," he said.

As he watched this exchange, Yuto could no longer contain himself.

"Uh . . . could I ask you something?"

Everyone turned in his direction. With all eyes upon him, he started to speak.

"What's the point of all this? You arrested a suspicious guy, right? What does *he* have to say for himself? Has he admitted to stabbing my father and stealing his wallet and briefcase?"

The detectives looked disconcerted. After a moment or two, a man in an ash-gray suit who seemed to be the most senior person there fixed Yuto with an earnest look.

"There's nothing we'd like to do more than question him, but unfortunately, we cannot."

"Why can't you just ask him?" Yuto asked.

"We can ask all the questions we want, but he's in no fit state to reply. He's in a coma and his condition is critical."

5

It was after eight p.m. by the time Kaori got back from the delicatessen where she worked part-time. Normally, she liked to immediately change out of her work clothes and into her sweatpants, but today, she waited for Fuyuki to come home.

He'd sent her a text just after five that afternoon. He'd found a lead on a job, so he was going for an interview. Kaori's plan was for the two of them to go and grab a celebratory drink at the pub if he'd gotten hired. *He can have a beer, his favorite, and I'll have oolong tea*, she thought.

She waited and waited, but Fuyuki didn't come home. Nine o'clock came and went, then ten. She tried calling him, but he didn't pick up. She sent a text. "I'm worried about you. Get in touch."

Perhaps the job interview hadn't turned out well. Something similar happened once before. Fuyuki left the house after announcing that he'd found a darts bar in Ikebukuro that was looking for waitstaff and then he didn't come back. Worried, she'd gone out to look for him, only to find him drunk out of his head in their local park. Beside him was a heap of empty beer cans. When she asked what had happened, he explained that he had been rejected because he "had a gloomy face." That had depressed him and he had bought a load of cheap beer at a convenience store and just started drinking. Kaori thought he was behaving like an idiot, but she knew how his mind worked. He didn't feel up to seeing her; he was furious at his own fecklessness.

Kaori didn't know what kind of job Fuyuki had gone for today. If it involved interacting with other people, things probably hadn't gone well. He wasn't very articulate and he wasn't very good at getting on with strangers. When he met someone new, he usually ended up tongue-tied.

Fuyuki often said that he preferred machines to people. In fact, most of his jobs had been at factories. And a factory job was the kind of job he was looking for this time too. But the staffing agency never had anything good for him.

Not being able to find a job is hardly the end of the world, thought Kaori as she looked at the time on her cell phone. The photo on her lock screen was of the two of them celebrating Christmas together.

A little after eleven p.m., the screen of her phone lit up with an incoming call. It was Fuyuki. She picked up immediately. "Hi, Fuyuki? Where are you?" she asked, the words tumbling out of her.

For a while, there was no response. She knew they hadn't

been cut off because she could hear what sounded like cars driving by. "Hello? Are you there?" she said.

"Kaori." At last, he spoke. "I don't know what to do. I've done something awful . . ." His voice was like a groan of pain.

"What? What do you mean?"

"Something terrible's happened. I don't know what to do."

"Hold on a second. What have you done? Talk to me."

The line cut out before Fuyuki could reply. Kaori hurriedly called him back. The phone rang, but no one picked up.

She had no idea what was going on. *What on earth has happened? What has Fuyuki gone and done?*

She was so anxious and distressed that she kept pressing Redial over and over. She must have called twenty or thirty times before she finally got through.

"Hello?" said the man at the other end of the line. The voice wasn't Fuyuki's. Startled, Kaori was at a complete loss for words. "Hello? Can you hear me?" reiterated the voice.

Kaori swallowed. "Uhm . . . who is that?" she asked. "That's Fuyuki's phone, right?"

The response was quite unexpected. So unexpected that Kaori initially thought she had misheard. "I'm a policeman," he said.

"You're the police?"

"Am I correct in thinking that this phone belongs to a Fuyuki Yashima? I checked his driver's license."

"Yes, that's right."

The man had checked Fuyuki's driver's license? Why?

"Mr. Yashima has been involved in an automobile accident. He is currently on his way to the hospital."

"What?" Her mind went blank. *An auto accident? How come?* They had been talking on the phone just a few moments earlier. It was all so incredible that she struggled to put her question into words.

"Excuse me asking, miss, but who are you? What is your relationship with Mr. Yashima?"

"We live together. What kind of accident was he in? How badly injured is he?"

"I'm afraid I can't give you detailed information. I would like to confirm your name. On the phone, your name comes up as Kaori. Is Kaori the correct name?"

"My name is Kaori Nakahara," she replied.

"All right, Ms. Nakahara, what I'd like you to do is to wait for me to call you back. I'll call you later. I'll be using a different phone, so don't let that put you off." He spoke quickly without giving her the opportunity to get a word in, then he hung up.

Kaori was stunned. She had no idea what was going on.

The only clue she had was what Fuyuki had said. *I've done something awful. Something terrible's happened,* he had said. Had he gone and messed up his interview again? But what connection could that have to an auto accident?

Suicide was a possibility. *No, that's crazy,* she thought. *No one would get that desperate from a bad job interview.* Still, on the phone he had sounded horribly dejected.

Kaori shook her head. Trying to imagine what might have happened wasn't getting her anywhere. Her main concern now had to be Fuyuki's well-being. He was in an accident and was being taken to the hospital. What condition was he in?

Despite not eating anything since getting off work, she wasn't hungry. Far from it, she felt nauseous and had stabbing pains in her stomach.

Her cell phone finally rang more than half an hour later. When she picked up, a different man answered. He too was a policeman.

He gave her the name of a hospital. It was in the Kyobashi area of Tokyo and specialized in accident and emergency. Fuyuki, who was unconscious and in critical condition, was being operated on at that very moment. The policeman asked her if she could come over immediately. "I'm on my way," she said and ended the call.

Leaving the apartment, she hailed a cab and climbed in. It was an unplanned-for expense. It would make things that little bit harder for the rest of the month. But now wasn't the time to worry about things like that.

There were a number of police cars parked in front of the hospital. As Kaori went into the building, a number of men came running up to her. Two of them were uniformed officers.

When she inquired how Fuyuki was getting on, they told her that he was still being operated on and that it was uncertain whether or not he would make it. Kaori almost fainted at the news. The men helped her over to a chair in the waiting room.

She had a thousand things she wanted to ask, but she

couldn't get a word in edgewise. Instead, she found herself being bombarded with questions. The police asked her everything imaginable about Fuyuki. She was so disoriented, she could barely give coherent answers. The men eventually left her alone. "Let's leave it till tomorrow," she heard the one who seemed to be in charge say as they left the room.

Sitting in the waiting room, she prayed frantically that Fuyuki would make it. There were so many things she didn't understand. She went back over what the policemen had said. Apparently, the police had wanted to question Fuyuki. He, however, had run away, dashed out into the road, and been hit by a truck. She had no idea why he would run away. But none of that mattered. If she could just ask Fuyuki himself what had happened, then everything could be sorted out. He was one of the few people she trusted implicitly. He would never lie to her; she was sure of that.

She sat with her feet up on the chair, hugging her knees as she buried her head between them. She didn't want to see anybody and she didn't want anybody to talk to her. The only thing she wanted to hear was the news that Fuyuki was okay.

If she screwed her eyes shut tight, she could imagine that Fuyuki was sitting there beside her. Any moment now he would put his arms around her shoulders. That's how they had made it this far together, by snuggling up close to one another.

They were both from Fukushima Prefecture. Kaori had been put in an orphanage after her parents were killed in an accident when she was a baby. Fuyuki's mother had been a neglectful parent. She had had him when she was eighteen, and the father had run off, leaving her an unmarried single mother. Fuyuki currently had no idea where his mother was or what she was doing.

After high school, Kaori got a job as a home care worker, while Fuyuki started working at a small building contractor's office. The firm went bust when they were both twenty. Fuyuki tried to find other work, but couldn't due to a shortage of jobs.

They could no longer remember which of them had first suggested moving down to Tokyo. They were both quite set on it. They had always dreamed of Tokyo. They were convinced that if they made it to the big city, there would be jobs aplenty, and with better pay too. They also didn't want to spend their whole lives living in the sticks.

Around five years ago, the two of them had pooled their modest savings, moved to Tokyo, rented a small apartment, and started living together. They were still poor, but they were optimistic and happy. Every night, they would share their hopes and dreams with one another. Fuyuki's dreams were simple—he wanted to find a good job.

But the economy was in a far worse state than they'd imagined. Their idea that finding work would be easy was quick to crumble. The only options for Fuyuki were either to work in a factory as an agency worker or to get day-laboring jobs. Kaori juggled a couple of part-time jobs. Between them, they just about managed to eke out a living. No matter how hard they worked, though, life was never easy.

Then something happened to make things even worse. Fuyuki had been working in a factory, but his contract was abruptly terminated about six months ago. To top it off, he was sick for quite a while afterward and couldn't find a new position. Kaori became the sole breadwinner, and lately, they hadn't been able to make rent.

"I'm so sorry, Kaori. I'm just a loser." Fuyuki had taken to apologizing like that at every opportunity. He would then go on, "But I won't give up. I promise I'll make you happy. I'll find a job soon and make things easier for you."

You do that. You do your best. Do your best and let me see your healthy, smiling face again—Kaori thought to herself, clasping her hands above her head in a gesture of prayer.

6

When Matsumiya got to the large room at the Nihonbashi precinct, he found Kobayashi and Sakagami smoking just outside the door. They both looked glum.

"Good morning," Matsumiya greeted them. He'd left them late the night before to grab a few hours of sleep.

"Just look at our faces. What do they tell you?" retorted Kobayashi, grinning to reveal the yellowing teeth of a heavy smoker.

"That it's not such a good morning after all?"

Kobayashi nodded and thrust out his lower lip.

"The guy's still unconscious and there's a good chance he won't make it. That'll suck. There I was thinking we could solve this one nice and easy."

"You identified him?"

"Believe so. The local guys were handling that."

Matsumiya nodded wordlessly and glanced at the door of the big room. The staff of the Nihonbashi precinct were rushing in and out, clearly under pressure to get the incident room up and running.

The notification about a suspicious person had come in while Matsumiya and the other detectives were busy gathering information around the area of Edobashi Bridge. The person in question fled when he caught sight of a policeman on patrol and ran out onto the road, where he'd been hit by a truck. They found a driver's license in a wallet he had on him, a wallet that belonged to Takeaki Aoyagi, the stabbing victim. The obvious conclusion was drawn.

There was a general sense of relief among the detectives at the news. Chances were that this was the man who had stabbed Aoyagi. He'd been carted off to the hospital, but once he regained consciousness and they could question him, the whole case could be wrapped up nice and easily. That's why they had been dismissed last night and Matsumiya had managed to make it home.

"Him dying won't be such a bad thing for us either, will it?" said Sakagami, lowering his voice and glancing around. "The fact that he had the victim's wallet on him proves that this was a simple crime with money as the motive. We can file it under 'suspect deceased,' and there we go, over and done with."

Kobayashi pulled a sour face.

"We need to assemble a certain amount of evidence even for that. The paperwork's got to be perfect. Figuring out how he got to the crime scene is a whole job in itself. If he lives, however, all we'll need to do is to confirm the details of his confession. Let's hope he pulls through," said Kobayashi as he stubbed out his cigarette.

The task of getting the incident room into shape was proceeding smoothly. Desks and chairs had been brought in, and radios, monitors, and a bank of dedicated phones were all in place. A raised platform had been installed at one end of the room. The top brass would sit there when the official investigation meetings were held.

Matsumiya and the other investigators were all assigned desks. When he went to the one with his name on it, he found someone he knew very well sitting at the desk beside his.

"Hey," said the other man, without bothering to get up. It was Kyoichiro Kaga.

Before Matsumiya could answer, Kobayashi came over.

"I just had a word with the unit chief. We've decided to pair you up with Kaga. Got a problem with that?"

"Not particularly." He shook his head, then looked down at Kaga. "Good to see you."

"Likewise."

Matsumiya waited for Kobayashi to move off before sitting down.

"Well, Kyo, seems the top brass are convinced that putting us together led to solving the case in Nerima."

"Any chance you can quit calling me that? Most people here have no idea we're cousins."

"What, then? Inspector Kaga."

"Too formal."

"How about just . . . Kaga?"

"That'll do nicely," said Matsumiya's handsome cousin with a nod. "Like I said when we were working on that last case, when TMPD Homicide swings into action, it's you guys who are the main act. Don't hold back: your wish is my command."

"Like you really mean that!" Matsumiya was screwing up his face sardonically when the atmosphere in the room underwent a sudden change. Glancing toward the door, they saw Unit Chief Ishigaki come in, followed by the top brass of the Homicide Division. The deputy commissioner and the director came in; the last of the four to join them was the chief of Nihonbashi Precinct.

When they had taken their places up on the dais, the investigation meeting got underway.

Ishigaki acted as facilitator and managed the meeting. The precinct chief of detectives, as well as someone from Forensics and someone from the mobile unit, delivered reports to bring the outlines of the case into focus.

The victim was Takeaki Aoyagi, fifty-five years old. Aoyagi worked for Kaneseki Metals, a building components manufacturer, where he was head of production. The company's head office was in Shinjuku; records there showed that Aoyagi had left the office at six p.m. the day before. His reasons for being in Nihonbashi, which was a good distance from both his office and his home, were currently unknown.

Estimates were that he was attacked somewhere between a quarter to nine and ten to nine in the night. Having been stabbed in an underground passage near Edobashi Bridge, he had then managed to stagger all the way to Nihonbashi Bridge.

That was where Patrolman Yasuda of the Nihonbashi Bridge police station had discovered him. He had subsequently been taken to the hospital, but he was pronounced dead soon after arrival. The murder weapon was a folding knife, eighteen centimeters in length, with an eight-centimeter blade. It had been thrust into Aoyagi's chest up to the hilt and left there by the attacker, perhaps because he found it difficult to extract. As the handle had a cloth covering, they had been unable to lift any prints.

At around eleven fifteen p.m., roughly two hours after the crime occurred, a policeman patrolling the neighborhood came across a man hiding in Hamacho Green Road, a small park in Nihonbashi. The man made a run for it but was hit by a passing truck and was rushed to the hospital. The discovery of Takeaki Aoyagi's wallet on him made it seem likely that he was involved in the murder. In addition, Aoyagi's briefcase was found in the park where he'd been hiding.

They established the man's name and address from a scooter license he'd had on him. Fuyuki Yashima, twenty-six years old. At around eleven p.m., Yashima had made a phone call to someone registered as "Kaori" in his contact list. When an investigator called the same number, a woman by the name of Kaori Nakahara, who said she lived with Yashima, answered. When the policeman explained the situation, the woman hurried to the hospital, but as she was in a state of shock, they hadn't yet been able to effectively question her.

They'd gotten Takeaki Aoyagi's family members to identify both the wallet found in Yashima's possession, as well as the briefcase found in Hamacho Green Road.

That summarized everything that they knew at this point. The direction of the inquiry would be determined based upon this information.

There was the inevitable nervousness that accompanies the start of any new case, but to Matsumiya, the mood of the meeting seemed mellower than normal. The deputy commissioner and the director interspersed their speeches with smiles, while the body language of all the top brass on the dais was on the relaxed side. The detectives sitting around Matsumiya also seemed to be quite laid-back. No one was expecting this case to cause them too much trouble.

After the meeting, the detectives divided into teams according to their different roles. Matsumiya was paired with Kaga under the supervision of Kobayashi. They were in charge of investigating the victim's personal background. On this occasion, however, Kobayashi seemed to have something a little different in mind.

"Matsumiya, I want you to investigate any link between Yashima and the victim," Kobayashi said. "I want you to go to the hospital where Yashima is. The woman he lives with has been there since last night. With luck, she'll have calmed down a bit and you'll be able to talk to her. The evidence team are heading that way by car, so get them to take you."

"Understood," said Matsumiya.

"The quickest solution would be for Yashima to regain consciousness. But there's a good chance he won't make it, so let's do everything we can," Kobayashi added.

The evidence team heading to the hospital consisted of Sakagami and a young investigator from Nihonbashi Precinct.

"I hope this case will sort itself out nice and easy," said Sakagami as soon as the car started moving. "We don't want anything too complicated, just a nice, simple financial motive. The old 'I was just hunting for someone who looked like they had money; anyone would do.'"

"I think money was the motive. I mean, he had the guy's wallet and briefcase," Matsumiya said.

"That'd be convenient, but there are problems with it. First of all, is it really normal to attack someone in a place like that? There's not a great deal of foot traffic there, but it's right in the center of Tokyo and it wasn't that late at night. There is always a lot of automobile traffic there and there'd be trouble if anybody saw him. A normal person wouldn't act like that."

"What if the attacker wasn't normal? Like if he was on drugs or something?"

"If that were the case, we'd have heard about it at the meeting just now. The guy must have had a blood test when he was admitted to the hospital. Maybe he did lose control and assault the other man. As a theory, that's plausible enough. But then there's the problem of the weapon. He had to have had it on him, meaning we're dealing with a premeditated crime, up to a point at least. Damn it. We really need Yashima to pull through." Sakagami scratched his head irritably.

Matsumiya contemplated the back of Kaga's head. He was sitting in silence in the front seat, looking straight ahead. He obviously had no intention of inserting himself into the homicide detectives' discussion.

Saeki, a Community Police Affairs officer, had been

stationed at the hospital overnight. As of now, nothing had changed, he reported. Yashima was in intensive care and not allowed any visitors.

"So where is this Ms. Nakahara?" Matsumiya asked.

"She was sitting in a corner of the waiting room. She said she was going to the local convenience store a minute ago. She should be back any minute."

"Was she here all night?"

"Looks like it."

"She can't see her boyfriend, so what's the point of her being here?"

"Technically, that's true, but . . ."

Matsumiya sighed and exchanged a look with his companions.

"They said she was in a state of shock and that it was impossible to get any sense out of her. She must be so shaken up that she doesn't know which way's up or down," Sakagami said, speaking under his breath.

They decided to have a word with Yashima's doctor while waiting for Kaori Nakahara to get back. The doctor was a thin man and appeared to be in his late forties. After five hours operating on Yashima, he was now monitoring him in between scheduled catnaps. He was clearly less than thrilled to see them.

"I'll spare you the technical jargon and explain things as simply as I can. The most serious issue is a complex skull fracture. That's affecting his brain, which is the reason why he isn't regaining consciousness."

"Is there a chance of him regaining consciousness? If there is, when might it happen?" Sakagami asked impatiently.

The doctor shook his head frostily.

"I just don't know. The state that he's in, frankly, it wouldn't surprise me if he never regained consciousness. At the same time, it wouldn't be that extraordinary for him to wake up now, right this minute. There are many cases of people miraculously coming around after spending months in a coma—but there are many more where people have simply drifted off without ever waking up."

Matsumiya saw the shoulders of his TMPD colleague slump suddenly. *Bet I look exactly the same,* he thought.

When the detectives returned to the first floor, Saeki brought a young woman over to them. She had to be Kaori Nakahara. Dressed in jeans, a shirt, and a cardigan, she was clutching a rolled-up down jacket and a rather large bag. Her face was pale and without makeup. Her hair was long and a little messy.

There was a café in one corner, so they decided to take her there. They explained the situation to the server and he let them use a couple of tables at the far end. Sakagami started hunting around for an ashtray, unaware that smoking wasn't permitted.

"How are you?" Matsumiya asked Kaori Nakahara. "Are you feeling a bit better?"

"A bit," she replied, without looking up.

"Has anyone taken you through the details of what happened?"

No response. Matsumiya ran his tongue over his lips.

"Last night, there was an incident at Nihonbashi Bridge in Chuo Ward. A man was stabbed. The police combed the area and located a suspicious person. When the officer tried to question this person, he made a run for it and was hit by a truck as he tried to get across a road. The person in question was Fuyuki Yashima."

Kaori Nakahara lifted her head, looked at all the detectives, then finally fixed her eyes on Matsumiya.

"I saw something about it on the TV news just now. My boyfriend would never do anything like that. He'd never stab anyone."

"He had the victim's wallet in his possession."

Her eyes widened. "That's got to be a mistake," she said feebly, before lowering her eyes again.

"We know you got a call from Yashima at around eleven o'clock last night. What was the call about?"

"Nothing in particular . . . wasn't anything important."

"Can you tell us what he said?"

"'I'll be—'" she stammered, before breaking into a cough. Perhaps her throat was bunged up. "'I'll be back soon. Sorry for staying out so late' . . . that's all it was."

"He didn't tell you where he was calling from or what he'd been doing?"

"No, he didn't."

"What time did Yashima leave the house yesterday?"

"I don't know. I was at work till eight. About five, he sent me a text saying that he was heading out for an interview."

"An interview?"

"A job interview. He'd found a place he thought might have a job for him and he was going to see someone there, he said."

Matsumiya sat upright with a jerk. "Yashima was unemployed, then?"

"Uh-huh," she said, before fixing him with a reproachful look. "That doesn't mean that he would attack someone and steal their wallet. He'd never do anything like that. The whole thing's a misunderstanding. Some kind of mistake." Her eyes were reddening visibly.

"All right. All right," said Matsumiya soothingly. "I want you to tell us about Fuyuki Yashima. Whatever you can. Shall we start with how the two of you met?"

"What's that got to do with anything?"

"Don't worry. Even if all this is just a misunderstanding, we still need to have all the facts in order to clear it up. I know you're tired, but we'd really appreciate your help."

Matsumiya ducked his head. With a slightly sulky expression, Kaori Nakahara began to explain their personal history. Matsumiya was surprised to hear they had both been raised in an orphanage.

"We never had any money, but we lived happily enough. At least, until Fuyuki got fired six months ago. He had no idea why he was let go; the reasons they gave him simply didn't make any sense."

"Where was he working?" Matsumiya asked.

"I don't know exactly. A firm that makes components of some kind. For office buildings, places like that."

"For office buildings?" A light bulb went off in Matsumiya's head. "What was the company's name?"

She frowned with concentration. "Kaneda . . . Kana . . . Kanamoto, maybe?" she murmured to herself.

"Kaneseki?"

"Yes, that's it."

Matsumiya exchanged a look with his colleagues. Sakagami whispered to the younger detective. With a tense expression on his face, he rose to his feet and left the café.

"What else did Yashima tell you about the firm? Did he mention any names?" Matsumiya asked.

A doubtful look on her face, Kaori Nakahara racked her brain. Eventually, she shook her head.

"I can't really remember. All he told me was that they'd fired him out of the blue. He's not very good at explaining things. Anyway, why are you asking? Has the firm got something to do with what happened?"

"No, nothing special."

Matsumiya tried to make light of the whole thing. She glowered at him, clearly dissatisfied.

"Tell me. It's not fair if you get to ask all the questions."

With Matsumiya clearly flustered, Kaga intervened. "You might as well tell her. She'll find out later anyway."

Kaga had a point. Matsumiya turned and looked Kaori Nakahara in the eye.

"The person who was stabbed on Nihonbashi Bridge was an employee of Kaneseki Metals."

Kaori didn't seem to grasp the significance of what he

said immediately. She blinked, took a deep breath, and only then began to speak.

"You're saying that's why he . . . why Fuyuki stabbed him? That's . . . that's completely irrelevant. Fuyuki would never do anything like that to anybody." The tears were streaming from her bloodshot eyes. She took a handkerchief out of her bag and wiped them.

"How has Yashima been behaving recently? Have you noticed anything different about him?"

"No, I have not. Nothing." She shook her head, her handkerchief still pressed to her eyes.

"Has anything changed in your personal lives? It could be a change for the better or for the worse, doesn't matter which."

"No, nothing's changed. Life is normal. Everything's normal."

She didn't seem to be thinking straight anymore. The pressure seemed to be getting to her.

"May I?" Sakagami broke in, placing a Polaroid in front of her. It was a picture of the knife. "Have you ever seen this before?"

Kaori looked down at the picture, keeping her handkerchief pressed to her cheek. The fear Matsumiya saw flash across her face had to be due to the dried blood on the blade of the knife.

"Have you ever seen something like this in your boyfriend's possession?" Sakagami asked for a second time.

Kaori shook her head. "No. I've never seen it before."

"Are you sure? Take a good look. Didn't he carry one of these around for self-defense purposes?"

"No, he did not. That's not the kind of person he is." Kaori moved to push the photograph away from her, but bumped her hand against the table. She yelped and burst into tears again.

7

The late-autumn sunlight came streaming in through a gap in the blackout curtains. *Why does it have to be so darn bright and sunny?* Yuto was thinking, despite being in the middle of a phone call.

"I understand the situation you're in. I'll handle all the paperwork at my end. You needn't worry about any of that." Sanada, Yuto's homeroom teacher, spoke in a slow and serious tone. "The important thing is that you take proper care of yourself. You've probably lost your appetite, but you must keep eating. If there's anything on your mind, no matter how small, feel free to come in and talk to me. I'll do everything I can. I know this isn't easy for you, but you've got to be a rock for your mother's sake. It's you she depends on now."

"Yes, sir."

"Good. Hang in there."

"Thank you," he said and ended the call. He'd always thought of his homeroom teacher as frivolous and flighty, but today, he'd sounded serious and sincere.

Yuto decided to send a quick email to one of his friends, Tatsuya Sugino. Not only had they attended the same junior high school, they'd also both been on the school swim team. Now that they were in high school, neither of them were doing any sports.

He thought for a moment, then typed the subject line: "My Dad's Dead."

"You probably got a shock when you saw the title of this email, but it's true. Must be plastered all over the TV by now. My dad was stabbed and killed, so I won't make it to school for a while. No idea if I'll be able to go on to university either. Put the word out that I don't want any messages of condolence. They'll just make things worse. Be in touch."

Yuto pressed Send and collapsed back onto his bed. He had no energy and his head felt heavy.

Had he managed to sleep at all the night before? He wasn't sure. He must have dozed off at some point, but he didn't feel any better for it. No big surprise there.

After a while, a reply to his email came in.

"I don't know what to say, Ao. I checked out the news online. It's awful! Anyway, I hear you loud and clear. I one-hundred-percent get why you don't want people pestering you with good wishes. If anyone comes and asks me about you, I'll tell them what you told me."

Yuto was surprised to find that emailing his friend made him feel the weight of the reality of his father's death all over again. *We've lost the breadwinner of the family. The old life we all took for granted could be gone for good.* He felt increasingly anxious.

Although Yuto still felt a certain heaviness in his head, he forced himself to get up, get dressed, and get out of his room. As he descended the stairs, he heard his mother's voice coming from the living room.

"It's all very well you asking me all these questions, but I have no idea what's going on myself . . . No, I haven't started thinking about the funeral yet . . . Like I said before, I've no idea . . . no, I know nothing about it."

Yuto opened the door. Fumiko had the landline receiver in her hand. From something in her manner, he knew she was talking to a relative.

"Listen, I'm going to hang up now. I'll be back in touch as soon as I hear anything . . . Okay . . . yes, bye, then." Fumiko sighed heavily after replacing the phone in its cradle.

"Who was it?" Yuto asked.

Fumiko grimaced. "Granny. Up in Sendai."

"Uh-huh," Yuto grunted. His mother's family came from Sendai. One of Yuto's uncles lived up there, as did his grandmother.

"I was just thinking I should call them when your uncle saw the TV news and called me. He put Granny on halfway through. She started asking me all sorts of questions, even though I told her I had no idea what was going on—" The ringing of the phone interrupted Fumiko. She scowled as she picked up the receiver, but her expression softened a little when she caught sight of the caller ID. "Yes, this is the Aoyagi house . . . I see . . . Any time you like is fine . . . Thank you . . . Great. We're looking forward to seeing you." Fumiko hung up. "That was Mr. Kotake," she said. "He asked if it would be okay for him to come around. He's going to be our point of contact with your father's firm."

Kotake was Takeaki's direct subordinate. He had known the children since infancy.

"Did you call Matsumoto?" Yuto asked. Takeaki had been born in Matsumoto, a city in Nagano Prefecture. Although the old family home had been sold and both Takeaki's parents were dead, they still had a few relatives living there.

"Uh-huh . . . I called Kyoko. She hadn't seen the news on TV, so I had to tell her what had happened. It wasn't easy. She burst into tears."

Kyoko was Takeaki's younger sister. Yuto hadn't seen her for three years or more, but his mental image of her was of a positive person always with a smile on her face. It was hard to imagine her crying.

Haruka quietly entered the room. The slight puffiness of the eyelids was the only sign that she'd been crying.

"Have you called your schools?" Fumiko asked.

"I did," said Yuto.

Haruka nodded. "My teacher had heard about what happened," she said. "She just never imagined it was Dad who was the victim. She was horrified."

Yuto reached for the remote, switched on the TV, and started flicking through the channels. A number of news and current affairs programs were on, but none of them were covering last night's incident.

"Just leave the TV on. It will come up on one of the channels," Haruka said.

Yuto felt mixed emotions. While he didn't really want to watch the news about his father's murder, he was curious to see how it was being reported. It was like wanting to fiddle with a rotten tooth even though you knew it would hurt.

The front doorbell rang. It was probably Kotake. Fumiko walked over to the intercom.

"Hello? . . . What? . . . Don't know what to say. Now's not the time . . . I'm sorry. I am afraid that won't be possible. Goodbye." Fumiko replaced the receiver, a flustered look on her face.

"Who was it?" Yuto asked.

"Some TV person. They asked me how I was feeling."

"That's outrageous. Was it one of the tabloid shows?"

"Guess so."

Haruka sprang to her feet and rushed out of the room. They could hear her feet pounding up the stairs.

Yuto sighed. "Seriously?"

"What are they thinking? I told them now's not the time."

Haruka reappeared in the room.

"There's a station wagon parked out front and a load of people looking like TV types wandering around."

Yuto went over to the glass door that overlooked the front garden. The street in front of the house wasn't visible from there, but he pulled the net curtain across nonetheless. He felt creeped out.

"I hate this. We can't even leave the house with that lot outside," Fumiko said. She sounded miserable.

That was when it happened. A snatch of music, simultaneously ominous and trite, burst from the television. Nihonbashi Bridge appeared as a screaming caption flashed up on the screen: "The capital's dead zone! Murder in the heart of Tokyo!"

It was a little after a quarter past eleven in the morning when Kotake reached the house. He had a couple of his junior colleagues with him. After a few polite expressions of condolence, they began to discuss with Fumiko the next steps. In fact, Fumiko just listened as the three men spoke at her. At his mother's request, Yuto joined the meeting, but for him his father's work life was a closed book.

One of the men brought up the subject of the funeral. There seemed little point in discussing that in any detail when the police hadn't yet released his body. They decided to push ahead with the basic preparations, but wait to settle on the day after hearing back from the police.

Kotake and his colleagues knew next to nothing about the incident. They also appeared to have no idea what Takeaki was doing in the Nihonbashi area in the first place.

"Someone from the Nihonbashi police contacted us a bit earlier this morning. They'll be sending a couple of detectives to our offices around midday. We may learn a bit more then," said Kotake soberly.

Several calls from relatives and friends came in while his father's three colleagues were in the house. Fumiko got Yuto to answer them. Although he knew the callers were motivated by genuine concern, he wished they had thought a bit more carefully about whether now was the best time to call. "No, we really don't know what happened." He got tired and resentful of having to say the same thing every time. To make things worse, he had to thank them for calling.

There was also a steady stream of people ringing the front doorbell. Mostly it was the TV reporters. Despite the family having made it clear they had nothing to say, one of the reporters had the gall to ask if they had a message for the attacker. Yuto flipped the switch to Off without bothering to reply.

"They want to sensationalize the murder because it happened right in the center of Tokyo. We'll go and see if we can't get them to back off," said Kotake as he was leaving.

He must have managed to negotiate some sort of truce because the reporters stopped buzzing the intercom.

Just before twelve, the family finally had something to eat. It was a simple meal: salad, bacon and eggs, and tinned tomato soup. None of them was hungry. They swallowed their food mechanically and almost wordlessly.

Yuto got a number of emails on his cell phone after lunch. They were messages of condolence from his old junior high school classmates and friends. Asking Tatsuya to head people off was clearly not enough. At least with emails, as opposed to phone calls, Yuto didn't have to reply right away.

"Yuto!" someone called. Haruka jerked her chin at the TV. There was a map on the screen. Yuto started when he realized it was the schematic diagram of a bridge with the caption "Nihonbashi Bridge" underneath it.

The newscaster was moving his pointer over the diagram.

"There is a short underground passage at the south end of Edo-bashi Bridge. The passage is about ten meters long. Traces of blood were found there that could well be Aoyagi's. What does that mean? Basically, that there's a strong likelihood Aoyagi was stabbed in this passage. It's thought that the man who's currently hospitalized and in a coma stole Aoyagi's wallet and briefcase, exited the underpass at the Edobashi Bridge end, crossed Edobashi Bridge, and then fled in an easterly direction. Aoyagi, despite being severely injured with a stab wound, managed to exit the underground passage from the other end and make for Nihonbashi Bridge. There are two possible reasons for him doing this. First, that he was trying to escape from the attacker; second, that he was looking for help."

Yuto found himself fascinated by the newscaster's slick, speedy delivery. He remembered what the detective last night had told them about Takeaki having staggered all the way to Nihonbashi Bridge after being stabbed elsewhere.

Could a stabbing victim really stagger all the way to Nihon-bashi Bridge without anyone noticing?

The newscaster's next remark made it seem that he had anticipated Yuto's question.

"People we spoke to in the area said that at nine p.m., the time the incident occurred, there were very few people around. That means it's quite possible that Aoyagi managed to get all the way to Nihonbashi Bridge without encountering anyone."

Yuto pictured the scene in his head. Trying to walk with a fatal stab wound in his chest must have been excruciating. His father was a stubborn, strong-willed man who never let pain or discomfort show, but this time must have been different. As he flickered in and out of consciousness, what was he thinking about? What was keeping him going like that?

And what about Nihonbashi?

What was Takeaki even doing there? The fact that Kotake and his colleagues had no idea meant it probably had nothing to do with work.

Yuto realized that Fumiko had come up beside him and was staring hard at the TV. She was clasping a hand towel. Haruka had started whimpering again.

The so-called expert commentators—a writer and a bunch of vacuous minor celebrities—all waded in with their opinions. "Things aren't what they used to be." "Society is angrier and coarser than before." "Life is no longer sacred." They riffed freely on their theme.

Yuto grabbed the remote control and changed the channel. A close-up of a face he vaguely recognized loomed up at him. The face belonged to a middle-aged woman. He was just wondering who she was when Fumiko murmured, "Oh, it's Mrs. Yamamoto. You know, from three doors down."

"Ah." Yuto remembered her now. He often bumped into her on the street.

"Oh yes, I think he was a very responsible man. Serious about his duties as a father, but able to have fun too. It's just too sad." Mrs. Yamamoto was responding to a microphone that the interviewer had thrust into her face.

Yuto switched off the TV and flung the remote onto the floor. Their neighbor probably meant no harm, but having strangers sound off about you and your family like that was horrible.

Haruka blew her nose into a tissue, crying the whole time.

"You're getting on my nerves. When are you going to stop blubbering?" Yuto snapped.

Haruka glared at him with bloodshot eyes.

"I can't help it. I'm actually sad. Unlike you."

"Bullshit. What's this 'unlike you' stuff? You mean because you're a girl or something?"

"That's nothing to do with it, you moron. Unlike you, I actually loved and respected our father. This is what a good daughter should do."

"Oh, please! When you spent all your time bad-mouthing him behind his back."

"Not all the time. Only when he went after me first. You hated his guts right up to the last day of his life. You always left home early to avoid him. That's what you did yesterday morning too, right?"

Yuto couldn't stand up to his sister's counterattack. She was right on target.

"Who says I didn't respect Dad? That's not true." His voice had lost its aggressive edge.

"Yes, but respect's not love, is it? You're just worried about what'll happen when he's not there to pay for everything."

"Oh, come on. As if you're not thinking the exact same thing."

"That's why I'm saying I'm not like you. I loved Dad." Haruka gave a toss of the head. "And that's why I'm crying."

"Why were you always so selfish, then?"

"I'm not selfish."

"Yes, you are."

"Cut it out, Yuto. And you too, Haruka," said Fumiko, groaning as she pressed her fingers to her temples. "Stop fighting. Please, can't you make an effort to get on?"

An uncomfortable silence settled on the room. Yuto reached for his phone and got to his feet. "I'm going out for a bit."

"Going where?" Fumiko asked.

"No idea. I just can't stand it in here anymore."

"Don't be stupid. God only knows what the neighbors will say if you go out for a casual stroll."

"Go outside, and the TV reporters from those tabloid news shows will harass you. I guarantee it." Haruka was looking up at him. "You fancy being on TV?"

Yuto picked up a cushion and slammed it down on the sofa. Just then, the phone rang again.

"Wonder who it is now." Fumiko picked up the phone. "Yes, this is the Aoyagi house . . . Uhm, yes, that will be okay . . . I see. Yes, in about half an hour. We'll see you then." She put down the phone, a bemused expression on her face, and turned to look at her children. "That was someone from the police. He says they want to talk to us."

There were two of them: Matsumiya, a young detective from the Tokyo Metropolitan Police Homicide Division, and Kaga, a detective from the Nihonbashi police. Kaga looked to be the older of the two. They had encountered Kaga the night before in the meeting room at the Nihonbashi Precinct station.

"How are you feeling?" asked Matsumiya.

After serving the two detectives green tea, Fumiko cocked her head to the side.

"Frankly, I still can't believe it's all real. Even when I see the reports on the TV, I can't help feeling as though it happened to someone else. It's only when one of our relatives calls that I think, 'Oh, something terrible's happened.'"

Matsumiya frowned sympathetically and tipped his head forward. "That can happen. Please accept our condolences."

"That man," Yuto broke in, "what's going on with him? The man who stabbed my father. They're saying he's still in a coma."

Kaga looked Yuto in the eye. "We can't yet be sure that he is responsible for the stabbing."

"Maybe, but still . . ."

"There's been no change in his condition," Matsumiya said. "He's still in a coma.

"The fact is, we've something here we'd like you to look at." Matsumiya slipped his hand into his suit jacket and extracted a photograph. It was a headshot of a young man. It looked like a color photocopy from a driver's license photo. "This is the suspect who's currently in a coma. His name's Fuyuki Yashima. It's written like this." He turned the photograph around to show the name and the characters with which it was written. He turned the picture back around so it was faceup again. "Have you ever seen him? Have you ever heard the name?"

Fumiko took the photograph from Matsumiya, while Yuto and Haruka looked on from either side. The man in the picture was looking straight at the camera. He was thin and his cheeks were hollow. His short hair was dyed brown and there was a certain sharpness in his eyes. He reminded Yuto of a boxer: pugnacious and up for a challenge.

"Do you recognize him? Has he ever been here to the house? Have you seen anyone who looks like this in the neighborhood?" Matsumiya asked again.

Fumiko looked inquiringly at Yuto and Haruka. They both shook their heads.

"We've never seen this man before," said Fumiko. She put the picture down on the table.

Matsumiya turned it upside down and pointed to the characters for Fuyuki Yashima on the back.

"What about the first name, Fuyuki, or the family name, Yashima? Do they ring any bells? Have you ever received anything in the mail from someone with that name? Or maybe a phone call? Did Mr. Aoyagi ever mention this name? The name doesn't have to be completely identical—Yajima with a *j* will do too."

Yuto stared at the name as he rooted through his memory. Despite his efforts, he came up with nothing.

"You don't need to be one hundred percent certain. It really doesn't matter if you think you remember something which later turns out to be wrong. Fuyuki Yashima. Twenty-six years old. Born in Fukushima Prefecture. Present address: Umeda in Adachi Ward. Was working at Kaneseki Metals in Kunitachi until six months ago. Well? Does any of that jog your memory?"

"Kaneseki Metals? Are you sure?" Fumiko asked.

"No doubt about it. We got confirmation from the head

office. He wasn't a full-time employee, but he's on record as having worked there."

Fumiko exchanged another look with her children, then shook her head again.

"As I told you yesterday, my husband hardly ever mentioned his work."

"I see." Matsumiya put the photograph back in his pocket.

"That man—did he work for my dad?" Yuto asked.

"He was a contract worker, so he wasn't a direct subordinate, though he did work in your father's division. We don't know if the two of them actually knew one another. That's what we want to find out."

"If they knew one another, would that mean the murder wasn't about money? That he had some kind of grievance against my dad?"

"We can't yet say."

"What are his family and friends saying?"

"Family? Whose family?"

"Him. That guy. He's got to have a family. What have they got to say about him?"

Yuto looked into each of the detectives' faces in turn. Neither said anything. "Thank you for this," Kaga eventually said, picking up his steaming teacup. He took his time as he swallowed a mouthful, then replaced the cup on the table.

Yuto was getting annoyed and he couldn't help showing it. "Just damn tell me," he snapped.

"Yuto!" Fumiko interrupted reproachfully.

"I'm very sorry," Matsumiya said. "We're not at liberty to discuss the details of the investigation."

"But we're the victim's family. Surely we have a right to know what the killer's family and friends are saying about him."

"As I've already said, we don't know for sure that he is the perpetrator. Right now, he's just the victim of an accident."

"I don't care what you call him. All I want is—"

"Look, I understand how you must feel," Kaga broke in. "We would like to give you an answer, but we're not at liberty to do so. Proper information management is an essential part of solving a crime. If leaks slow us down or even prevent us from discovering the truth, then ultimately that's not good for you either. We'd really appreciate it if you could see your way to being patient for a while."

Kaga gave a formal bow and Matsumiya followed suit. In the face of such respectful treatment from two grown men, there wasn't a thing Yuto could do. He crossed his arms and shut his mouth.

"Please, please, that's enough bowing," Fumiko said. "Will you at least tell us when you find out what happened? The truth: that's what we want to know. The reason my husband was killed."

"When the time is right, of course we'll tell you," Matsumiya said.

"You mean it? You promise?"

"Absolutely." Matsumiya nodded forcefully.

"Actually, I have a question of my own." Kaga turned to look at Yuto. "I think you're the best person to ask."

"What is it?"

Kaga flipped open his notebook. "You graduated from a junior high school called Shubunkan Junior High?"

Yuto was dumbfounded. That was the last thing he had been expecting to hear.

"Yes, I did, but so what?"

"There's a record of a call to the school in the recent call log on your father's cell phone. The call was made three days ago. Any idea what it was about?"

"My dad? He called the school?" Yuto looked at his mother. "Did he mention it to you?"

Fumiko made a noncommittal sound and tipped her head to one side. "Why would he have called Yuto's junior high?"

"So you didn't know anything about it either, Mrs. Aoyagi?"

"No, this is the first I've heard of it."

"Okay, I'll try asking the school, then."

"Uhm . . . could you tell us if you learn anything?"

"Certainly." Kaga shut his notebook. "Oh yes. There's just one more thing. Did your husband often visit the Nihonbashi area?"

"None of us really know," Fumiko sheepishly replied. "What he was doing there, I mean."

"Of course, Nihonbashi is made up of several different districts. Did your husband ever mention any of them?"

Fumiko shot a questioning glance at Yuto and Haruka. They both shook their heads in silence.

"I see." Kaga gave a smile of acknowledgment and the two of them took their leave.

After the detectives had left, Yuto felt a sense of lingering malaise. He had hoped for some clear and concrete news from them, but, if anything, their visit had only increased his sense of frustration.

With just the three of them in the room, the atmosphere once again grew tense. "This is hopeless," Haruka muttered. *"We're* hopeless."

"Why?" Yuto asked. "What's so wrong with us?"

"What's wrong with us?" Haruka replied. "We know nothing about Dad. We couldn't provide a single decent answer to even one of the detectives' questions. 'I don't know.' 'Never heard of it.' 'Never seen it before.' That was the best we could do. They must think we're complete fools."

"You're out of li—" Yuto began, but his voice trailed off. He shared his sister's overwhelming sense of impotence.

Without a word, Fumiko went into the kitchen.

Haruka went back to crying and Yuto no longer had it in him to criticize her.

8

It was a little after seven in the evening by the time Matsumiya and Kaga got back to Nihonbashi Precinct. In the incident room, a cluster of detectives was standing in a circle around Ishigaki, giving him their latest reports.

"We have managed to verify the victim's movements. He was spotted at a café not far from the crime scene," said Nakase, the detective in charge of the crime-scene vicinity.

"A café? He was inside it?"

"Yes." Nakase unfolded a map on the table. "It's one block to the west, about two hundred meters from the crime scene. One of the staff recognized Aoyagi from the photo, because he paid with a two-thousand-yen note."

"A two-thousand-yen note? They're pretty unusual these days."

"According to the café, Aoyagi pulled out the note,

grinned at him, and said, 'Don't see too many of these now, do you?' More important is that the server said he couldn't recall what the victim ordered, but he was sure that he ordered two of them."

"Two? He ordered two drinks?"

"That's right. In other words, there was someone with him. Unfortunately, the server didn't see the other person."

"When are we talking?"

"He's not sure. The best he could add to it was somewhere between seven and nine p.m."

Ishigaki crossed his arms on his chest.

"If the person with Aoyagi was Yashima, then what? The girl who lives with Yashima told us that he was going for a job interview. Have you found out where that interview was?"

Nakase shook his head.

"We've visited all the bars and restaurants in the vicinity of the crime scene but haven't yet found the place. We went through the call log on Yashima's cell, but there wasn't anything that fit the bill there either."

"Which could mean that this meeting with the victim in that café was in fact a job interview?"

"It's a possibility. According to the live-in girlfriend, his text said that he'd found a lead on a job and he was going to see someone."

Ishigaki turned and looked at Matsumiya and Kaga. "Have you found out anything about possible links between Yashima and the victim?"

Matsumiya glanced over at Kaga. Kaga gave a slight nod as if to say, *Go on, you tell him.*

"We can't yet say with any assurance whether the two men were acquainted. The victim spent most of his time in the Shinjuku head office and seldom went to the factory in Kunitachi. I'm not saying never, though, because there are regular shop floor inspections. We can't rule out the possibility that they had some sort of contact then."

Ishigaki stroked his chin.

"If, hypothetically, the two of them did meet in the café, then it's hard to see money as the sole motive for the crime. And if it wasn't money, then what could the motive be?"

"I've my own ideas about that," Matsumiya said. "We know from Kaori Nakahara that Yashima wasn't happy about the way Kaneseki Metals terminated his contract. When we put that to the HR person at the head office, he claimed that the contract had simply run its course and that there wasn't anything especially problematic about it."

"You mean the two accounts don't match up? The company could have been laying off contract workers in a heavy-handed way. It's hardly unheard of, recently."

"And Yashima's response was to argue unfair dismissal and he was meeting with Takeaki Aoyagi to ask for his job back—that seems a plausible enough interpretation of events, don't you think? Of course, this is all predicated on there being some sort of connection between the two men in the first place."

"That scenario would certainly explain why they met—plus it dovetails nicely with the text Yashima sent his girlfriend. What it fails to account for is the knife. Why would Yashima be carrying a concealed weapon?"

"To threaten Aoyagi would be my guess." It was Kobayashi who said that. "Yashima never intended to kill Aoyagi. He just brought the knife along to make sure that he was taken seriously. When their discussion broke down, something happened, Yashima snapped and stabbed the victim on impulse. Or do you disagree?"

"Hmm." Ishigaki emitted a pensive groan and looked at each of his subordinates in turn. "Have you learned anything about the knife?"

Sakagami cleared his throat before he spoke.

"It's a foreign-made knife. A fairly common model. We've visited all the stores in Tokyo that stock it, but none of the employees recalls seeing Yashima. These days, of course, you can buy anything online, so he may have gotten it that way."

"Kaori Nakahara told us that she'd never seen the knife before," said Matsumiya.

Sakagami snorted contemptuously. "What, and you believe her?"

"We need confirmation on this point," Ishigaki said. "Things will get complicated if Yashima regains consciousness and claims that the knife was the victim's, not his. We need to get our hands on objective evidence that proves the knife belongs to Yashima, and we need to do so pronto. You handle that, Sakagami."

"Yes, sir."

Ishigaki looked at his watch.

"Whether we like it or not, we're just going to have to wait for Yashima to come around. Let's knock off for the day. Everyone, go home and get a decent night's sleep."

"Yes, sir," Ishigaki's men chorused enthusiastically.

As Matsumiya was preparing to leave, Kaga began looking through the file containing photographs of the evidence. He seemed to find the contents of Takeaki Aoyagi's briefcase particularly intriguing.

"Come across something interesting?" Matsumiya asked.

Kaga jabbed a finger at one of the pictures. It was of the eyeglasses case. Made of cloth, the case was decorated with traditional comic masks of a man and a woman along with some hiragana lettering.

"What's so special about that?"

Without replying, Kaga reached for his phone and made a call.

"Hello? This is Inspector Kaga of the Nihonbashi police . . . Yes, that's right . . . It certainly has been a while. I've actually got something I want to ask you. I was wondering if I could come around . . . Oh no, it's nothing terribly important. I just need you to confirm something for me . . . Oh, really? Thanks very much. Appreciate it." After ending the call, Kaga slipped the photo of the eyeglasses case out of the file and stood up.

Matsumiya hastily got to his feet. "Where are you off to?"

"Just checking up on something. The chances are it's not connected with the case. Probably not worth your while tagging along."

"No, I'm coming with you. 'The more fool's errands you go on, the more cases you solve.'"

Kaga grinned wryly.

"That's a saying I've heard before. You really like it, huh?" Matsumiya asked.

"Yeah, well, you know."

You're the man's son. You should be the one who quotes his one-liners, not me, Matsumiya thought as he followed Kaga out of the room.

Kaga hailed a cab in front of the police station. "Amazaké Alley," he said to the driver. "Sorry it's so close by."

"Amazaké Alley? Why do you want to go there?" Matsumiya asked.

"You'll see when we get there," Kaga said, turning to look out the window.

Matsumiya felt the urge to get back at his cousin.

"That reminds me, how're things going with the service for the second anniversary of your father's death? Don't tell me you've forgotten?"

Kaga turned to face his cousin. He looked thoroughly fed up.

"No. I'm going to hold the service. Mainly because you and your mother won't stop going on about it. I saw Ms. Kanamori yesterday, and she's going to help me organize things. She and I were in the middle of discussing it when I got called in for this case."

"I'm very glad to hear it. Mom was worried sick. She thought you couldn't care less."

"Personally, I don't see the point of memorial services."

"Because you're looking at it all wrong. It's not something you do just for yourself. You're not the only person in your father's family, Kyo. If you don't organize the service, then we don't get the chance to remember Uncle Takamasa."

"Okay, okay. I'm going to do it, so stop giving me a hard time." Kaga was waving an annoyed hand in front of his face.

The taxi turned onto Ningyocho Boulevard. Kaga instructed the driver to stop just before Amazaké Alley.

"It's a one-way street. We'll walk from here."

Kaga marched off down the alley and Matsumiya had to scuttle after him to catch up. Amazaké Alley was lined with small shops, most of which were already closed.

There was a palpable atmosphere of old Edo. The shop signs with ideograms for things like wicker baskets, shamisens, and wholesale tea weren't anywhere else in Tokyo.

It would be a thoroughly enjoyable place to visit in the daytime, Matsumiya thought.

"The rice crackers at this place are truly something special." Omakara, the rice cracker shop, had its metal shutter down.

"I envy you. Getting to hang around places like this."

"What can I say? One of the perks of the job."

There had been a murder at Kodenmacho not long after Kaga had been transferred to Nihonbashi. Although Matsumiya didn't know the full story, he'd heard that Kaga made a major contribution to solving it. Clearly, his cousin was making this district his own.

Up ahead, light was streaming through the door of a store. The *noren* half-curtain had been taken down. The sign said "Hozuki-ya" and the place seemed to specialize in handmade crafts.

"This is the place," said Kaga, pushing the door open.

"Well, hello there. How nice to see you. Been ages." A woman came to the front of the store, smiling broadly. Matsumiya put her in her fifties. She had a round face and eyes that slanted downward at a slight angle from her nose.

"Sorry to barge in so late like this," Kaga said.

"Don't worry. Not as if I'm run off my feet. Another crime?"

"Afraid so," Kaga replied.

The woman grimaced. "How horrid! When and how did the world become such a wicked place, eh?" she said as she turned to Matsumiya, who had never met her before, for confirmation. He managed a half hearted grunt.

"I'm here to see if you could have a look at this." Kaga showed the woman the photograph of the eyeglasses case.

She glanced at it, gave an emphatic nod, said, "Just wait a minute, will you?" and headed into the back. The shop was narrow, but it went back a long way. Woven fabric bags and pouches and little furry toys were all crammed together on the shelves. There were also some beautifully painted spinning tops along with other old-fashioned toys.

The woman came back. "Here you go," she said, holding out a cloth eyeglasses case. It was identical to the one in the photograph.

"So it did come from here. I knew I'd seen this pattern here more than once, so I thought, *Just maybe*."

"You were right. The pattern is quite unusual."

The woman explained that the pattern on the cloth was known as *jidai komon* and that, come to think of it, she had several other items in the shop decorated with it.

Kaga then showed her a second photograph. This time it was a head-and-shoulders shot of Takeaki Aoyagi.

"Oh, I remember this gentleman," she said, nodding her head up and down. "He's definitely been here."

"When was that?"

"Let's see . . ." Keeping hold of the photograph, she rolled her black eyes up toward the ceiling. "I'd say probably a month or so back. And the time before, it was definitely summer. I remember because it was swelteringly hot."

"Summer? So he was here more than once?"

"That's right. I never forget the face of a repeat customer," she said breezily as she handed the photograph back to Kaga.

"Did you talk to him?"

"Not so much. I gave him the usual spiel about the products in the store. You know, the same speech I gave you when you first came here. That one."

"Your impression of him?"

"Let me think. He seemed to enjoy hearing what I had to say as much as anybody else. Who knows, perhaps all along he was thinking: 'Why won't this old bat just shut up and leave me the heck alone!'" The woman laughed uproariously.

Kaga and Matsumiya said their farewells and left Hozuki-ya. Rather than retrace his steps, Kaga walked farther down Amazaké Alley. Realizing that his cousin must have something else on his agenda, Matsumiya kept his mouth shut and tagged along. Clearly, Kaga had been exploring the district's every nook and cranny since being posted there, hence his immediate association between the pattern on an eyeglasses case and one particular little local retailer. That must have been what prompted him to ask the family about Takeaki Aoyagi's links to Nihonbashi.

After crossing a wide road, they found themselves at the entrance of a long, narrow park decorated with a statue of Benkei, the warrior monk. Squeezed in between two roads, the park was more of an oversized median strip than anything else. Kaga went in. A meandering path with leafless trees on either side stretched into the distance.

Kaga stopped and dropped down onto a bench. Matsumiya remained on his feet and looked around.

"Is this where I think it is?"

"It's Hamacho Green Road," said Kaga. "The place where Fuyuki Yashima tried to hide."

"He made it all the way here?"

"It's not actually that far from the crime scene. Two kilometers at the most is my guess. Cross Edobashi Bridge, keep going straight, and you'll end up here. Yashima must have been on the lookout for somewhere he could lie low and ended up here." Kaga pointed up the path. "The exit at the other end of the park opens onto the road Yashima ran out into—straight into the arms of a passing truck."

Matsumiya nodded. He now understood how the different locations fitted together.

"I wonder what Aoyagi was doing around here," Kaga said. "I find it hard to believe that he was only here to shop. If anything, I imagine he probably dropped into the store while doing something else entirely. But what was his main reason for being here."

"The fact that he didn't mention it to his family is certainly suspicious, but does it actually have any connection to his murder?"

"No idea. There's also the fact that his camera didn't have a single photograph saved on it."

They left the park and headed back toward Amazaké Alley. A number of empty taxis drove past; Kaga didn't give them a second glance. On his right, Matsumiya spotted the signboard of Tamahide, a restaurant famous for its chicken and rice bowls. As they passed the restaurant, Matsumiya finally realized what Kaga was doing: he was making his way to the crime scene.

The elevated metropolitan expressway, which goes over Nihonbashi Bridge, appeared in front of them. They soon reached Edobashi Bridge. Crossing the street and heading straight would take them to the north end of Nihonbashi Bridge. Instead, they went over Edobashi Bridge. Because *that* underpass was at the far end of it.

They were following the route that Yashima was likely to have taken for his escape, but in reverse.

The underpass had been reopened to the public. After they emerged from it, Kaga paused, and, his back to Edobashi Bridge, pointed to the south.

"The café Aoyagi went to was over that way, right?"

"That's right. One street up from Showa Boulevard."

Kaga just stood there, tilting his head to one side in puzzlement.

"Does that matter?" Matsumiya asked.

"I'm just wondering where on earth Aoyagi was heading. If he was planning to go home, there's an entrance to Nihonbashi Station right there beside the café. He had no reason to go through this passage."

Matsumiya looked along Showa Boulevard, then turned to look back at Edobashi Bridge. Kaga was right.

"Maybe Yashima lured him down here. If he was planning to stab him, then this underpass was about the only suitable place."

"Yes, but what would he say to get him to come down here? 'Fancy a stroll around the neighborhood?'"

"I . . . I don't know."

Kaga resumed walking. Now he was heading in the direction of Nihonbashi Bridge. Down the same street that Takeaki Aoyagi had walked, fighting the agony of a stab wound.

"I wasn't expecting to have to walk quite so much," Matsumiya said.

"You don't have to stick around."

"That's not what I meant and you know it."

Kaga came to an abrupt halt and directed a stern look at Matsumiya.

"I'll only say this once. If Fuyuki Yashima doesn't regain consciousness, then I'm prepared to walk one hundred times as far as this. If you don't like it, have Ishigaki and Kobayashi assign you a different partner."

"You're overreacting," shot back Matsumiya. He was marching off when his cell phone began vibrating in the inside pocket of his jacket. He pulled it out to see who was calling. It was Kobayashi, their squad leader.

"On your way back home?" Kobayashi asked.

"No, we're in the immediate vicinity of the crime scene."

"Perfect. I want you to go to the hospital. The one Yashima's in."

"Why? Has he regained consciousness?"

"No such luck. It's his girlfriend. She's collapsed."

"Kaori Nakahara?"

"They say it's nothing serious, just anemia. Anyway, the hospital has some news for us. I'm heading over there now, but I'd like you to join me for the meeting."

"Yes, sir. I'm on my way."

Matsumiya ended the call and explained the situation to Kaga.

"Do you want me to come with you?"

"No, Kyo, you're better off going home and getting some rest. You're the one who's planning to walk a hundred times as far, starting tomorrow." Matsumiya raised his hand and hailed an approaching taxi as he said this.

When Matsumiya reached the hospital, he found Kobayashi in conversation with a uniformed policeman. He directed the two men to a consulting room where a man in a white lab coat was sitting. It was a different doctor from the one who had explained Fuyuki Yashima's condition to them that morning.

"How's Ms. Nakahara doing," Matsumiya asked.

"We've put her in an empty room to recuperate. It was a shock to hear she'd collapsed in the waiting area," the doctor said. "She hasn't slept at all since last night, apparently. I understand that she wants to be with her boyfriend, but it's a surefire route to total exhaustion. We're going to have to send her home." The doctor lowered his voice. "In fact, she's got a condition of her own. She's pregnant."

Matsumiya's eyes widened. "Are you sure?"

"I was worried she might have hit her head when she fell so I recommended her to get x-rayed. She was violently opposed to the idea and refused outright. That was when she told me. Apparently, she's in her third month."

Matsumiya and Kobayashi exchanged a look. They weren't sure how to deal with this development.

"Since there are privacy issues at stake, it's not the sort of thing I would normally reveal to a third party. Given the situation, though, withholding the information didn't seem the smartest thing to do. I discussed the matter with the hospital director, and we made a joint decision to inform the police. I also told Ms. Nakahara what we were going to do," said the doctor, choosing his words with care.

"Can we have a word with her?" Kobayashi asked.

"That should be all right. She's okay to get up now. I'd be grateful if you could persuade her to go home."

Kobayashi said nothing and pondered for a moment. "Let's go see her," he said to Matsumiya.

"What about Yashima? Any change in his condition?" Matsumiya asked the doctor.

"The doctor in charge thinks he's out of the danger zone, but it's still very much touch and go."

"Any idea when he might come to?"

"I can't answer that," came the brusque reply.

The doctor led them to the room where Kaori was. He went in alone, leaving them to wait in the corridor. He re-emerged a few minutes later.

"She's made a good recovery. There's nothing to worry about here."

Matsumiya and Kobayashi stepped past the doctor and into the room. Kaori Nakahara was sitting on the side of the bed. Her head was slumping forward—possibly the result of the treatment—but her face was a far healthier color than that morning.

"The doctor's briefed us on the situation," Matsumiya said. "You've had a tough time of it. We're glad the baby wasn't harmed."

Kaori nodded her head feebly. Her lips remained clamped shut.

"This morning when we asked you if there'd been any major changes in your life recently, you said no. Why did you conceal the fact that you were pregnant?"

She didn't reply. She clasped her hands on her lap and started rubbing one against the other.

"Your boyfriend . . . I assume he knows?" asked Kobayashi, speaking gently.

Kaori stiffened convulsively, then gave a small nod.

"You aren't yet married. Are you planning to file your marriage papers?"

She stuck out the tip of her tongue and ran it over her lips. "We're going to do that," she said. "I told Fuyuki we should do it before the baby arrives."

"Practically speaking, though, life isn't easy for you, is it?

For example, we've heard that your boyfriend is struggling to find work."

"No, life's not . . . easy. Fuyuki's always saying that once he gets his health back, he'll be able to work as hard as ever."

"Oh, that's right. I heard he was in poor health a couple of months ago. What was the problem?"

"He . . . uhm . . . his neck."

"His neck?"

"He'd had this problem with a stiff neck for a while, then, two months ago, it suddenly got worse. He ended up losing all feeling and movement in his left hand."

"That's worrying. What caused it?"

"We don't know. Fuyuki won't go to the hospital. Recently, though, it was getting a lot better. That's why he was going to start looking for a job seriously. Then this . . ." She pressed her lips together. She was obviously battling to keep her feelings in check.

"Having a baby costs money. Happy-go-lucky really won't cut it." Kobayashi's tone was deliberately callous. "I wonder what your boyfriend was planning to do?"

Kaori took a deep breath and glowered at Kobayashi.

"Things will work out. Provided we stick together, we'll figure something out. That's how it's always been for us. We made a promise when we moved down here to Tokyo: that we'd stick together through even the toughest times."

Which is why Fuyuki Yashima would never kill anyone for money—that was what her defiant eyes seemed to be saying. Kobayashi nodded in silence, anxious not to rile her further.

"Listen, we really think you'd be better off at home,"

Matsumiya said. "Doing what you're doing isn't good for your health. Or for your unborn baby either. I'll take you home."

"I don't want to be a bother."

"One of our duties is to escort witnesses we've kept late back home," Kobayashi said. "Besides, staying here's not going to help your boyfriend get better."

Harsh though the remark was, it was also true. Kaori must have known that, because she nodded submissively.

Outside the hospital, Matsumiya wished Kobayashi good night. He was going to see Kaori home. The two of them climbed into a taxi.

For a while, neither of them said anything. Eventually, Kaori summoned up the courage to speak. "I heard that the man who died managed to walk all the way to Nihonbashi Bridge—and that he had a knife stuck in his chest the whole time."

"That's right."

"Nihonbashi Bridge is the famous one, right? The starting point of all the roads in Japan."

"'Kilometer zero' . . . is the phrase, I think. Yes, that's the one. Why do you ask?"

Kaori took several shallow breaths, then peered sideways down at the floor.

"That's where we got out when we hitchhiked to Tokyo."

"You hitchhiked here? When was this?"

There must have been something comical about Matsumiya's surprise. Kaori smiled.

"Funny, isn't it? I mean, *no one* hitchhikes in the twenty-first century anymore! We didn't have any money, so we couldn't think of anything else to do. Luckily, there are some kind people out there, so we managed to get a lift—several, in fact. When the people who picked us up asked us where in Tokyo we wanted to go, we always gave them the same answer: 'The place where this road ends.' The last fellow who gave us a lift, a truck driver, he dropped us off at one end of Nihonbashi Bridge. We stood on the bridge and cheered, 'Yatta!'" She took a handkerchief out of her bag and pressed it beneath her eyes. "Sorry."

Not quite sure what to say, Matsumiya turned and looked straight ahead.

9

There was a team meeting first thing in the morning. The investigators gathered around Ishigaki and one after another made their reports. Much of what they said didn't come as news to Matsumiya.

When it was Matsumiya's turn, he got to his feet and gave an account of what they'd found out the day before. He chose not to mention Takeaki Aoyagi having made a purchase at Hozuki-ya. Kaga had advised him to keep it under wraps for the time being, since they didn't yet know whether it had any connection to the case.

When Matsumiya announced the news of Kaori Nakahara's pregnancy, a frisson ran through the room. "Kids today—got no money but still can't wait to make babies," grumbled an old detective sitting nearby.

The main meeting was followed by a smaller one just

for the top people from Forensics. Matsumiya and Kaga were sent to the Kaneseki Metals factory.

As they stepped out onto the street, Kaga spoke in a rather formal tone. "Detective Matsumiya, I don't see much point in your taking a detective from the Nihonbashi police along to make inquiries at the factory in Kunitachi, so I will let you handle that alone."

"What are you going to do, Kyo . . . I mean, Kaga?"

"Like I said yesterday, I think I'll do a bit of walking around."

"What? Go back to Amazaké Alley?"

"Not just there. A wider area. I can't stop thinking about why Aoyagi was in that neighborhood on the night of the crime." Kaga fixed his eyes on Matsumiya and grinned.

"I think you're just about capable of conducting an interview by yourself."

Matsumiya scowled at his cousin.

"I've got one condition. Report anything you find to me. Whether relevant to the case or not."

Kaga nodded, his face serious again. "Of course. That's a promise."

"Fine, then. I'll call after I'm done with my inquiries at Kaneseki Metals."

"Roger that." Kaga turned smartly on his heel and strode off. He clearly wasn't going to take a taxi.

It looked as though Kaga meant to check if Takeaki Aoyagi had been spotted at any other shops in the area. Even though part of him wanted to make the rounds with his cousin, he thought it best to leave him to it.

Matsumiya caught a train at Tokyo Station. The journey took almost an hour. From the station, he caught a cab to the Kunitachi plant.

On the way, he was struck by the number of vacant lots. There were only a few private houses; mostly, it was small factories, warehouses, and other industrial buildings. Here and there, there were enormous blocks of public housing arranged in orderly rows.

They approached a building with a fence around it. The taxi stopped in front of the gate emblazoned with the words "Kaneseki Metals Kunitachi Plant." As soon as Matsumiya climbed out of the cab, he heard the clang of machinery.

Upon giving his name at the guard booth, he was presented with a visitor's pass and instructed to make his way to the office.

He went in through the first-floor entrance. Somewhere between ten and twenty people were working at desks arranged in rows. The blue jackets they were all wearing had to be the factory uniform.

A short, middle-aged man came up to him and bowed politely. His name was Yamaoka. The guard must have informed him that the detective had arrived. His business card gave his job title as "Manager, 2nd Production Department."

"The head office was in touch. You're here about Fuyuki Yashima?" Yamaoka said.

"That's right. Fuyuki Yashima and Mr. Aoyagi too."

"Of course. Look, let me just call in the person with the most knowledge of the situation." Yamaoka briefly returned to his desk to make a couple of phone calls, then rejoined Matsumiya. "He won't be a minute. Will you follow me?"

Yamaoka led Matsumiya to a meeting area and a female employee brought in tea.

Yamaoka sipped his tea and sighed ostentatiously.

"Let me tell you, this was quite a shock. Who would ever have thought it? It's just too sad."

"Mr. Yamaoka, did you have much to do with Mr. Aoyagi?"

"Absolutely, I did. Back when Mr. Aoyagi was the manager of the plant, we saw each other almost every day. Even later on, he still came around on a pretty regular basis. He was the overall head of production. That made him a sort of supreme commander for everyone who works in the factory, myself included."

"His sudden death must make things difficult?"

Yamaoka enthusiastically concurred. "Difficult isn't the half of it. Mr. Aoyagi knew the factory floor better than anyone else. When something went wrong or we were unsure what to do, he was always our first port of call."

From the warmth in Yamaoka's voice, Matsumiya got the sense that Aoyagi's colleagues liked and trusted him.

A man dressed in work overalls came in through the gap in the partitions. He looked around forty, was sturdily built, and on the dark-skinned side. He removed his cap and gave a brisk nod of greeting.

"Thanks for coming." Yamaoka got to his feet. "This gentleman is a detective from the Tokyo Metropolitan Police."

Matsumiya also stood up. "The name's Matsumiya. I appreciate you taking the time to talk to me."

With his thick fingers, the man extracted a business card from the wallet he pulled out of the back pocket of his pants. According to the rather dog-eared card, his name was Onoda and he was team leader of Unit 1 in the 2nd Production Department.

"Yashima worked in Onoda's unit," explained Yamaoka once the three of them were all sitting down.

"What exactly do you do in this factory?" Matsumiya asked Onoda.

"We make metal components for the construction industry," Onoda replied. His voice was guttural and unclear. "I used Yashima to restock materials and transport completed components."

"What was he like as a worker?"

"What was he like?" murmured Onoda, cocking his head to one side. "Honestly, I don't know. He wasn't one of us and I barely spoke to him. I just told him what job to do—*and that was it.*"

"It's like that with a lot of the temp workers," broke in Yamaoka, eager to clarify things. "The temp agency instructs them not to do anything they haven't been told to do and never to talk any more than is strictly necessary. The whole arrangement is very businesslike, you might say."

"How about his attitude to work? Was Yashima a good worker?"

"Yes. Or rather . . ." Onoda scratched behind his ear and looked a little nonplussed. "I suppose I'd say he was just normal. It's like Mr. Yamaoka said, the guy did what he was told."

"Did he make any major screwups?"

"Uhm . . . No, he didn't make any serious mistakes."

Matsumiya consulted his notebook.

"As I understand it, Yashima was on a rolling three-month contract and was terminated after nine months here. What was the reason?"

Onoda stammered something incoherent and looked over at Yamaoka.

"It was just a simple matter of downsizing," Yamaoka replied. "We were producing less, so we reduced our worker numbers in proportion. It's that simple. Check our records and you'll see."

It was true. As far as they could tell from consulting the records at the head office, there was no evidence of unfair dismissal. Why, then, had Yashima grumbled to Kaori Nakahara?

Matsumiya looked at the two men's faces.

"What are your personal views on the incident? I should add that we don't yet know for sure that Fuyuki Yashima is the culprit."

Onoda said nothing and looked at the floor. Once again it was Yamaoka who did the talking.

"The whole manufacturing sector is having a hard time of it right now. I get how these contract workers must feel, but still, there's no way that having your contract terminated justifies stabbing one of our full-time employees."

"Assuming that Yashima was the attacker, can you think of any motive other than the termination of his contract?"

"Nah." Yamaoka cocked his head to one side. "I mean, we just don't know what the temp workers think about things. We have next to nothing to do with them."

This was what Matsumiya had been expecting. Neither of them wanted to get dragged into the case. He shut his notebook. "Can you show me around the factory? The place where Yashima actually worked?"

Yamaoka and Onoda both looked disconcerted.

"I suppose we can, but things have changed. The products we're making now are different," Yamaoka explained.

"That's not a problem," said Matsumiya, getting to his feet.

He followed the two men as they led the way to the factory. On the way out of the office, someone handed him a hard hat.

"If something happens to you, Detective, it's our responsibility," said Yamaoka, grave-faced.

The unremitting din of machinery came from the factory. As soon as they stepped inside, the same noise echoed off the walls and the roof and assaulted their eardrums at several times the volume. Along with motors and machine presses, there was also the hiss of compressed air being released at a high velocity.

The factory contained lines of machine tools with workers performing their tasks in the spaces between. There was also an assembly line with a conveyor belt. A forklift carrying a load with wooden pallets drove past them down the narrow walkway.

Yamaoka and Onoda came to a halt in front of an assembly line for small metal components. The workers stood, faces turned toward the conveyor belt, executing their allotted tasks in solemn silence.

"This is where Yashima worked," said Yamaoka, shouting into Matsumiya's ear.

Matsumiya nodded as he watched the movements of the workers. The components were fed to them in an endless stream and their hands were in perpetual motion. They were placed at intervals from one another, so any sort of chitchat was impossible.

Talk about cogs in the machine, Matsumiya thought.

The worker closest to them suddenly jerked away from the conveyer belt. There was a look of alarm on his face. Now he was crouching on the ground scrabbling for something.

"Oi!" Onoda bellowed. The worker turned toward them. His eyes widened in alarm behind his safety goggles. A moment later, he pressed a nearby red button. The conveyor belt juddered to a stop with the sound of compressed air escaping. The worker looked at Onoda and Yamaoka and ducked his head apologetically.

"What's the problem?" Matsumiya asked.

"Oh, it's nothing," Yamaoka said. "Is there anything else you'd like to see?"

"Let me think." A chime sounded inside the factory before Matsumiya could answer. One after another, the machines fell silent and the workers began to drift away from their stations.

"It's lunch break," Yamaoka said. Matsumiya looked at his watch. It was noon.

"Perfect timing for me. I want to speak to anyone who worked directly with Yashima."

"What!" Yamaoka's face wore a look of obvious displeasure.

"I don't think he was particularly chummy with any of his workmates." Onoda looked equally glum.

"That's okay. I'd really appreciate it."

Matsumiya ducked his head. Yamaoka grimaced and sighed.

The workers were about to start their lunch in one corner of the factory that was kitted out with a few old office tables and steel pipe chairs. Most of them had brought in lunch boxes or convenience-store sandwiches.

After introducing himself, Matsumiya said, "Feel free to eat while you listen to what I have to say." None of them touched their food.

Matsumiya threw out a series of questions. Was anyone there friendly with Yashima? Had Yashima ever made any comments about the company or about Mr. Aoyagi in particular? Had anything out of the ordinary happened while Yashima was working there?

Not one of his questions elicited a response. The workers were so silent and stone-faced that he started wondering if they could even hear him. All sitting there in the same posture in complete silence with their food in front of them, they reminded him of well-trained dogs who had been given the command to wait.

"See. I told you so," Yamaoka said beside him. "They don't really get to know one another, so there's not much point in asking them anything."

Matsumiya said nothing but scanned the crowd of workers a second time. While most of them were looking firmly at the floor, there was one who was willing to meet Matsumiya's eye. A towel draped around his neck, and probably in his mid-twenties, Matsumiya reckoned. After an instant, he too looked away.

"Okay," Matsumiya said to his two chaperones. "If someone does happen to remember anything, I'd be grateful if you could contact me."

"Yes, certainly. I'm sorry we couldn't be more helpful." Relief was written all over Yamaoka's face.

"Oh, darn it!" Matsumiya came to an abrupt stop as soon as they were out of the factory building.

"Is something wrong?" Yamaoka asked warily.

"I put my notebook down on a shelf when you were showing me the assembly line, then forgot all about it. I'll just nip back in and get it."

"Do you remember where it is?"

"Sure I do. I'll swing by your office on my way out," Matsumiya said. He darted back into the factory without waiting for their response.

What he had said about forgetting his notebook was, of course, a lie. He was thinking about the young man with the towel draped around his neck. He wanted to get his phone number. From the look in his eyes, it was clear that he had something he wanted to say.

At that moment, the young man appeared at the far end of the walkway. Spotting Matsumiya, he glanced furtively around, then darted toward him.

"Something you want to tell me?" Matsumiya asked.

The young man nodded. "Go out of the compound, turn right, and there's a parking lot after about thirty meters. Wait there. I'll be along soon."

"Got it. Your name?"

"I'll tell you later," the young man said, speaking rapidly. He wiped his mouth with the towel and sped off.

Matsumiya left the factory building and dropped in at the office. Yamaoka was in conversation with a square-faced man in a brown suit. He came over to Matsumiya, bringing the other man with him.

"Let me introduce you. This is the factory manager."

"I'm Kotake," said the square-faced man, proffering his business card. It was printed with the name Yoshinobu Kotake.

"Mr. Aoyagi was good to me ever since I first joined the firm. I'm close to the whole family. I was at their house only this morning. What's happened really is too sad," Kotake said, looking downcast. He might have been sincere, but the speech came off as theatrical.

"Did you know Yashima, a contract worker here?"

"No. Why—" Kotake scowled and planted his hands on his hips. "I have no recollection of him. We have quite a large workforce here and there's a lot of turnover among the contract workers. It's impossible to keep track of them all."

"As the factory manager, Kotake is responsible for keeping the show on the road, you see," chimed in Yamaoka. Glancing at him, Matsumiya wondered if Yamaoka had appointed himself as Kotake's full-time bootlicker.

He thanked them and left the office. Passing through

the main gate, he turned right and strolled over to the metered parking lot. The young man from the factory wasn't yet there. Since there was a vending machine, Matsumiya bought himself a Coke.

He had just finished the can when the young man appeared. The towel was now wrapped around his head.

"Fancy a drink?" Matsumiya pointed at the vending machine.

"No. I've got to get right back," the young man said. He paused a moment. "Actually, I'd be happy if you got me one, provided I don't have to drink it here and now."

It took Matsumiya a moment to grasp exactly what the young man meant, but the slightly embarrassed look on his face helped him figure it out. He gave a wry smile and took out his wallet. "What would you like?"

"I'll have a green tea."

The green tea was available in 350 ml and 500 ml bottles. Matsumiya bought one of the bigger bottles, which he handed to the young man, who said, "Thanks. That's a lifesaver." *Life can't be easy for him,* Matsumiya thought.

There was a bench in one corner of the parking lot. The two men sat down, side by side. The young man's name was Yokota, he said.

"I started working here about the same time as Yashima. We used to talk to each other a lot. Yamaoka, the department manager, told you that we don't get to know one another, but that's not true. For contract workers like us, life's tough and we share information."

"But no one said a word back there."

Yokota shrugged.

"They don't want to attract the attention of management. They'll fire you just like that."

"Did Yashima do something that attracted attention?"

"It wasn't like that. He was in an accident."

"In an accident? You mean he caused an accident?"

Yokota nodded. "Know what an interlock is?"

"Interlock? No, never heard of it."

"It's a kind of safety device. When you're on the production line, accidentally touching a machine that's in operation can be dangerous, okay? So all the machines are protected with a cover guard. Lift up the cover guard and the machine automatically switches itself off. That's what an interlock does."

"Oh, I get it. Sounds necessary."

"Yeah—but loads of the interlocks at our place have been disabled."

"Disabled?"

"Switched off. It's hard to get any work done if the machines are always switching themselves off at the slightest little thing. That's doubly true on a production line where multiple machines are connected to one another. Stop one of them and all the other operations are forced to halt. Imagine that a component gets stuck inside a machine. It's our job to stick our hand in while it's still running and pull the thing out."

"Seriously? Isn't that dangerous?"

"It *is* dangerous. We may think it's wrong, but temp workers like me are in no position to object. If someone refuses to follow the company's unwritten rules, we'll be fired. We're between a rock and a hard place."

Matsumiya recalled what he had seen in the factory. The worker who was crouching down and was about to do something until Onoda yelled at him and he pressed the machine's kill switch. Maybe that had been a case of a disabled interlock. It was only when the worker realized an outsider was there that he had hurriedly shut the machine down.

"Is there a link to Yashima's accident?"

"More than a link. It's one hundred percent." Yokota gave the bottle of tea a little shake. "You're supposed to turn the machines off whenever you restock them with materials. But we have this cheat: what we do is climb up onto a nearby work surface, straddle the conveyor belt while it's still moving, and restock the machine that way."

Matsumiya frowned.

"And that's how the accident occurred?"

"Yes. The hem of Yashima's trousers got caught in the conveyor belt and he was dragged down onto the floor. I was right there. I saw the whole thing."

"Was he hurt?"

"No visible injuries, but he must have hit his head pretty hard, because he didn't move for a while. I reckon he was out for five minutes. Even after coming around, he was still woozy. Onoda and Yamaoka came rushing over, had a word with him, and sent him home early. He was off for, oh, about a week after that. Later, when I asked, he said his neck hurt so bad he could hardly move it."

"Did he go to the hospital?"

Yokota smiled sardonically and shook his head. "Apparently not."

"Why?"

"Too much hassle, he said. The temp agency told him he was welcome to go to the hospital, but that if he did, they didn't want him saying anything about an accident at work. They wanted him to come up with some other story. They also told him not to file a workplace accident report."

"How come?"

"It happens all the time. Kaneseki Metals puts pressure on the temp agency. If someone files an accident report, the factory will be inspected and the inspectors will discover that the interlocks are disabled, right? Because accidents here are never treated as workplace accidents, people have to pay out of their own pocket if they do go to the hospital. It's no wonder everyone just thinks, 'Why bother?'"

"I'm guessing that's the reason Yashima's contract wasn't renewed. They thought that he might start complaining, which would lead to trouble." Yokota then asked: "What's the time?"

Matsumiya consulted his watch. "Nearly twelve forty."

"Uh-oh," said Yokota. He got to his feet. "I have to go. Thanks for this." He held up the plastic bottle.

Matsumiya also got up. "Thank you for talking to me."

"I knew that I had to tell someone about this as soon as I heard about Yashima stabbing the boss. I've got a pretty good idea how he felt myself."

"Thanks. It was helpful."

"Be seeing you," said Yokota and he dashed off. Matsumiya watched him until he was out of sight then set off himself.

He phoned Kaga once he was back at Tokyo Station.

"How did you get on? Did your visit to the Kunitachi factory produce any results?" Kaga asked.

"I learned some interesting things. How about you?"

"Not bad. I found another place that Takeaki Aoyagi used to go."

"Seriously? What kind of place?"

"An old-fashioned coffeehouse. I'm actually having a coffee there right now."

"Well, I'll come and join you. Give me the name and address."

The coffeehouse was on Amazaké Alley and Matsumiya was struck by the brick façade and wood-framed windows. To him, it looked like something from the reign of Emperor Showa, but the signboard included the date 1919, putting it in the reign of the previous emperor.

Kaga was at a table by the window. Matsumiya ordered a coffee and sat down.

"I like the atmosphere," he said, running an eye over the place. As well as a few businessman types, there were some old folks, presumably locals.

"It's a famous place. It's in all the guidebooks," Kaga said. "One of the waitstaff told me that Takeaki Aoyagi was last here about two weeks ago. Used to come regularly, about once a month or so. They're not sure when he first started coming, but reckon it was probably this summer."

"Further proof that Aoyagi was a frequent visitor to this part of the world. What on earth was he up to?"

"I don't know. Could have been something he did for fun."

"For fun?"

"The person here told me that Aoyagi would often consult a map as he drank his coffee. A map of the neighborhood. This is a nice district for a stroll. Something must have led him to discover the charm of the place."

"That's plausible. But Aoyagi's work was in Shinjuku and he lived out in Meguro. As a place to casually drop in on, it's rather out of his way."

Matsumiya's coffee arrived. The fragrant aroma made his nostrils quiver. He took a sip, without adding milk or sugar. The perfectly balanced bitterness stimulated every cell in his body. "God, that's good," he burst out.

"You said you'd learned something interesting," Kaga said, after ordering a second cup of coffee for himself.

"It was well worth going. I got an insight into the background of the crime." Matsumiya looked around to check that no one nearby was listening, then leaned over the table.

With perfect timing, Kaga's coffee was brought to the table just as Matsumiya was winding up his account. Kaga added milk, slowly stirred it in, and lifted the cup to his lips. Matsumiya recognized the expression on his face: he was thinking.

"A classic workplace accident cover-up . . . ," Kaga murmured as he put his cup back down. "A lot of companies are at it these days."

"According to Kaori Nakahara, Yashima lost the feeling in his left hand because of something that had happened to his neck. If that was one of the long-term effects of his accident at the factory, then he'd have every reason to bear a grudge against Kaneseki Metals. And Takeaki Aoyagi was the person in overall charge of the factory then. My guess is that Yashima was meeting with Aoyagi to get his old job back in return for not exposing the factory. When their negotiations broke down, Yashima lost his temper and stabbed the other man . . . Or is that too far-fetched?"

"Sounds believable enough to me. There is one snag, though."

"That he had a knife with him? That was bugging me too."

"There's the knife, yes, but this is what worries me." Kaga held up his coffee cup.

"Coffee's worrying you?"

"In the café, Aoyagi purchased drinks for two. In the scenario you've just described, Yashima was the initiator, while Aoyagi had no motivation to talk to Yashima. Wouldn't you normally expect the person who'd initiated the meeting to be the one who pays for the drinks?"

It was an ingenious point, but Matsumiya didn't take long to think of an objection.

"Of the two, Aoyagi was the one at a disadvantage. I can see him paying for the drinks in an effort to ingratiate himself with Yashima."

"That would mean the topic of the workplace accident would have to have been broached already."

"You're right. It's hard to believe that Aoyagi would have agreed to go to a café with Yashima without knowing what it was all about in advance."

"Let's try to imagine Aoyagi's state of mind. A young man has suddenly confronted him with the issue of a workplace accident cover-up. My guess is that he would be pretty flustered and uncomfortable. Thoughts?"

"I agree. It wouldn't be comfortable for him."

"And yet Aoyagi hands a two-thousand-yen note to the server while casually commenting on how rare they are. Is that really the behavior of a man who's under pressure?"

No, it definitely isn't, Matsumiya thought with a start. This time he couldn't think of an objection.

"Takes all sorts to make a world. It's hard to generalize about what's odd and what's not." Kaga sipped his coffee with evident pleasure before putting the cup back down. "Either way, you got some good info from your Kunitachi visit. You should get straight back to the incident room and give them an update."

"What are you going to do, Kyo? Wander around the neighborhood some more?"

"No, there's a place I need to go." Kaga checked the time on his watch. "A junior high school. The one Aoyagi's son graduated from—Shubunkan Junior High, I think it is."

"Ah." Matsumiya nodded.

"It was one of the numbers called on Aoyagi's phone."

"Do you seriously think that's connected with the incident? It was quite a few days before."

"It may well have no connection. That doesn't mean I

shouldn't follow it up. We don't need highfliers from the Homicide Division like you getting involved in banal inquiries like this. I'll deal with it." Kaga drained the last of his coffee and got to his feet.

10

In the portrait displayed on the family altar, Takeaki Aoyagi was wearing his golfing clothes and had a smile on his face. The family had chosen it after a discussion because they thought "he looks happiest in this one." In actuality, though, Takeaki wasn't that enthusiastic a golfer.

The wake started at six p.m. As the Buddhist priest chanted the sutra, the mourners lined up to offer incense, one after another.

The body had been returned to the family sooner than expected and they had been very busy since early in the morning. The undertaker from the firm that Kotake, his coworker, had found came to the house. Fumiko, as usual, had been incapable of making up her mind about anything. Things had got only worse when Kotake, who was helping out, had to leave midmorning when the news came that a detective had shown up at the plant. After that, every decision Fumiko made was in line with the advice of the sly-looking, bespectacled undertaker. While Yuto had no idea what a funeral would normally cost, as he listened in, he couldn't help feeling that his mother was being taken for a ride.

Once the meeting was finished and the undertaker got down to work, Yuto had to admit that he was a true professional. All the different tasks proceeded with assembly-line efficiency, and by the time Yuto and the rest of the family had changed and taken themselves to the funeral hall, the body was already in the coffin. The body was beautifully laid out and there was no visible evidence of the autopsy. Yuto even thought that his face had a better color than when they'd last seen him in the hospital.

Relatives and a number of Takeaki's work colleagues were there to help with various tasks. Listening to their discussions, Yuto realized that determining who gets to offer incense first at a funeral was a far more difficult question than he'd thought.

Kotake reappeared in the late afternoon. He put his subordinates to work, and they handled reception and gift duties briskly and efficiently. Fumiko followed the instructions of the undertaking staff to the letter. As he watched his mother, Yuto remembered having read somewhere that the whole point of funerals was to keep the family so busy they wouldn't have the time to grieve.

Yuto spotted various of his high school friends, including Tatsuya Sugino, among the mourners. He had sent a text to Sanada and Sugino, letting them know about the wake.

When they shuffled past him to offer incense, Yuto bowed at them both, feeling a surge of genuine gratitude.

Some of his junior high school friends had also shown up. Most of them were friends from the swim team. Standing behind them in line was Itokawa, who was the coach. As usual his hair, prematurely flecked with gray, was cropped short. He still looked as lean and muscular as when Yuto and his friends had graduated.

After the offering of the incense was completed, Fumiko thanked everyone for coming, bringing the wake to an end. The relatives and Takeaki's colleagues moved to the next-door room where drinks and a simple meal had been laid out for them. Yuto was on his way there when he bumped into Itokawa and his old swim team buddies in the corridor. Sugino was with them too.

"You doing okay, Ao? Are you eating enough?" Sugino asked, rushing up to him. Something about the expression on his face made him look surprisingly mature.

"Don't worry about me. I'm fine. Just got to get on with it. Nothing I can do will bring the dead back to life."

"What's happened to that guy? Is he still in a coma?"

Yuto guessed he meant Yashima.

"Think so. The police aren't telling us anything."

"No? What's his status? Is he going to regain consciousness?"

"I've no idea. Honestly, they don't tell us anything."

The other boys from the swim team came over and offered him their condolences. Yuto thanked them all again.

His friend Kurosawa pulled a face.

"It's too bad. The attacker still being unconscious like that. Him getting run over serves him right, but we don't want him to die on us. When it comes to payback, dying's no good."

"I don't care so much about revenge, but I'd like to hear what he's got to say for himself. Like why did he target my dad. I still can't figure that out."

"Right. That's what we wondered. Why your dad of all people? The world's full of middle-aged men no one would miss."

Kurosawa's indignation sounded heartfelt. *Good to have friends at a time like this,* thought Yuto, responding to the other boy's anger.

"Bad luck, Aoyagi." Itokawa came up to him.

"Thanks for coming, sir." Yuto bowed to his favorite junior high school teacher.

"I was horrified when Sugino gave me the news. I'm so sorry for you. You've got to keep your chin up. We're all here for you. Any problem you have, just let us know. We'll all do whatever we can."

Itokawa spoke with obvious sincerity. Back when Yuto was on the swim team, the coach had always had their backs, no matter what.

"Thank you, sir," he repeated.

Sugino aside, Yuto hadn't seen his old swim team buddies in ages. There had been ten boys from Yuto's year on the team and most of them had shown up. He wanted to hang out and catch up with them, but tonight wasn't the time. Instead, he just escorted them to the door of the funeral hall.

Yuto's friends went home, but Itokawa, the teacher, stayed behind. He shot Yuto a glance. "Could I have a word with you?" he asked. Yuto had a strange, queasy feeling as he agreed.

They moved to a corner of the lobby and sat down side by side on a couch there.

"How had you been getting along with your father lately? Did you two talk?"

"Talk?"

"Uh-huh. When you were at junior high, you told me that you almost never saw your dad."

"That's because he was working in a factory out in Kunitachi. Some days he didn't even make it back home."

"I'm asking what things were like *recently*. Have you two talked?"

Yuto said nothing. He didn't know how to reply. Why on earth should Itokawa be asking him such a question?

"Your father called the school a few days ago. Said he wanted to talk to me about you."

"Ah . . . Well, now you mention it . . ."

"What?"

"The detective who came by the house yesterday said the same thing: that the Shubunkan Junior High School number was among the recent calls on Dad's cell phone."

Itokawa nodded.

"That's what they told me too. A detective from the Nihonbashi police came today to speak to me."

"Really?"

"'I'm worried. My son and I haven't been getting on recently.' That's what your father said to me."

"Dad said that?"

"Your father believed that I knew you better than either your current high school teachers or your old homeroom teacher at junior high. That's why he wanted to talk to me. I guess I should be flattered."

Takeaki wasn't far off the mark, Yuto thought. None of his homeroom teachers had ever understood him—and he had never wanted them to.

"All he said was that he wanted to see me so we could discuss the matter. In the end, we never got that chance. That's why I can't get it out of my head. Did you and your father have a problem? Come on, Aoyagi, tell me. Perhaps it's too late to do anything, but if there's something there, why not make a clean breast of it?"

"No, it's not like that." Yuto shook his head and smiled. "It's really no big deal. My dad and me not getting along—it's hardly like it only started yesterday. There's no big secret what was behind it: my dad wasn't happy because my school grades were crap. And I didn't enjoy the way he threw that in my face every chance he got. That's all it was."

Itokawa nodded, grunted, and looked intently at Yuto. His piercing eyes transmitted a silent, menacing message: *I'll see right through any of your half-baked lies.*

Suddenly, all the intensity evaporated from Itokawa's gaze.

"Your father is no longer with us. Now it's up to you to

make the most of your life. I just wanted to let you know that your father was worried about you. Perhaps I shouldn't have said anything."

"No, sir. I appreciate it."

"Okay. Well, hang in there." Itokawa patted Yuto on the shoulder and headed for the exit. Yuto made his way to the room where the reception was already underway. Everyone was busy eating sushi and drinking beer.

Fumiko was flanked by Yuto's grandmother and one of his uncles, who were both saying comforting things to her. Haruka was at the same table. Yuto joined them.

"Things aren't going to be easy, Yuto, but you've got to be brave and soldier on. We're all there for you," his uncle said, pouring juice into Yuto's glass. "I know you're worried about your future, but we'll sort things out. There's no need to worry."

He must be talking about college. "Thank you," said Yuto, bowing to his uncle.

Kotake and a load of other people from his father's work came over to their table to express their grief. They vied with one another in their declarations of all that they owed to Takeaki. A guy called Yamaoka even claimed that he'd probably have quit his job long ago if Aoyagi hadn't been his boss.

The other mourners eventually went home, leaving only Yuto, Fumiko, and Haruka. The three of them were going to spend the night at the funeral home and had even brought along a change of clothes for that purpose.

When Haruka announced that she wanted to go and take another look at the altar, Yuto went with her. The coffin stood at the far end of the dark hall. In front of it, spiral coils of incense sent up smoke.

"I wasn't looking forward to this. I thought wakes and funerals were really boring, but everyone's been so sweet, I sort of enjoyed it—plus loads of my school friends came," Haruka said, looking up at Takeaki's portrait photograph. "It was good to hear what Dad's colleagues had to say about him. They really looked up to him."

"They can hardly bad-mouth him here, can they?"

"I'm not stupid. I can tell when people are being sincere." Haruka frowned. "I should have spent more time talking with Dad. He must have had all sorts of good points I knew nothing about."

Thanks for the speech, Miss Goody Two-Shoes. The words were on the tip of his tongue, but Yuto reined himself in. Maybe his sister had a point.

They were busy from first thing in the morning the next day. With the chief executive and board of directors of Takeaki's firm coming, there were twice as many mourners at the funeral as at the wake the day before. Sanada, Yuto's high school homeroom teacher, also showed up and encouraged him to hang in there. He saw people from the neighborhood he hadn't seen for ages. Even if their words of encouragement were no more than a formality, Yuto was still touched by their kindness.

After Fumiko had delivered her speech, it was time for the funeral procession. Yuto picked up the framed photograph of Takeaki and took his position at the head of the bearers. It was his uncles who carried the coffin.

Only the immediate family and relatives accompanied the coffin to the crematorium. When the coffin disappeared into the furnace, Yuto felt as though a load had been lifted off his heart. Now he could finally accept the reality of his father's death. *I've got to be strong,* he thought.

He wondered if Fumiko and Haruka felt the same sense of relief. As they stood around chatting with the other family members waiting for the cremation to end, their faces were untroubled, serene. Fumiko broke into tears from time to time, but she smiled often enough too.

After transferring Takeaki's cremated remains to an urn, they went back to the funeral hall to hold the *shonanoka* memorial service and the shojin otoshi banquet. Fumiko made yet another speech, thanking the mourners. "From today, we three will do our best to get on with our lives. I will take full responsibility for bringing up our children, and I look forward to receiving your help and support," she said by way of conclusion. She radiated dignity and strength. The wake and the funeral aren't just about helping the immediate family and the relatives let go of their grief, thought Yuto, they also provide spiritual succor.

The three of them said farewell to their relatives, and then it was time to go home. There were many things to be done, but the first order of business was getting an altar set up in the house. One of the undertakers would bring the necessary things around later.

Yuto was busy cramming things into his bag when he heard voices from down the corridor. One was Fumiko's; he didn't recognize the others.

He opened the door and peered out. Fumiko was standing there talking to a couple of youngish men. One had a camera hanging off his neck.

"I already told you. I don't know anything about it. You need to ask someone at the firm." Fumiko's voice had an edge to it.

"So, Mrs. Aoyagi, can I confirm that your husband never mentioned this matter to you?" asked the man without the camera.

"No, he didn't. I've already told you. I don't know anything about my husband's work."

"Right. How do you feel about what I just told you? Does it affect your feelings toward the killer?"

"I don't know . . . It's difficult when you spring questions on me. I'd like you to leave. Or I'll call the police."

"Fine. We're going. Please understand, though, that all we want is for the family to know the truth." So saying, the man darted a look at his companion and they moved off.

Fumiko pressed both hands to her temples as if she had a headache.

She sighed wearily when Yuto asked her what was going on.

"Those men were making weird claims. Did I know that the man who stabbed your father had been fired to cover up an accident at work? Did I know that he had suffered long-term effects from the accident? Stuff like that."

"What are they on about? What's that got to do with Dad?"

"They suggested that Dad was the person who ordered

the cover-up. And that that's why the young man hated him enough to stab him."

Yuto took a deep breath. Words were inadequate to express his anger.

A sense of unease was roiling his chest.

11

"The high school Yashima graduated from was notorious in Fukushima for being a wild place. Plenty of the students, even if they weren't in a gang, carried knives for self-defense. I spoke to someone at his orphanage. He assured me they would never let the kids in their care have anything so dangerous, but Yashima could easily have had one without the orphanage staff knowing."

Listening to the investigator make his report, Ishigaki looked less than pleased. He scratched the back of his head noisily, then cocked his chin.

"We've still got no proof that Yashima was the owner of the knife. How are we doing with tracing the purchasing route?"

Sakagami got to his feet. He looked even unhappier than Ishigaki.

"The knife used in the assault has been on the market for five years. If Yashima did acquire one, that means he must have done so *after* moving to Tokyo. I found a firm in Gifu Prefecture that sells this particular model online. They sent me a list of the people who've purchased one and Yashima's name wasn't on it. Of course, it's always possible that someone who bought the knife went on to resell it in an online auction—something which makes determining the path of the weapon that much harder."

Ishigaki frowned and stuck out his lower lip.

"Connecting Yashima to the knife is the best option we have. That way, we can wrap up the case, even if he never comes out of his coma."

As usual, the investigators who had come back from the field came up to Ishigaki to update him. It was a little after eight.

Matsumiya and Kaga had spent the whole day canvassing the area between Edobashi Bridge and Hamacho Green Road. Their plan was to pinpoint Yashima's escape route by gathering eyewitness statements. They hadn't managed to get so much as one. It was a district with plenty of people around at night, making the likelihood of anyone remembering him on the low side.

Their efforts, however, hadn't been wholly unrewarded. At the same time as looking for eyewitnesses who had seen Yashima, they had also been looking for places frequented by Takeaki Aoyagi. They had found one more: a soba noodle restaurant.

According to the member of the staff they spoke to, Aoyagi had been there at least twice. He couldn't recall precisely what Aoyagi had ordered, but he remembered him because he said something complimentary about the food. Since they had the opportunity, Matsumiya and Kaga decided to eat lunch there themselves. Matsumiya had cold soba noodles. They were nicely al dente while the broth was delicious with a real depth of flavor.

It was pretty clear that Aoyagi was a regular visitor to the Ningyocho area. But they still had no idea why.

Next, the investigator who had been sent to keep an eye on proceedings at the funeral hall launched into his report. He was still dressed in a charcoal-gray suit. He said nothing out of the ordinary had occurred.

It was the same with all the other investigators' reports. Nothing they said helped drive the investigation forward in any significant way.

"So Yashima's condition is the same as before? Frankly, I wish the fellow would stop sitting on the fence. He should either wake up or just damn die," said Ishigaki with a half sigh. It wasn't the most tactful comment, but Matsumiya secretly sympathized. The other investigators nodded without saying anything.

"What about Yashima's motive? Are we okay with the grudge notion?" Kobayashi asked.

"Seems plausible to me. That story Matsumiya dug up struck me as convincing. Efforts probably were made to cover up Yashima's accident. We'll need evidence, but that's something the professionals should be able to get their hands on. We can work with what they give us."

The professionals Ishigaki was referring to were the people at the Labor Standards Inspection Office. The previous day, Ishigaki had officially reported their suspicions that a workplace accident that had taken place at the Kunitachi plant of Kaneseki Metals had been covered up. The LSIO had assured them that the incident would be investigated as a top priority.

"Yashima's girlfriend was pregnant. He couldn't find a job. He felt desperate and so he exploited the cover-up as a means to blackmail the victim into giving him his old job back. Is that the idea?" Kobayashi murmured, looking up at the ceiling. "I don't know . . . It just seems a little too convenient to me. Besides, is covering up a workplace accident even a serious crime in the first place?"

"The punishment is a fine up to five hundred thousand yen," Matsumiya replied. He had looked into the matter the day before.

Kobayashi snorted.

"And Yashima really thought that he could scare someone with that? I guess we'll never know until we ask the guy."

"Exactly. When it comes to motive, talking to the man himself is the only option we have," Ishigaki said. "That makes the knife all the more crucial. Tomorrow, I want you all to stay focused on gathering witness statements and investigating the knife. Everybody got that?"

"Yes, sir," chorused Matsumiya and the other investigators. Matsumiya glanced over at his partner. Kaga was away from the group, seated at his desk, looking through the evidence file and checking things on his computer.

A moment later, Kaga sprang to his feet and shot out of the incident room. Alarmed, Matsumiya dashed out after him.

"Kaga!" he yelled down the passage. "Are you going straight home?"

Kaga shrugged and looked ambivalent. "What if I'm not?"

"Where's the planned detour?"

"It's not really a detour. I mean to grab some dinner en route."

"That's it? Really?"

"Well, there is an ulterior motive." Kaga scratched the side of his prominent nose.

"I thought as much. I'm coming with you."

The two men headed north after exiting the police station. They went down through the underpass and across Edobashi Bridge. Normally, they would have headed east at that point, but this time Kaga kept going north.

"Why are we going this way?"

"Just shut up and follow me, okay."

At the second street on the right, there was a shop specializing in traditional Japanese *washi* paper. It had some sort of little museum up on the second floor. Matsumiya was once again struck by the sheer number of old-established stores in the neighborhood.

They went a little farther down the street. On the left, there was a miniature shrine with a torii gate in front. Nihonbashi is littered with shrines.

Kaga stopped in front of a building. Matsumiya was surprised when he saw the signboard.

"Another noodle place?"

"If Aoyagi was a fan of soba noodles, there's nothing odd about him wanting to try different restaurants."

"Does that make it worth our while to come all the way here?"

"If you don't like it, you're free to leave."

The restaurant was called Kobaian. Kaga opened the door and went in. Matsumiya followed. About one-third of the tables in the spacious interior were occupied. Most of the customers were just having beer or sake. *They must round off the drinks with a bowl of noodles afterward,* Matsumiya thought.

The detectives were ushered to a corner table where they ordered beer and some nibbles. There was only one server, a woman who was bustling around, clearly very busy. It didn't look as though she would have the time to talk with them.

Their beer and appetizers were brought to the table. Kaga promptly reached for the bottle and filled up both their glasses. "Cheers." They clinked glasses and drank.

"So, Kyo, what do you think?"

"About what?"

"The case, of course. Do you buy the notion that Yashima's the killer and the motive's what Kobayashi said at the station just now? Seems the higher-ups are pretty keen for us to wrap the whole thing up neatly along those lines."

Kaga split his disposable wooden chopsticks and picked up some salted fish guts. "Ooh, that's good," he murmured, and took a swig of beer.

"It's not the job of people at the bottom to worry about the opinions of people at the top. Our job is to uncover the facts. When you clear your mind of preconceptions and stereotypes and simply focus on finding the facts, you occasionally unearth things you could never have imagined."

"You think the truth behind this crime could be something no one expects?"

"Who knows?" Kaga tilted his head to one side, then leaned across the table.

"You might not understand the situation, so let me make something clear. I also think that the likeliest solution is that Yashima is the culprit. The motive Squad Leader Kobayashi proposed seems plausible enough too. But even if we manage to prove all that, can we honestly claim to have solved the case? I don't think so. Unless we can find out why Aoyagi visited this district so regularly, then this case won't be closed, not for the family at least," Kaga said, then leaned back.

"But is that part of our job as detectives?" asked Matsumiya.

"Personally, I think it is. But I'm not going to force you to think the same."

Their food was brought to the table. "Looks delicious," said Kaga, his eyes sparkling. Matsumiya used his chopsticks to help himself to a piece of lotus root deep-fried with pollock roe. The taste and texture were in perfect balance.

"There's one thing that's bothering me," Kaga said. "Did I tell you what happened when I went to the junior high school yesterday?"

"The junior high of the victim's son? Come to think of it, no, you didn't. What was it? Shu . . ."

"Shubunkan Junior High School. I figured out who

Aoyagi wanted to speak to there. It was a teacher by the name of Itokawa, who's also the swim coach. Aoyagi's son was on the school swim team. The father hadn't been getting on with his son recently and he called to discuss the problem with Itokawa."

"Oh, I didn't know Aoyagi was worried about that," Matsumiya said, then drank the remaining beer in his glass.

Kaga refilled his glass. "Don't you think it's odd? Normally, if you were worried about your relationship with your kid, there's someone else you'd consult first."

"You mean the boy's homeroom teacher? Not necessarily. Coaches are important figures for kids who are seriously into sports."

Kaga made a dismissive gesture.

"I don't need you to tell me that. Besides, that's not what I'm getting at. I'm saying that normally the first person you'd talk to is the boy's mother—in other words, your own wife."

"Ah!" Matsumiya exclaimed. "I guess you would."

"The wife hasn't said a word about this to us. More than that, the impression I get from talking to Aoyagi's family is that he had no interest in them whatsoever. How to explain this inconsistency?"

Matsumiya stared off into space. "It's certainly odd."

"Why did Aoyagi suddenly get the urge to discuss his son with his old teacher a few days ago? And why didn't he mention it to his wife?"

"I see what you mean. Yuto . . . was that his name? How about asking him directly?"

"That's one way of going about it. Personally, I think it's

better to stand back for a while and see how things develop. If the boy knows something and he's deliberately keeping it secret, there's got to be a reason. If I confront him, he might clam up completely. He's at a difficult age."

How the hell would you know? Matsumiya wanted to sneer, until he remembered that Kaga had been a teacher at a junior high school.

"Let's order some soba noodles," said Kaga, and called the waitress over. As they ordered chilled soba with dipping sauce, they showed her a photograph of Takeaki Aoyagi.

The middle-aged waitress cocked her head and had a good, hard think. "I'm not sure. I don't remember what all our customers look like."

They showed her a picture of Fuyuki Yashima for good measure. She didn't recognize him either.

Matsumiya paid and they left the restaurant.

"Show me the receipt," Kaga said.

"Here you go," Matsumiya said, handing it to him. The printing was poor and the restaurant name was smudged and partly unreadable. The phone number was faint to the point of invisibility.

"Despite coming all this way, we seem to have struck out," Matsumiya said, a note of mockery in his voice.

Kaga didn't reply. He was staring at the receipt.

"No, we didn't strike out. We got a base hit. The woman doesn't remember Aoyagi, that's all." As he spoke, he took out his cell phone and started operating it. When he found the image he was looking for, he showed it to Matsumiya, alongside the paper receipt.

Matsumiya gasped. On the screen was an identical receipt, though with a different date and amount.

"I found this receipt in Aoyagi's office desk. It had been bothering me. I had a hunch it was from a soba restaurant, so I trawled through the internet and found this place. No doubt about it: Aoyagi came here."

Matsumiya looked up at the sign above the door.

"Why would he come all this way? It's quite a way from Amazaké Alley."

"Indeed it is. That's another riddle for us," said Kaga, gazing down the street that stretched away into the distance.

12

Yuto switched off the alarm clock and rubbed his face. His head was a little heavy, but he still felt more wide-awake than he had for several days. He climbed out of bed, did a full-body stretch, and began to get dressed. Today was going to be his first day at school since his father's murder. While he was looking forward to seeing his friends, the thought of classes depressed him. What did it matter? The teachers would be sure to look the other way even if he dozed off, attributing it to fatigue from the wake and the funeral.

He went down to the first floor. Fumiko was in the living room, with her apron tied around her waist. The TV was on and her eyes were glued to the screen.

He didn't need to ask her why. There was a graphic on the screen which read: "Unexpected Truth Behind the Nihonbashi Bridge Murder."

The image changed. A man was sitting in a dark room. You could tell that he was wearing a suit, but his face was completely obscured. Beneath him was the caption: "Former employee of Kaneseki Metals."

"Oh yes, that sort of thing was going on all the time," the man was saying in a voice artificially deepened to disguise his identity. "As far as they're concerned, contract workers like me are a disposable commodity. Say you bump into something, cut yourself, and you start bleeding. They're just like, 'Wrap a towel around that.' They don't actually do anything for you. Acknowledge workplace accidents? Doing that would just show up the complete lack of any health and safety provision, not to mention someone having to take responsibility. That's why they never want to report them."

"Nonetheless, reporting workplace accidents isn't the responsibility of the company, it's actually the responsibility of the agency that sends you there, isn't it?" the female reporter asked.

"The agency won't defy the company they're supplying workers to. If the company says not to file reports, the agencies will suck it up."

"Some of these workplace accidents have long-term effects. What are people supposed to do in that case?"

"Long-term effects? There are people who have *died*. The fact that the accidents are not reported means that no improvements are ever made to the workplace, right? And that results in more accidents. But everything gets brushed under the carpet."

The image changed. The screen now showed a close-up

of the male reporter, frowning gravely. "That's the reality of what you face. I see."

The camera drew back. The female reporter who had conducted the interview was with the host in the studio.

"Our investigation has shown us that Yashima, who's suspected of the murder, had to take at least five days off work due to the fall that we mentioned earlier in the program. Since companies are legally required to file a report if any-one is off work for four or more days, there can be no doubt that this was a cover-up of a workplace accident. The agency instructed Yashima not to reveal the cause of his injury if he went to the hospital, and they told him that he would have to cover all the costs of treatment himself."

The male host emitted a disapproving grunt.

"While it hasn't yet been established for certain that Yashima is indeed the culprit, it's hard not to think that there's a problem that's bigger than any single individual behind this incident."

Following the formula of these sorts of programs, the host then began soliciting opinions from a range of so-called commentators.

Social inequality, the law of the jungle, power harass-ment—as he listened to all the smug-looking minor TV per-sonalities reeling off the talking points the host had been fishing for, Yuto began to get annoyed. Fumiko, however, was a step ahead of him. She grabbed the remote and turned off the TV.

"What nonsense," she declared, and disappeared into the kitchen.

Yuto realized that Haruka was standing right behind him. Her face was pale.

"Don't let them get to you," he said.

When Yuto got to school, his friends came over, one after another, to have a word or two with him. Yuto once again thanked the ones who had come to the wake or the funeral. He had mentally prepared himself just in case anyone who had seen the TV program made a nasty remark, but nobody even mentioned it. Perhaps no one had actually seen the show.

First period, then second period. As the day advanced, Yuto felt himself sinking back into the familiar rhythms of school life. Although he was going through the sorrow of having lost a father, that made little difference to his fellow students. For them, life was going on as usual. *The sooner I get back into the flow of things, the better,* he thought.

Yuto was in the lunchroom with Sugino when he noticed a group of boys looking at him and speaking in hushed tones.

"Those guys, what's their problem? Why're they being so creepy?" Sugino said. He went over, exchanged a few quick words with them, and came back. He looked deflated.

"What did they say?" Yuto asked.

"I don't really know. Something about the factory manager making an apology. It's on the internet."

"Factory manager? What's that about?"

"Hang on. I'll have a look." A puzzled expression on his face, Sugino pulled out his phone. He made a few deft swipes with his fingers, then grimaced at what came up on the screen.

"What's wrong?"

Sugino silently handed his phone to Yuto. Yuto peered at the screen.

A block of text screamed out at him. "Did Aoyagi order the cover-up of workplace accidents? Factory manager reveals all."

13

Matsumiya recognized the square face on the TV screen. It was Kotake, the factory manager at Kaneseki's plant. Whether it was nerves or the heat of the lights for the TV cameras, his forehead was glistening with sweat. He bowed repeatedly while dabbing at himself with a handkerchief.

"I didn't think it was the right thing to do. Of course I didn't. But he kept going on and on about the reputational damage. In the end, I couldn't say no. I had to do what he ordered."

Kotake was briefly replaced by text on a monochrome background. It was a question: "Was Aoyagi responsible for covering up accidents at the workplace?"

The image switched back to Kotake.

"Yes, he was. I got my orders from Aoyagi, the head of

production. As to whether he in turn was getting orders from someone higher up, that's something I cannot speak to," Kotake said as a microphone was thrust in his face.

The image switched to a close-up on the newsreader's face.

"In view of the possibility that Kaneseki Metals carried out frequent and egregious workplace accident cover-ups, the Tachikawa Labor Standards Inspection Office has launched a formal inquiry. Now, moving on to today's stock market and foreign exchange news—"

Matsumiya looked away from the TV screen and sighed.

"The media certainly move fast. They've already sniffed out the accident cover-up."

Putting down his chopsticks, Kaga reached for his cup of tea.

"Oh, they didn't sniff it out. It's much more likely that the director or the deputy commissioner leaked it to them. In this way, even if the worst happens with Yashima, it's easier to push the whole 'suspect deceased' angle."

"You're probably right." Matsumiya resumed eating.

After finishing their meal, they looked around to verify that there were no other diners, then called over the female manager. As per usual, Kaga showed her a photograph of Takeaki Aoyagi. Had he ever been there? he asked.

The manager, who looked around fifty, took the photograph. Conflicting emotions appeared on her face. She was clearly reluctant to verbalize whatever it was that had occurred to her.

"Is there something wrong?" Kaga asked.

"A bit, maybe . . . This man, it's the man from the murder, isn't it?" she asked diffidently.

"He's the victim in the Nihonbashi Bridge murder case. Do you know him?"

"No, I haven't seen him myself, but we had a customer in yesterday who was talking about having seen . . ." Her voice trailed off.

"Having seen him? Did he say where?"

"At the O-Inari-san over there."

"Sorry, the O-Inari-san?"

"You must know the place? The full name's Kasama Inari."

"Yes, it's a shrine in Hamacho. You're saying your customer saw the victim there?"

"Says he was a frequent and enthusiastic visitor. That's why he remembered his face."

"Does that customer come here often?"

"Off and on, yes. The thing is, I don't know his name. I think he's a businessman. He usually brings along some of what look like junior staff with him."

Kaga nodded and extracted a business card from his breast pocket.

"I'd be grateful if you could contact me the next time he shows up. My phone number's on the back of the card. I guarantee we won't cause any inconvenience either to him or to your restaurant."

The woman took his card, but there was still an expression of uncertainty on her face.

"I'll take your card, but I've got no idea when he might show up next."

Kaga smiled.

"Just do what you can."

The manager grunted, smiled half heartedly, and nodded.

"The way she was carrying on, she's bound to forget," said Matsumiya once they were out in the street. "She's too laid-back, not a true Tokyoite at all. I'm surprised to find someone like her here in Ningyocho."

"Takes all sorts, you know. That business of Kasama Inari Shrine was a surprise. Things are finally starting to line up." Kaga nodded his head several times with evident satisfaction.

"What is it? Come on, tell me."

"Why don't you just come with me?" Kaga grinned at him meaningfully and stalked off.

They advanced eastward along Amazaké Alley until they got to Hamacho Green Road, the little park to which Fuyuki Yashima had fled. This time, however, they walked straight across it, then took a left at the next corner.

A broad road appeared in front of them. Kaga stopped just short of it. On the corner, there was a small but dignified-looking shrine behind a fence and a torii gate. A number of vertical red banners with the words "Kasama Inari Daimyo-jin Shrine" were dotted around.

Matsumiya followed Kaga into the shrine. As he looked around, he was struck by the number of stone fox statues.

They all had red cloth bibs tied around their necks. There was a small table next to the shrine building, on which a selection of amulets, good-luck talismans, and pamphlets were displayed. It looked for all the world like a shoplifter's dream—or was no one foolhardy enough to steal from the gods?

"This is one of the three most important fox shrines of Japan," Kaga said. "The main shrine is in Ibaraki Prefecture and this is the Tokyo branch."

"So Aoyagi made a point of coming to worship here," Matsumiya said as he looked at the shrine building.

"My guess is that this wasn't the only place."

"What are you trying to say?"

Kaga picked up a pamphlet from the table.

"There's a coffee shop right next door. I'll explain over a cup."

The coffee shop was an old-fashioned-looking place with rows of little tables. After they had ordered a couple of coffees, Kaga opened the pamphlet.

"As you know, Nihonbashi is full of shrines. There are almost too many to count, if you include all the smaller branch shrines. Did you know that there's a miniature shrine just next to the Meijiza Theater? That's yet another branch shrine of the Kasama Inari," said Kaga. He spoke with complete authority about the area, despite having only been stationed there for a couple of years.

"I know. But so what?"

Kaga pointed to the map in the pamphlet. On it, all the most important shrines were marked. Kasama Inari Shrine was one of them.

"There's something called the Seven Lucky Gods of Ni-honbashi. It's a seasonal ritual: around New Year's, people visit all the shrines in that particular group. In baseball terms, it's like the Major League of Shrines. Now, the Seven Lucky Gods includes . . ."

Kaga finger darted around the map as he reeled off the names. "There's Koami Shrine, Chanoki Shrine, Suitengu Shrine, Matsushima Shrine, Suehiro Shrine, Kasama Inari Shrine, Suginomori Shrine, and Takarada Ebisu Shrine. That makes eight in all."

"*Eight?* Even though it's the Seven Lucky Gods?"

"Ebisu, the same god, is enshrined at both Suginomori Shrine and Takarada Ebisu Shrine. I don't know why they both make it onto the list. Anyway, for our purposes, that's neither here nor there. It's the location of those two shrines that's the issue for us. They're different from all the other shrines. Take a good look."

Matsumiya duly scrutinized the map. Their coffee was brought to the table while he was doing so. He drank it black without bothering to look up.

Eventually, he gave a start. He had figured it out.

"This Takarada Ebisu Shrine, is it last night . . . ?"

"Very good," Kaga said approvingly, a self-satisfied look on his face. "Takarada Ebisu is the shrine that's closest to the Kobaian soba noodle restaurant. Six of the eight shrines are relatively close to Amazaké Alley, but the Suginomori and Ta-karada Ebisu Shrines are a ways away. That's particularly true of Takarada Ebisu Shrine. We couldn't figure out why Aoyagi was going to a soba noodle restaurant all the way over there.

But if he was doing the Seven Lucky Gods circuit, then we have our explanation. When you think about it, the locations of the shops and restaurants where Aoyagi was seen more or less correspond with the Seven Lucky Gods route."

Raising his face from the map, Matsumiya looked at Kaga and nodded his head.

"Bull's-eye. I think you've nailed it. This explains why Aoyagi was coming to Nihonbashi. He was doing the Seven Lucky Gods pilgrimage." Without him being aware of it, Matsumiya's voice had grown more strident.

"If we're right about that, the next mystery is why he was doing the shrine circuit in the first place. The tradition is to do it around New Year's. But to do the pilgrimage repeatedly during the year—he's got to have had a very special reason for that."

"I'd guess that he was praying for something in particular. That's the only possible explanation for him doing the pilgrimage so fanatically."

"You're probably right." Kaga picked up his coffee cup. "What would you do, Shuhei? If there was something you wanted really badly, would it occur to you to visit a shrine?"

"Let's say it wouldn't *not* occur to me. Like, when I had my university entrance exams, I did actually make a shrine visit."

"But I'll bet you did it as part of your regular New Year's shrine visiting. Or did you make multiple visits to a specific shrine just for your entrance exams?"

"Well, no, I didn't . . ."

Kaga took a sip of coffee with a bemused look on his face, then put his cup down.

"It's always hard when you're dealing with tastes and attitudes at the individual level, but I wonder what percentage of people truly believe that praying to the gods delivers benefits. I know some older folks are very religious, but Aoyagi's not of that generation."

"That's just your opinion, Kyo. There's no shortage of young people who believe the gods can do something for them. There was this one guy in college who used to go to church every week."

Kaga tipped his head to one side.

"Attending church regularly and doing the Seven Lucky Gods pilgrimage strike me as two fundamentally different things."

"Okay, then how would you explain why Aoyagi did what he did? What other reason is there for going to a shrine than to pray for something?"

Kaga knitted his brows and frowned down at the pamphlet. "Why Nihonbashi?"

"Huh?"

"If he was praying for something, then why pick the Nihonbashi Seven Lucky Gods? There've got to be plenty of other shrines much closer to his house or his office. Maybe even shrines of the same Seven Lucky Gods. So why did he come all this way across town?"

"Maybe . . . maybe because he thought these specific shrines would get him what he was after?"

"You mean give him exactly what he asked for? He'd have to be very religious to be so fussy."

"Maybe he was."

Kaga gulped down the last of his coffee and started folding up the pamphlet. "Let's get verification."

They left the coffee shop and walked to the nearest train station. It took them around thirty minutes to get to the station about ten minutes' walk from the Aoyagi house. It was in a warren of small streets where a single careless turn could leave you stuck in a dead end.

As they approached the house, they noticed a group of reporters on the opposite side of the street. *What a bore,* Matsumiya thought. Kaga, however, didn't slow down, so Matsumiya followed along behind him.

Sure enough, as they reached the garden gate, one of the reporters came rushing up to them. He was a weaselly-looking little man in glasses.

"Are you going in? What for, if you don't mind my asking?"

Matsumiya held up one hand to keep the man back, while tapping his own chest with the other. The implication was: *I've got a police badge under here.* The message must have gotten across, as the reporter flinched and stopped in his tracks.

Kaga pressed the doorbell on the intercom. Fumiko was in. "Come through the gate and right up to the front door," she said. She didn't want to let the media people see her, Matsumiya realized.

When they reached the front door, it was discreetly opened for them. Fumiko's slightly gaunt face appeared.

She was the only one at home. The children were back at school from today, she explained.

"Things are still lively out front, I see," Kaga said, lowering himself onto the living room sofa.

"They're out there in the morning too. I think they're hoping I'll go out." Fumiko had returned from the kitchen carrying a tray with teacups. "They asked me via the intercom what I thought about the whole workplace accident cover-up business. What do they expect me to say? I don't *know* anything and I can't *say* anything. The first I heard about my husband's involvement was from watching the TV news." She put one teacup in front of Matsumiya and another in front of Kaga. The smell of roasted green tea wafted through the air.

"You've already said that your husband didn't talk about his work at home, yes?"

Fumiko responded to Matsumiya with an emphatic nod and fixed him with a pleading look.

"Do you think that what they're saying on the news is true? Do you think that a workplace accident cover-up is what got my husband killed?"

"Well, uhm . . ." Matsumiya shot Kaga a glance.

"We do seem to have a witness with regard to the accident cover-up," Kaga said. "We don't yet know the nature of your husband's involvement, though. Nor has a link yet been established between the cover-up and the murder."

Fumiko's shoulders slumped. "I see," she whispered.

"We're actually here today to ask you a very specific

question. It's about your husband, of course," Kaga said. "Would you describe him as a religious man?"

Fumiko gasped and her eyes widened. The question had clearly surprised her. "What exactly do you mean?"

"Let's say that your husband wanted things to turn out a certain way or was worried about something—did he turn to religion at such moments? Did he believe in the power of prayer? Did he have a collection of amulets?"

"No," Fumiko said, slowly shaking her head. "If anything, I'd say he didn't take religion seriously at all. When the shrines were jam-packed with people making their first visit of the year, he would make fun of them: 'I don't know why they bother.' Why do you ask?"

"No particular reason. We're just checking up on something," said Kaga, darting a glance at Matsumiya. Now, apparently, wasn't the time or place to reveal that Takeaki Aoyagi had been doing the Seven Lucky Gods pilgrimage on a regular basis.

Matsumiya put his cup on the table and rose to his feet. "Thank you very much for your time."

"Is that all?" Fumiko asked. She sounded confused.

"Yes, that's all. Thanks for the tea," Kaga said.

"Could you tell me . . ." Fumiko also stood up and looked from one man to the other.

"Is covering up a workplace accident such a bad thing to do? Is it something a person deserves to be despised and knifed to death for?"

Matsumiya looked at Kaga.

"Mrs. Aoyagi," said Kaga quietly. "The cover-up of a

workplace accident is a crime. It's definitely not a good thing to do. Still, there is nobody—nobody at all—in this world of ours who *deserves* to be killed."

Fumiko pressed her lips together and looked Kaga full in the face. There were tears in her eyes.

"Let's go," Kaga said to Matsumiya.

14

The lights were much brighter than she had expected. They reached into the nooks and crannies that were normally in shadow and revealed just how grubby they were. *I'd have given the place a proper cleaning if I'd known it was going to be like this,* Kaori thought. But it was too late now. She knew they were going to pixelate her face, but she could hardly ask them to pixelate her apartment as well. From the discussions she had overheard earlier, showing her apartment was one of the aims of the exercise.

"Let me get this straight. You didn't know that your boyfriend had even had an accident at his workplace, did you?" asked the female TV reporter. She had a forceful face and long hair pulled back behind her head.

"No, I didn't know. What he told me was that he'd fallen

down a flight of stairs on his way home from work," said Kaori. That was how she remembered things.

"Can you describe his original injuries?"

Kaori tilted her head to one side.

"Fuyuki insisted they were nothing serious, but he looked pretty uncomfortable to me. When I urged him to go to the hospital, he said that rest should do the trick and then spent the next few days in bed."

"Did he say anything about having had an accident at work at that time?"

"Nothing."

Kaori realized that the camera was pointed at her belly. She had already told them she was pregnant. The faces of the TV crew had lit up at the news.

"Not long after, the agency told Fuyuki that his contract had been terminated. What did he tell you about the reasons behind his termination?"

"That they were a load of nonsense, but there wasn't anything he could do."

"He subsequently started to suffer from aftereffects. What sort of symptoms were they exactly?"

"Severe stiffness in the neck and shoulders . . . then he lost all sensation in his left hand. The symptoms might have been there earlier. He could have been keeping quiet about them to avoid worrying me."

The female interviewer gave an emphatic nod. Kaori must have given her the answer she had been hoping for.

"The aftereffects made it very difficult for Fuyuki to find

other work. It was the company that was responsible for the original accident, and it was the company's determination to cover up the accident that ultimately prevented Fuyuki from going to the hospital. What do you think about that?"

"That's something I only just found out about. If it's true, then I think it's awful, really awful. If he'd gone to the hospital, things wouldn't have turned out the way they did."

"Turned out the way they did? You mean that the murder wouldn't have taken place?" A microphone was thrust in Kaori's face.

"No, I, uh, I just mean that he wouldn't have suffered so much physically."

"But what about the murder? Takeaki Aoyagi, the head of production, was the person who masterminded the cover-up of workplace accidents at Kaneseki Metals. Don't you think there's got to be a link between that and the murder?"

"The murder . . ." Kaori, who was starting to get confused, shook her head. "I don't know. I certainly don't think Fuyuki had anything to do with the murder. He's simply not capable of doing anything like that."

The reporter's face clouded. She frowned and raised a hand.

"*Cut!* Do we want her to say that?" she asked her staff.

There was a whispered discussion and a man in glasses came over to Kaori.

"A word, Ms. Nakahara? You want to think the best of your boyfriend, we get that. The fact is that he stole the victim's wallet and fled the scene. Surely, it's hard to believe that he's *not* involved in the crime?"

"Well . . . I suppose so."

"So you do think he was involved in the crime, then?"

She grunted in assent.

"Well, then, could you make that the starting point of your answers? Why did Fuyuki end up involved in a crime? Surely you've got to admit that him being the victim of a malicious accident cover-up was what led directly to this crime?"

Kaori was feeling confused all over again. She agreed with what the man said: Fuyuki was the victim of a workplace accident cover-up. He felt cornered and then one thing led to another. His words from that evening echoed in her head: "I've done something terrible—"

"You . . . you could say that."

"You bet you can! All we want you to do is to tell us what you really think. You don't need to say anything fancy or flowery. Just exactly what you think. Good. Now we're going to retake that part."

"Okay." The whole crew sprang into motion as Kaori said the word. There was something predatory about the look on the female reporter's face. *This time give us the proper answers or else!* Kaori felt intimidated.

"I'd like to ask you about the murder. Takeaki Aoyagi, the victim, was the mastermind behind the cover-up at Kaneseki Metals. Do you think there's a link between the two things? Let me be very clear here that murder, whatever the motivation for it, can never be condoned."

The question had been bulked up. Kaori was at a loss what to say. Should she ask them to cut to give her time to think? She shrank from the piercing gaze of the interviewer.

She didn't dare make such a request. She had to come up with some kind of answer.

"I think that . . . that what took place happened because my boyfriend was the victim of a workplace accident cover-up."

"So you're saying that he was responsible for the crime?"

"Yes," agreed Kaori, feeling dazed.

"Lovely. That's a wrap," a voice immediately said. The female reporter sprang to her feet with a look of triumph on her face. She didn't give Kaori a second glance.

Kaori sat in her dilapidated apartment as the equipment was packed up and the TV crew prepared to leave. She felt bewildered. After she had seen them off, she was left holding twenty thousand yen in cash. Money was the reason she had agreed to do the interview. Money was what she needed right now.

Yesterday, the boss of the delicatessen where she worked had told her he wouldn't be needing her for a while.

"I hear that your live-in boyfriend is the suspect in the Nihonbashi Bridge murder case."

Her boss was as soft and plump as a loaf of bread. He had made the comment diffidently enough, but Kaori still recoiled.

"How do you . . . ?"

She hadn't told any of her delicatessen coworkers that she lived with Fuyuki.

An anxious frown appeared on his face.

"I got a phone call. This woman. She said she was a regular customer of ours. Lives near you and sees you around all the time, she said. Told me how the police searched your place. She was out in the street, watching."

Kaori lowered her eyes. Her memory of the search was all too vivid. Her boss was right: a group of bystanders had gathered to watch. And one of them was a customer here. The world was full of people who loved spreading nasty gossip, people who did nothing when you needed help most.

"We're a customer-facing business, Kaori. We don't need nasty rumors circulating. You can understand that."

Kaori had no reply. She would probably have done the same thing herself in the boss's shoes.

Kaori sighed as she looked at the twenty thousand yen. Right now, it represented a considerable sum of money, but it wasn't as if it really solved anything. She needed to figure out a way to earn money. She had once been approached by a fellow in a black suit who was recruiting for a sleazy hostess club. She still had his business card. Knowing Fuyuki wouldn't like it, she hadn't seriously thought about it at the time; now she wondered about giving him a call.

It's no good. She patted her belly. *The state I'm in, I won't be able to work for very long. Who knows if they'd even give me a job in the first place—*

That was when it happened. Her cell phone, which was lying on the low table, started to ring.

"Hello?"

"Hello, is this Kaori Nakahara?"

"Speaking. Who's this?"

"This is Kyobashi Central Hospital. There's been a

change in Fuyuki Yashima's condition. We'd like you to come as fast as you can."

Kaori's heart was in her throat. Her whole body grew warm and the hand with which she was holding the phone began to tremble.

15

When Matsumiya finished delivering his report, Ishigaki nodded.

"The Nihonbashi Seven Lucky Gods pilgrimage circuit? That's an interesting angle you've come up with."

"It came to light by pure chance while we were looking for eyewitnesses who had seen Fuyuki Yashima."

Ishigaki snorted. "I'm not so sure about it being a matter of chance—" He shifted his gaze from Matsumiya to Kaga, then back again to Matsumiya. "Anyway, that's neither here nor there. We now know why the victim was in the Nihonbashi district. If he did arrange to meet Yashima, then it would make sense for him to choose a café in the same part of town.

"Good job," Ishigaki added as an afterthought.

"The next question is why Aoyagi was doing the Seven Lucky Gods pilgrimage."

Ishigaki gave a dismissive wave of the hand.

"That's not something you need to worry about. It's got nothing to do with our case. Aoyagi's son's got his university entrance exams next year and he was probably praying for him to pass or something."

"According to his wife, the victim wasn't a very religious man—" At that point, Matsumiya felt a poke in his side. It was Kaga, jabbing him with his elbow. *Don't tell him any more than you already have,* his eyes said. *Let's get out of here.*

"I'm not a religious man either, but I'm always praying for something," Ishigaki said. "A lower uric acid count, or for my daughter not to go out with idiots—stuff like that. People are capricious creatures. They can suddenly get serious about religion when it suits them to do so. It's important to look into the victim's background, but don't get too caught up by the small stuff."

If we were talking about once, fine. But I don't think doing the Seven Lucky Gods pilgrimage circuit repeatedly can be put down to caprice. Matsumiya swallowed his objection and meekly sat down.

"Okay, how are we doing with the murder weapon?" Ishigaki ran his eye over the group of investigators around him.

Sakagami raised his hand to shoulder height.

"We've managed to contact around ninety percent of the people who bought the same brand of knife online. That includes people our investigators couldn't meet with personally because they live far away. We got the ones who still had their knives to take a photo and email it to us. Some no longer had them in their possession. In most of those cases, they had either lost the knives or damaged them and thrown them away. Anyway, we couldn't get any statements that linked these knives to Yashima."

Ishigaki scowled and groaned loudly.

"Same old story, then. Zero results. Can't someone clear up the mystery of how the perpetrator procured the weapon?"

"Is that really a problem? Does it actually matter that much?" Kobayashi said. "The knife isn't an unusual model. Yashima could well have bought it himself at an outdoor gear shop. There's nothing strange about the store clerks failing to remember a customer."

"The way things are now, we have zero physical evidence. Not even a statement from someone that the knife belonged to Yashima."

"Shall I have another word with Kaori Nakahara?"

"That's certainly an option." Ishigaki frowned pensively, then jerked his head abruptly to one side as if to clear his thoughts. "We're certainly not going to solve anything by sitting around here looking miserable. Let's call it a day. Good night."

"Good night," replied a few of the investigators. The meeting broke up.

A phone started ringing in the far corner of the room. The detective closest by picked it up. There was a short exchange, during which his face went pale; he turned to look at Ishigaki. "Chief, it's the officer on duty at the hospital." There was a note of urgency in his voice.

A sense of foreboding flooded Matsumiya. "What's happened?" Ishigaki asked.

"Fuyuki Yashima died without ever regaining conscious-ness," answered the detective.

When Ishigaki announced that someone would need to go to the hospital to verify Yashima's death, Matsumiya volunteered. Kaga caught up with him as he left the room. "I'll come with you."

Matsumiya sighed as they walked along side by side.

"So now we won't be able to get the truth directly from Yashima."

"The higher-ups will definitely see the case as being in the bag now. As far as they're concerned, all that needs to be done is to send the paperwork to the Public Prosecutor's Office under 'suspect deceased.' The lack of evidence won't matter anymore. The case won't even go to prosecution. Even if Yashima didn't actually do it, dead men tell no tales. Nobody's going to complain."

"And the mysteries remain more or less unsolved. Including why Aoyagi was doing the Seven Lucky Gods circuit. Perhaps that counts as good police work—"

"It's not good," Kaga shot back brusquely. "It's no use to anybody to close a case in such a half-assed way. I'm going to do whatever it takes to get to the truth." Although his voice was barely more than a murmur, it was full of determination.

When the taxi reached the hospital, they were surprised to see a gaggle of TV reporters outside. Someone at the hospital must be leaking information. As Matsumiya went inside, he was wondering how the media was planning to spin Yashima's death.

In the waiting room, a man in a white coat stood talking to a uniformed cop. The doctor was the one responsible for Yashima, the same one Matsumiya had met on his first visit. He nodded a greeting.

"A regrettable outcome," the doctor said. He was quite calm.

"He took a sudden turn for the worse?" Matsumiya said.

The doctor nodded.

"We suspect that the hematoma became acute. He did well to last as long as he did, given the severity of the cerebral contusion."

"That's thanks to your hard work. Where is the body?"

"Go to the nurses' station on the third floor. They'll have moved him from the ICU to another room. Oh yes, that girl—you know who I mean—got here a minute ago. The girlfriend."

"Thank you," Matsumiya said.

He and Kaga left the waiting room and took the elevator up to the third floor. He had located the nurses' station and was about to ask where Yashima had been moved to when Kaga called out to him. Matsumiya turned around and Kaga jerked his chin down the corridor. Kaori Nakahara was sitting on a couch halfway down, hunched forward and with a towel draped over her face.

With no idea what he was going to say, Matsumiya made to walk toward her. Before he could take a step, he felt a hand on his shoulder.

"Tonight at least, we should leave her be," Kaga said. "We've verified that Yashima is dead. From what the doctor told us, there's nothing suspicious about it. Surely that's good enough? Leave the woman alone."

Matsumiya nodded wordlessly.

Before getting back into the elevator, Matsumiya took another look at Kaori Nakahara. There was something dangling off the handle of the bag that was beside her on the couch. It hadn't been there last time.

Squinting, Matsumiya realized that it was an amulet. The girl must have picked it up at a shrine when she was praying for Fuyuki Yashima's recovery. What if it was one of the Seven Lucky Gods of Nihonbashi!

Kaga's right, thought Matsumiya. *No one will get closure or comfort if the case ends like this. Not the Aoyagi family and not Kaori Nakahara—*

16

Yuto could feel that the tide had turned against him in a matter of a few days. The other boys were not actively ignoring him, but they were certainly keeping their distance. Nobody at the school would come over and talk to him. And if he tried to talk to them, they were very standoffish.

There was a group of boys standing in a small circle not far away. Their faces were close together and they were whispering conspiratorially. Every now and then, they would turn and look at him with a disgusted frown or a cruel sneer.

He knew what was behind the change. Kaneseki Metals' practice of covering up workplace accidents had been all over the news the last few days.

The day before, the Kaneseki CEO held his first press conference on the subject. A small man with glasses too big for his face, he apologized for the scandal and announced that he had been completely ignorant of what was going on. Company policy was to leave the running of the factory in the hands of the factory staff. It was their responsibility to manage health and safety properly, and, in the unlikely instance of an employee having an accident, to respond swiftly and appropriately and do their best to make sure that it didn't happen again. Of course, what he meant by "employee" wasn't just full-time employees but also employees on short-term contracts and temp workers. The company planned to launch a thoroughgoing investigation into how such a thing could have happened.

Kotake, the factory manager, had already confessed that it was Aoyagi, the head of production, who ordered the cover-up of all workplace accidents. Kotake claimed to have been threatened by Aoyagi. "If push comes to shove, it's you, as factory manager, who'll be in the firing line."

Everyone above Aoyagi in the hierarchy claimed to have been kept in the dark. They were all singing from the same hymn sheet: the person with ultimate responsibility for the factory was the head of production.

In other words, Takeaki Aoyagi was to blame for everything.

Because of deficiencies in the company's safety management, a contract worker had had an accident. Nonetheless, Takeaki Aoyagi's policies meant that the incident hadn't been recorded as a workplace accident nor had the worker been permitted to go to the hospital. To make things even worse, the worker had lost his job and then been unable to find a new one because of the aftereffects.

The worker—Fuyuki Yashima—was living with a girl who was three months' pregnant and he needed to find a job, fast.

It was unclear what sort of interactions there had been between Fuyuki Yashima, who was understandably frustrated, and Takeaki Aoyagi. It seemed likely that Yashima laid responsibility for the cover-up at Aoyagi's door. Things could plausibly have escalated into a full-blown shouting match from there. This was how the tabloid shows on TV had been presenting the Nihonbashi Bridge murder case in their coverage over the last few days.

One TV channel had broadcast an interview with Fuyuki Yashima's girlfriend.

The woman's face was pixelated, but you could tell from her clothes she was just scraping by. The camera spent a lot of time lingering on her belly.

The reporter conducting the interview got the girlfriend to talk about her life and the difficulties she had been having since getting pregnant. She also asked her quite a few questions about Fuyuki Yashima's accident. The interview concluded with this question.

"I'd like to ask you about the murder. Takeaki Aoyagi, the victim, was the mastermind behind the cover-up at Kaneseki Metals. Do you think there's a link between the two things? Let me be very clear here that murder, whatever the motivation for it, can never be condoned."

The girlfriend's response to the question was:

"I think that . . . that what took place happened because my boyfriend was the victim of a workplace accident cover-up."

"So you're saying that he was responsible for the crime?"

"Yes," said Fuyuki Yashima's girlfriend almost inaudibly.

In the tradition of such programs, this segment was followed by feckless comments from a range of talking heads. "Yashima must have felt cornered." "No one has the right to take another human life." "Why couldn't anybody reach out to him?" The commentators were clearly on the perpetrator's side. Yashima's death seemed to have further aroused their sympathy.

The sequence of events had subtly changed the mood at school. Yuto felt an acute sense of injustice at the cold and contemptuous glances he got. *We're the real victims here. Why are we being treated like this?*

Yuto was isolated at breaks and during the lunch hour. No one came near him. Even Sugino seemed to be avoiding him. In a way, it was a relief. The state he was in, Yuto was well aware that even the smallest thing could trigger his anger.

Of course, Yuto wasn't the only one who was suffering.

Arriving back home, he heard shrill voices coming from the living room.

"What am I supposed to do? I can't stand another day of this."

It was Haruka. There was genuine rage in her voice.

"It's all very well your saying that, but I've no more idea of what's going on than you do. It's not like the police have told us anything." Fumiko sounded shaken.

"Listen to what they're saying on TV. That it was all

Dad's fault. On the internet, people are saying that Dad simply got what he deserved. Did you know?"

"I can't believe it."

"Well, it's true. Go look for yourself. There are so many awful comments about him," Haruka wailed through her tears. "Today, a girl at school said she regretted having shown me any sympathy. And she made sure I could hear her."

Yuto pushed open the living room door. The two women wheeled around. They must not have realized that he was back and surprise was all over their faces. Haruka was red around the eyes.

"This is such a mess," he snarled. "Dad was rotten. You reap what you sow."

Haruka glowered at him. Pressing her lips together angrily, she marched out of the room with her schoolbag. They heard her running full tilt up the stairs. *She's going to lock herself up in her room and bawl her eyes out*, Yuto thought.

"God, it's just too depressing."

"Has anyone said anything to you at school?" Fumiko asked him.

"Not really. The atmosphere's weird, though. No one will talk to me anymore."

"School too, huh . . ." Fumiko's voice trailed off.

"What do you mean, 'school too'? Has something happened here?"

After a moment's hesitation, Fumiko reached into the trash can in a corner of the room. She pulled out a piece of paper that was scrunched up into a ball and handed it to Yuto.

"I found this when I went to check the mailbox a few minutes ago."

Yuto unfolded the piece of paper. "Return the condolence money," someone had written in thick black marker.

He crumpled up the note and threw it back into the trash can. *God, some people are pathetic!* It was probably a neighbor, but whether they had really attended the wake or the funeral was anybody's guess. Chances were, they had written the note for the pleasure of making them miserable.

Walking to the far end of the room, Yuto opened the sliding doors that divided the living room from the Japanese-style room next door. It was there that the altar with Takeaki's memorial photograph stood.

"Let's take this crap down. It's just an eyesore."

"How can you say that!"

"It's *my* dad who got murdered and everyone's giving *me* the cold shoulder! It makes no damn sense."

"It can't last forever. Give it time, people will forget. Mr. Kotake—"

"Kotake?" Yuto wheeled around. "Have you spoken to him?"

"He called around lunchtime. He said he had done something he was sorry for."

"Oh yeah? What was it he was so sorry about?"

"Going on the news, of course. When the authorities started digging around, his superiors told him to tell the truth. He had to make a clean breast of things."

"What? That when he behaved fraudulently, he did so under orders from Dad and had no choice in the matter?"

Fumiko nodded glumly. Then, with a sudden jerk of the head, she looked up at her son.

"No, but listen. Kotake says it's not actually as bad as all that. The fine is only about five hundred thousand yen. Covering up workplace accidents is something that all businesses do, he says. It's not such a big deal. It's not a serious crime or misdemeanor."

"Great. Why don't you go and proclaim the good news from the rooftops?" Yuto stamped his foot on the tatami mat. "Yeah, come to my school and tell the other kids. 'What Dad did wasn't so bad after all.' Saying it in here doesn't make a jot of difference. People have already made up their minds: Dad was a wicked man who deserved to be killed. Come on, they're even saying that on the TV."

"Kotake said we'd caught a bad break. The whole thing got blown out of proportion because Dad was killed in such a famous location . . . Kotake said that he couldn't believe anyone would stab someone over such an insignificant matter."

"What's the man even talking about? What sort of consolation is that supposed to be? Saying crap like that at this stage is useless."

Yuto pictured Kotake. That friendly, smiling face of his could be a mask he was hiding behind. He was probably thinking, *Thank God it wasn't me who got stabbed.*

Self-pity and anger churned in Yuto's chest. The fact that both men responsible for this state of affairs were dead only reinforced his rage.

Yuto grabbed the photograph of Takeaki and raised his arm as if to fling it into the family altar.

"No, Yuto, don't!" Fumiko cried.

Yuto lowered his arm. The hand holding the photograph was shaking. With a final glance at Takeaki's smiling face, he replaced the picture on the altar. Facedown.

17

This is all that's left of him—that was the first thought that came into Kaori's head as she contemplated the little jumble of bone fragments. She had cried herself dry. She seemed to have exhausted her capacity for grief.

Following the crematorium attendant's instructions, she started picking up the pieces of bone with the chopsticks. She struggled to reconcile the bones, which looked like so many dried-up white twigs, with the healthy Fuyuki.

She got the hospital to hold on to Fuyuki's body for just one night after his death. The next day, a female administrator at the hospital had given her advice on the proper procedures to follow. If Kaori spoke to the authorities, they would pay for the cremation. She went straight to the ward office and explained the situation. The person in charge understood immediately. Something in his manner gave Kaori the impression he had heard about Fuyuki.

Everyone—the hospital administrators, the people at the ward office—was so nice to her. Since arriving in Tokyo with Fuyuki, she had never felt so grateful for the kindness of strangers.

By the time she left the crematorium, the sky was starting to redden. A very special day was coming to an end, she felt. What would her life be like tomorrow? The people at the ward office had encouraged her to apply for welfare. She would be able to live, albeit very frugally. But simply staying alive—how meaningful was that? Fuyuki was gone. All that was waiting for her back in their apartment was cold, stale air.

As she got close to home, she noticed a couple of men loitering in front of her little apartment block. She felt a pang of anxiety. Was it more TV people? She appreciated the money, but she didn't want to be on TV again.

Taking a closer look, she realized that she knew them. One of them was the detective called Matsumiya. Kaori relaxed a little. The man looked tough, but his eyes were sweet and kind. She recognized the other detective, the taller one too. He'd been at the hospital right after the accident. She couldn't recall his name; perhaps he had never told her.

As she walked toward them, the men spotted her and bowed their heads in greeting.

"Cremation?" Matsumiya was looking at the bundle Kaori was carrying.

"That's right," she replied.

"We're sorry to bother you at a time like this. We just have a couple of questions. Do you mind?"

"That's fine. The apartment's rather messy, I'm afraid."

After they stepped inside, Kaori placed the box containing the urn with Fuyuki's ashes beside a framed photograph showing the two of them at Tokyo Disneyland.

She sat herself down at the low table across from the two detectives. The taller one reintroduced himself. His name was Kaga and he was based at the Nihonbashi precinct. His gaze was more penetrating than his partner's and Kaori could hardly bring herself to make eye contact.

"I see you've had visitors," Kaga commented. He was looking at a paper carrier bag that was sitting in front of the refrigerator. It bore the logo of a famous cake shop and contained a box of cookies.

"The TV people were in here the other day. They brought me that . . . Oh, that reminds me, I didn't offer you tea." She started getting to her feet.

"We're fine. Don't worry about us," Matsumiya said hastily. "We just have a couple of questions."

Kaori straightened her back and shifted around to find a comfortable position. "What do you want to know?"

"You've probably been asked this so often that you're sick of it. Still, I need to reconfirm something. It's to do with the knife."

"Again?" She felt the energy drain out of her. Another detective had subjected her to exhaustive questioning about the exact same thing. She had told the man that she had never seen a knife like that before in her life.

"Did Yashima previously own a knife, even one that wasn't exactly the same as the one we showed you? Maybe he was looking after a knife for someone he knew? Could he have borrowed one?"

"No, no, and no." Kaori shook her head, her eyes fastened on the floor. She was mortified. She'd told them the same thing umpteen times. Why wouldn't they believe her?

Matsumiya took a photograph from the inside breast pocket of his jacket and placed it on the low table. It was a picture of a knife: a folding knife with a brown handle. It was different from the one she had been shown at her previous questioning.

"Do you recognize this?"

"No. I've never seen it before. What is it?"

"Yashima worked for a small building contractor after graduating high school. Apparently, this is the knife he used at that time."

"Fuyuki? No, I don't think so." She looked Matsumiya right in the face. "It's not true. He's never owned anything like that, anything so vicious."

Matsumiya gave a wry smile.

"There's nothing vicious about this. It's a tool, nothing more."

He explained that it something called a cable-stripping knife and was used by professional electricians.

"A guy working at the same contractor bought a couple and gave Yashima one of them. The knife in this photo is the other guy's."

"I didn't know. What's it supposed to mean?"

"We know for certain that Yashima owned this knife. You, however, were unaware of that fact. That suggests that your knowledge of his things is less than comprehensive. It's possible that he kept dangerous objects—knives and things like that—out of sight."

"I don't accept that. Okay, I'm prepared to admit I didn't know about that knife, but everything else I knew about: what he had and what he didn't have. Fuyuki was hopeless without me. He was clueless about where his stuff was. On that day, he really struggled to find a pair of socks without holes in them."

"Knives and socks are not quite the same thing," said Matsumiya, tucking the picture away.

Kaori placed both her hands palms down on the tatami mat and leaned forward into a bow.

"Please believe me, Detective. Fuyuki wasn't capable of murder. That's just not the kind of person he was. This whole thing is some kind of ghastly mistake. Maybe he did steal the man's wallet on an impulse, but there's no way that he killed him." Her voice echoed in the small room. After that, the only sound was the buzz of the aging fluorescent light.

"I'm sorry," she said in a muffled voice. "It doesn't matter how many times I tell you. You just won't listen, will you?"

Kaga leaned toward her.

"You got a call from Yashima the night of the incident, didn't you? 'I'll be back soon. Sorry to be so late,' he said, then abruptly rang off. At least, that's what you told us. Are you quite sure that's correct?"

"Yeah, uhm . . ."

"The phone records show that the call was made *after* the crime occurred. Since Yashima ended up in possession of the victim's wallet and briefcase, he must have been aware of the crime in some form or other. Despite that, he didn't mention it to you—you, the one person in this world he felt he could trust. Why do you think that is?"

"I . . . ah . . . I don't know."

"I'll tell you what we think: we think it was so serious, he couldn't bring himself to talk about it. It wasn't some piffling, low-level crime like theft or common assault, this was murder and robbery—"

"You're wrong!" Kaori half shouted. Startled and upset by the loudness of her own voice, she burst into tears. She wiped her eyes with the back of her hand.

"Ms. Nakahara," Kaga addressed her, speaking in the gentlest tone he could muster. "Please tell us the truth. Nothing good comes of lying. You believe in your boyfriend. I know that."

Kaori pressed a hand to her temples. She didn't know what to do.

"He said he'd done something awful . . . ," she murmured.

"What?" Matsumiya seized on her words. "Repeat that, but clearly this time."

Kaori inhaled deeply.

"'I've done something awful . . . Something terrible's happened. I don't know what to do.' Those were his exact words . . . He sounded hysterical."

"That's crucial information," Matsumiya said in a whisper.

"I'm sorry. The first time you asked, I thought the best thing I could do for Fuyuki was to cover for him. I thought the best thing wasn't to say anything that tied him to the crime." She was crying uncontrollably now. She wanted to collapse onto the table, but just managed to stop herself.

The two detectives waited in silence for Kaori to regain her composure. She took a number of deep breaths, then nodded several times in succession. "Sorry about that. I'm okay now."

It was Kaga who spoke.

"You mentioned Fuyuki's socks a moment ago. You said that on that day he'd really struggled to find a pair of socks with no holes in them. By 'that day,' I assume you mean the day the incident took place?"

"Yes. When I got back that night, the drawer containing his socks and underwear was sitting in the middle of the room . . . Fuyuki's not a great one for cutting his toenails, so he gets holes in the toes of his socks. Normally, he's quite happy to wear socks with holes."

"I see." Kaga looked thoughtful. "There's one more thing I want to ask you." He held up an index finger. "You went to work on the day of the incident. Did you and your boyfriend discuss anything before you left the house?"

"On the day of the incident? No, we didn't. He was usually still asleep when I left for work. That day was no exception."

"How about the day before? What did the two of you discuss, either before you went to work or after you got back home?"

"You're talking about the day before? In the morning, I

think he was asleep, like I said. Then, when I got back from work . . ." She rummaged around in her memory. She always got home by around eight, but that day had been different. "Of course. We went to see a movie."

"A movie? The two of you?"

"Yes. I'd gotten a pair of tickets. I arranged to meet Fuyuki at a theater in Ginza at eight o'clock, and we watched the movie together." She gave them the name of the theater and the movie.

"You'd been at work until that time. But what about Fuyuki? Where was he? What had he been up to?"

"I'm not sure . . . Oh, I remember now. He arrived late."

"He was late? He didn't make it for eight?"

"He'd actually arrived early. He went for a wander around the neighborhood and ended straying too far. We nearly missed the start of the feature. I was getting panicked."

"You went straight into the theater when he showed up?"

"Yes."

"And after the movie?"

"We went straight home. We can't afford to eat out."

"You probably discussed the movie after getting home?"

"We certainly did. It was a pretty good film, so it was a lively chat. Fuyuki opened up a canned cocktail . . ." The memory triggered a feeling of heaviness in her chest. It was so recent, but it already felt like the remote past; almost like a dream, in fact. "Sorry, but why are you asking me about this? What does the day before the incident have to do with anything?"

"I'm just asking for reference purposes. Did you discuss anything other than the movie that night?"

"Uhm, no, I don't think we did. Fuyuki got a bit tipsy and went off to bed. He looks like a little child when he's asleep . . . Fun times."

We'll never have another day like that again, she thought, and the tears welled up. She tried and failed to hold them back.

Kaori took the handkerchief that Matsumiya was holding out to her.

18

It was a little after eight p.m. when Matsumiya and Kaga got back to the task force room. This time, however, there was no cluster of investigators standing around Ishigaki. The unit chief was contemplating a number of reports strewn over his desk, with a pensive and unhappy look on his face.

Work had begun to send the case to the public prosecutor as a "suspect deceased" case, since that was what the top brass wanted. Ishigaki, highly experienced chief inspector that he was, was far from satisfied with the case.

Matsumiya reported their latest findings: that Kaori Nakahara hadn't known about Yashima having an electrician's knife; and the truth about the final phone call from Yashima.

"'I've done something awful. Something terrible's happened.' That's it? Sounds a reasonable enough thing to say in the circumstances." The furrow above Ishigaki's nose stayed firmly in place. "It's circumstantial evidence, sure, but it's on the weak side. It's not like he came straight out and said, 'I killed the guy.'"

"Well, no . . ."

"It's weak," repeated Ishigaki.

"There is one more thing," Matsumiya said after turning to glance at Kaga. "In the last text Fuyuki Yashima sent Kaori Nakahara, he said he was going to a job interview. Everyone currently sees that as referring to Yashima asking the victim for his old job back, but I wonder if that's really the case."

"Huh? What are you getting at?"

"That rather than meeting the victim, perhaps Yashima went out because he was going to have an interview at a bar or restaurant or some other kind of business."

Ishigaki looked skeptical.

"Don't you pay any attention in the darn meetings? We've contacted all the nearby establishments that were advertising for staff and didn't find a single one that Yashima had applied to or visited in person. There aren't any phone numbers of bars, restaurants, or other businesses in Yashima's phone. You can't seriously believe that someone who was going in for an interview wouldn't have had any advance contact?"

"I'm quite sure he was in touch with them—just without using a phone."

"How's he supposed to contact them without using his phone? There's nothing in his email or texts either."

Matsumiya shook his head and looked at his boss's narrow eyes.

"You can do it without calling, emailing, or texting. You just show up in person."

"Show up in person? Why would he do that?"

"It's faster than using the phone. Imagine that Yashima saw a help-wanted ad and the place that was hiring was right there in front of his eyes—don't you think he'd go in and try his luck?"

"In front of his eyes?" The expression on Ishigaki's face had switched from sullen to comprehending. "You think Yashima came across a help-wanted flyer stuck up on a wall somewhere?"

"Exactly. The kind that businesses post on their own doors. The flyer catches Yashima's eye, so he goes in and asks about the job. The other party comes back with, 'Today, no can do, but come back for an interview tomorrow.' What do you think? In that scenario, there's nothing strange about the lack of a call record in the log."

Ishigaki crossed his arms on his chest and looked up at Matsumiya.

"That certainly hangs together. Still, don't you think Yashima would have said something to his live-in girlfriend? Or did he keep quiet because he didn't want to count his chickens before they were hatched?"

"That's a possibility—but I suspect he just forgot. The day prior to the incident, Yashima and Kaori Nakahara went to a movie for the first time in ages. Net result: they didn't discuss work at all. Oh, and by the way, they went to see their movie in the Ginza area and Yashima went for an extensive ramble to kill time before they met. If he did stumble upon a job advert, it would have happened then."

His arms still crossed over his chest, Ishigaki puffed himself out.

"What triggered this?"

"Sir?"

"What set you on this train of thought? Was there a specific trigger?"

"Uhm, it was . . . his socks."

"Yashima's socks? Enlighten me."

Matsumiya relayed what Kaori Nakahara had told them.

"The fact that Yashima went to so much trouble to find a pair of socks without holes suggests that he knew he was going to have to take off his shoes somewhere later. At a business in Ginza, for example. If the plan was only to meet Aoyagi in a café, then the state of his socks would be neither here nor there."

Ishigaki sighed wearily. His eyes, which had been fixed on Matsumiya, now moved past him. Matsumiya had a pretty good idea who he was looking at now. Kaga must be standing behind him.

Kaga was the one who had come up with the theory Matsumiya had just put forward. Matsumiya had absolutely no clue why Kaga was questioning Kaori Nakahara about the day before the incident until he explained his reasons.

"That's some pretty impressive reasoning," said Ishigaki. "Okay. We'll take your idea on board. I'll instruct the detectives handling the investigation of the crime scene environs accordingly. If Yashima was planning to go to an interview, or if he really had one, that could change the whole thrust of the investigation. Whether it'll be a change for the better is another matter."

Something in Ishigaki's tone suggested he was preparing himself for a worst-case scenario where the whole investigation would be forced to go back to square one.

Matsumiya was getting ready to leave for the day when Kaga came up beside him.

"Ishigaki liked your idea."

"It's your idea, Kyo. You should have been the one to tell him. It's not like the chief doesn't know who figured it all out anyway."

"There's a right and a wrong way of doing things," Kaga said as he pulled out his cell phone. He had an incoming call. "Hello . . . Yes, Kaga here. Oh, thanks for calling . . . Oh, really? I see. Thank you very much for letting me know . . . Yes, that'll be fine. I'll be there soon." He spoke in a jaunty tone and his face had brightened.

"Anything you want to share?" Matsumiya asked.

"It was the restaurant owner. The customer who saw Aoyagi at Kasama Inari Shrine has just shown up at her place. He's in there, drinking, right now."

The two of them hurried off to the prix fixe restaurant. They caught the owner's eye and nodded good evening.

A group of four typical businessmen were drinking at a table for six. They had sashimi, a rolled Japanese-style omelet, and deep-fried chicken in front of them.

The owner went to have a word with a fat man seated at the end of the table nearest to the open passage area. Indicating Matsumiya and Kaga with her eyes, she whispered something. Unsurprisingly, his three companions stopped talking.

The fat man nodded his head. They could read his lips. "Sure, no problem."

The owner went over to Matsumiya and Kaga. "He's happy to talk to you."

Kaga approached the men's table, holding up his police badge. "Sorry to disturb your meal, gentlemen."

"It's fine. It's no big deal." The fat man looked a little unsure.

Kaga asked for his details. His name was Iwai and he worked for a company based in Yokohama.

"This is quite a surprise, I tell you. Never expected things to go this far. Just mentioned the fellow in passing. It's not like I really know anything."

"All I need you to do is tell me the facts. The person you say you saw, is this him?"

Iwai inspected the photograph that Kaga produced, then nodded his head. "Yes, that's definitely him."

"And when was it?"

"Uhm. A couple of months or so ago."

"At Kasama Inari Shrine?"

"That's right."

Iwai's mother had turned eighty this year. When she got sick, he had started dropping into the shrine regularly on his way back from work. Whether it was in answer to his prayers he couldn't well say, but his mother had staged a rapid recovery.

"When I pray, I'm more just going through the motions, but that guy in the photo, he had brought some serious kit with him. That's why I spoke to him."

"What do you mean by 'serious kit'?"

"Cranes. Origami cranes on strings." Iwai took a swig of beer. "He didn't have a thousand of the things, but I'd guess he had at least a hundred. They were this lovely purple color. He put them on the offertory chest, then pressed his palms together like this. You can see why I might want to talk to him, can't you?"

"Purple, you say? Normally, people make their thousand paper cranes from different-colored paper, but his were all purple?"

Iwai frowned slightly.

"Don't expect me to remember every little detail. I glanced at the things and the impression I got was, 'Wow, what a gorgeous purple.' Maybe there were some other colors in there. I'm not sure."

"That's not a problem. So what did you say to him?" Kaga asked.

"'You're very serious about this. You must have a real thing for this shrine.'"

"What did he say?"

"The man looked rather embarrassed and started putting the cranes away rather hastily. He told me that he was only there because he happened to be nearby."

"Happened to be nearby?"

"I thought it was an odd thing to say too. How could he seriously claim he was only there by chance when he'd prepared so many paper cranes? I guess that's why I remembered the fellow. When I saw the news about this case, his photo bugged me; it was a face I'd seen before. Then, out of nowhere, it came to me and I started shooting my mouth off, here among many other places. Sorry if I've been disturbing the peace." Iwai's tone was glib. He was probably a little tipsy.

"You said that he quickly tidied away the cranes after finishing his prayers. What exactly did he do?"

"What did he do? He put them away. Stuffed them into a paper carrier bag he had on him. At least, I think he did. Sorry, the old memory's a little hazy."

Kaga nodded. "I see. Well, my apologies for disturbing your meal. We're very grateful for your help." He bowed in thanks.

"Isn't the case closed?" Iwai said. "I mean, the guy who did it is dead. At least, that's what they're saying on TV."

There was a pause. Kaga grinned at the man.

"We're just the rank and file. We don't get to decide if a case is closed or not. We just investigate what our superiors order us to investigate."

"That's how it goes, eh? Life's hard, whatever your line of business." Iwai directed this final comment at his three companions.

"Let's go," Kaga said to Matsumiya. Matsumiya nodded goodbye to the restaurant owner and pushed the door open.

"Surprised to hear about the origami cranes," he said as they walked along. "That's not your run-of-the-mill praying. That's serious stuff."

"Aoyagi claimed to be there by chance; that his visit to

Kasama Inari Shrine was unplanned. My takeaway from that is that Kasama Inari wasn't the shrine where he really wanted to do his praying, but that, since the opportunity had presented itself, he was visiting all the Seven Lucky Gods shrines."

"I agree. The question is: which of the shrines was his favorite."

Kaga had turned and they were on a different street from their usual route. Matsumiya followed, wondering where on earth his cousin was off to now, when he suddenly noticed a small torii gate. It was half inside a small modern office building, and seemed the last place where you would expect to find a shrine, until you were right on top of it.

"Matsushima Shrine. One of the Seven Lucky Gods shrines," said Kaga, passing under the torii gate.

Matsumiya went in after him. At night, they must pull a fence across to protect the shrine building. The offertory chest would be on the inside of the fence too.

"The god of this shrine is Daikoku. Daikoku's the god of agriculture and trade. Aoyagi was a businessman, so it would be normal enough for him to come here to pray for the success of his business, but that doesn't fit with what we've been told about the origami cranes. The thousand paper cranes are used when praying for long life and recovery from illness. Kasama Inari Shrine fits that bill perfectly." Kaga extracted his notebook from the inside breast pocket of his jacket. "Kasama Inari Shrine is dedicated to Jurojin, the god of longevity. Now, how about the other shrines? . . . Koami Shrine is similar. The god there is Fukurokuju; he's a symbol of longevity."

"Is Koami far?"

"Not at all. Let's go."

They then headed west, past the old coffee shop that Takeaki Aoyagi had visited.

The road snaked around the back of Nihonbashi Elementary School. At one corner of a three-way intersection crowded with office buildings, there was a small open area with greenery, inside which stood a modest torii gate and shrine. Paper lanterns hung on either side of the gate.

"Wonder if this shrine was his favorite?" Matsumiya said.

Kaga looked unhappy.

"There's any number of shrines dedicated to long life and good health. There's no reason for this to be his favorite."

"Perhaps it had special associations for him. Maybe his prayers were answered when he came here before."

"Have you forgotten what his wife said? Aoyagi wasn't a religious man."

"It's all very well saying that, but he did come to pray at all these shrines. That's a fact. He even made those origami cranes."

"That's the real mystery. Why the origami cranes?"

"Nobody we've questioned has mentioned Aoyagi making paper cranes. When did he make the things? It's not like he made just one or two of them."

"Exactly," Kaga said. "And where have all those paper cranes disappeared to?"

"Search me." Matsumiya shrugged.

"The man just now told us that he put the cranes away after having placed them on the offertory box. Did he take them somewhere? Or did he just throw them away?"

"I can't see him treating origami cranes he'd made for prayer like ordinary trash. So what would he do with them?" Kaga said. He was silent for a while, then slowly he began nodding his head. There was a faint smile on his lips. "Yep, I've got it. I think this will do it."

"What? Why are you looking so smug?"

"I've figured out a way to find Aoyagi's favorite shrine. The origami cranes will reveal all," Kaga said as he contemplated the shrine building half-enveloped in darkness.

19

Just after ten o'clock the next morning, Matsumiya and Kaga were in the administrative office of Suitengu Shrine.

"Origami cranes? You're sure about that?" Matsumiya asked forcefully.

The man they were talking to, who was dressed in a white shirt with a gray cardigan on top, nodded.

"At the rate of about once a month, I reckon. Someone put them on top of the offertory box, along with a white envelope with a thousand-yen note inside and 'For the cost of ritual burning' written on the front."

"Have you got any of the cranes?"

"No . . . I mean, we burned them," said the man, sounding apologetic.

"When did the crane offerings start?"

"Maybe . . . six or so months ago."

The main gate of Suitengu Shrine shuts at five o'clock, but there is a nighttime entrance that is open until seven. One evening, around six months ago, the man had been checking the shrine precincts before locking up for the night when he noticed a big bunch of paper cranes sitting on the offertory box.

"I say 'big bunch,' but there weren't a thousand cranes. There turned out to be exactly one hundred of them when I counted. A nice yellow color."

"Yellow?" Matsumiya and Kaga exchanged a look. "All of them?"

"Yes. All the same matching yellow. The color would change every month."

"Yes?"

"There was green, there was blue, there was purple, but always one color at a time. And there were always exactly one hundred of them."

Kaga took a step forward. "Was this always the same day? The same day every month?"

"I don't think so. It wasn't that systematic."

"Was it on the weekend?"

"No, weekdays, I think. When there aren't many worshippers around."

"Didn't anyone here see who was offering the cranes?"

"My impression is that the person deliberately targeted times when no one else was about. I don't know why they had to be so furtive. It's not like they were doing anything wrong," the man said with a rueful smile.

The two detectives thanked him and left the shrine

office. Even though it was a weekday morning, there were quite a few people in the shrine precincts.

What had Takeaki Aoyagi done with the origami cranes he used when praying at the shrines of the Seven Lucky Gods?

Kaga reckoned that he must have had them burned. Shrines have regular ritual bonfires they use to get rid of old amulets and talismans, and strings of origami cranes are often thrown onto the fire. That was the reason why Matsumiya and Kaga were visiting all the Seven Lucky Gods shrines this morning. Before going to Suitengu Shrine, they had tried their luck at Koami Shrine. They had been told that no one had been offering paper cranes there and that the shrine didn't conduct the ritual burning of lucky charms either.

"Is it fair to assume that praying at Suitengu Shrine was Aoyagi's main goal?"

"We can't yet say for sure. We still need proof that Aoyagi was the person offering the cranes there."

"That's easy enough to say, but how are we supposed to do it, now that all the darn things have been burned. My gut tells me we're right. The paper cranes here match the ones Aoyagi was seen with at Kasama Inari Shrine. The color was different, but we now know he changed that every month."

"That's it! Why do you think he changed the color?"

"I don't think it means much. Though it's actually harder to get that many sheets of paper all in the same color."

Kaga stopped.

"Paper, huh? How would you go about it, Shuhei? If you were going to make a string of origami cranes, where would you get the paper?"

"Oh, come on. You can find paper anywhere. They even sell origami paper at your local convenience store."

"Fine, then. Let's check it out."

They left the shrine and started roaming around the neighborhood. They came across a stationery store where they were shown several varieties of origami paper in response to their inquiries. It came in packs, either with a hundred sheets of the same color or with mixed colors. There were also different textures and sizes of paper. They bought several of the most popular assortments and left the shop.

"And the point of buying all this crap is . . . ?" asked Matsumiya. He was the one holding the paper carrier bag. And even origami paper is heavy when you have several hundred sheets of the stuff.

"Duh! We're going to make some origami cranes."

"You're kidding me."

"This is as good as anywhere." Kaga had stopped in front of a diner-style restaurant.

Ignoring the waitress's sour looks, Matsumiya and Kaga set about making cranes. Matsumiya hadn't done any origami for twenty-odd years. Despite that, he still remembered how to fold the paper.

Once they had completed a decent number and had some lunch, they left the restaurant. They went straight back to Suitengu Shrine and got the same man at the shrine office to inspect their handiwork.

"I reckon this one's the most like his. Yes, this is the same kind of paper he used."

The crane the man was holding up was made of traditional Japanese *washi* paper. It was one of the ones Matsumiya had made.

"But the size is wrong. His were smaller. More like this." As he said this, he picked up a crane made from a ten-centimeter-square sheet of paper.

Matsumiya and Kaga exchanged a look. The stationery shop didn't have any ten-centimeter-square traditional Japanese *washi* paper for origami. Standard origami paper was typically fifteen centimeters square.

"Ten-centimeter-square traditional Japanese *washi* paper. That's handy to know," said Kaga as they went down the stairs leading out of the shrine. "Aoyagi's office was in Shinjuku. If he was after traditional Japanese *washi* paper, chances are he'd go to one of the local department stores there. We should be able to find the place if we visit a few of them."

"A traditional Japanese *washi* paper store . . ." A light bulb went off in Matsumiya's head as he murmured to himself. He gasped, missed his footing, and almost tumbled down the stairs.

"What's wrong? Are you okay?"

"I know a place, Kyo. A traditional Japanese *washi* paper store. Very close to here."

"Close by? Where?"

"What was that soba noodle restaurant we went to the other day . . . Kobaian? Just near there. It specializes in traditional Japanese *washi* paper."

Kaga's eyes widened. He pointed a finger at Matsumiya's face. "Let's go take a look."

They decided to take a cab. First, though, they would

need to do something with all their spare origami paper. A woman with a child in tow had just come down the steps. They explained the situation and got her to take the paper off their hands. Her pleasure was so genuine that it was written on her face.

The traditional Japanese *washi* paper store was in an office building in Nihonbashi. There was a store on the first floor and offices upstairs. As they went through the glass doors, there was some papermaking equipment, and panels on the walls explaining the process of making Japanese paper, off to the right. According to the store plan on the wall, there was an exhibition space, a history museum, and a small gallery up on the second floor.

The store was spacious with items of every imaginable color on display. As well as traditional Japanese *washi* paper itself, they had numerous products made from paper. Hunting down the origami paper was going to be a challenge.

Matsumiya called over the female store clerk standing nearby. Did they have any origami paper? he asked.

She beamed at him and produced something called Traditional Paper in Ten Colors. It proclaimed itself to be handmade. The sheets were ten centimeters square and came in packs of one hundred. There were ten sheets each in pink, red, orange, brown, yellow, green, light blue, dark blue, purple, and lilac. The pack cost 1,050 yen, including consumption tax.

"This must be it." Matsumiya showed it to Kaga. "I'm guessing he bought ten packs of this, then used a hundred sheets in the same color for his cranes."

Kaga nodded, turned to the female store clerk, and flashed his police badge.

"Has anyone been buying this origami paper in large quantities? We're talking roughly six months ago."

The store clerk looked discombobulated. "Could you wait a moment, please, sir?" she said and walked off briskly.

Matsumiya took another look at the pack of paper. It was so light and thin that it was hard to believe that it contained one hundred sheets of paper. The paper was packaged with the edges of the different color sheets not quite flush, so that you could see all ten colors at once. Looking at all the vibrant colors next to one another, Matsumiya felt it was too good to use for origami.

The store clerk eventually reappeared. She had brought an older woman, presumably her manager, with her.

"I'm told you've been asking about our origami paper?" she asked.

Kaga repeated his question. The woman nodded solemnly.

"We certainly have some such customers. It's not unusual for people to buy this particular item in bulk."

"How about this gentleman? Has he ever been here?" Kaga showed the two women a photograph of Takeaki Aoyagi.

A change came over the older woman's face. She blinked rapidly, then looked at Kaga and Matsumiya one after another.

"Yes, he's been here. And I'm pretty sure he purchased ten packs of this brand."

Matsumiya felt a surge of heat in his body.

"Was this around six months ago?" Kaga confirmed, keeping a studiedly neutral tone.

"That's right. I remember it because we had some problems with it."

"What sort of problems?"

"The first time he came in, we didn't have enough stock. We had to ask him to come back again a week later."

Kaga nodded. "I see. Thank you very much indeed."

They bought a pack of Traditional Paper in Ten Colors and exited the store. They agreed to walk back to Suitengu Shrine. On their way, they passed Takarada Ebisu Shrine.

"Aoyagi must have come across that paper shop while he was doing the Seven Lucky Gods circuit," Matsumiya said.

"Which means that when he started doing the circuit, he hadn't yet incorporated bunches of origami cranes into his prayer ritual. I wonder what prompted him to do so?"

"No special reason is my guess. I say it was just a whim."

"What? You think someone can make one hundred origami cranes on a whim? On a monthly basis?"

"Fair point."

At Suitengu Shrine, they asked the man in the shrine office to take a good look at a crane they had made using paper from the Traditional Paper in Ten Colors pack. He placed the yellow crane on the palm of his hand and squinted at it.

"This is the one. No doubt about it. It's identical."

Matsumiya and Kaga exchanged a satisfied nod.

"We now know for sure that it was Aoyagi who was making the crane offerings. And we were right about Suitengu being his favorite shrine." As they emerged into the shrine yard, Matsumiya looked over at the main shrine building.

"Those are both reasonable assumptions. But we're still left with the mystery of why Aoyagi got so religious all of a sudden . . . ," Kaga said, a tinge of frustration on his face.

Suitengu Shrine was a place you go to pray for safe childbirth. Who was Takeaki Aoyagi praying for on his visits there?

The shrine hall exuded majesty. Just in front of it, there was a small, roofed structure where you could wash. Kaga explained the protocol: you were supposed to purify your hands and mouth there before you went on to worship at the shrine.

There was a little sales booth with a display of good luck charms and talismans off to the right of the shrine hall.

A woman was sitting inside the booth. She looked unsure when Matsumiya showed her a photograph of Takeaki Aoyagi. She could well have seen someone who looked like that, but then again she could just be imagining it, she said. It was a reasonable enough response. She must deal with a large number of people every day.

To the left of the shrine, there was a copper statue of two dogs, a mother and puppy. The dogs were sitting on a hemisphere decorated with carvings of the twelve signs of the Chinese zodiac. Rubbing your star sign was supposed to bring you good luck, but evidently, the part that got rubbed the most was the puppy's head. It was the only place that shone with a goldish tint.

Matsumiya noticed a little group of worshippers, a man and two women. The man and one of the women were in late middle age, while the younger woman's belly was swollen. Parents with their pregnant daughter, obviously. All three looked quite joyful.

The sight of them made Matsumiya think of another young woman.

"Could Aoyagi have been coming here for Kaori Naka-hara?" Then he stopped and shook his head. "No, that's impossible. Aoyagi and Yashima would have had to be really close for that to happen. It doesn't fit with what we've learned so far."

"What have we learned so far?" Kaga said. "All we've got is a scenario concocted by the investigation team that's very loosely based on whatever they managed to find out. We don't need our findings to dovetail with theirs. The only thing that matters here is the truth."

"Okay, then, Kyo, do you think that Aoyagi was coming here for Kaori Nakahara?"

"There's a more-than-zero possibility. But you're forgetting one very important thing."

"What? Tell me."

"Kaori Nakahara told us that she's three months' pregnant—and Takeaki Aoyagi started visiting the Seven Lucky Gods shrines much more than three months ago."

"Oh . . ." Kaga was right. Matsumiya could have kicked himself for his sloppy thinking.

"Why don't we start by talking to Aoyagi's family," Kaga said, heading for the exit.

This time there were no suspicious-looking characters hanging around the Aoyagi house. Not even the tabloid TV shows were giving much coverage to the Nihonbashi Bridge murder case anymore. Following the death of Fuyuki Yashima, there was a general feeling that the case was over and done with. The TV stations must have realized that they had wrung all the ratings mileage they could out of a workplace accident cover-up, which was hardly the most atrocious of crimes.

Matsumiya pressed the bell on the intercom. It was Fumiko Aoyagi who answered. As soon as he announced himself, a note of irritation became audible in her voice. She was nonetheless willing to meet with them.

Just like the time before, she ushered them into the living room. Matsumiya and Kaga sat down, side by side. Fumiko served green tea despite their protestations. The teacups were the same as the last time too.

"So, what is it today?" Fumiko asked, her eyes fixed firmly on the floor.

"The fact is, we've learned something intriguing," Kaga began. "Your husband seems to have been telling people in his circle something about there being a baby on the way. Would you know anything about that?"

Fumiko looked mystified. "Sorry . . . a baby?"

"That's right. Your husband was planning some sort of celebration for the birth, apparently."

Kaga had decided not to reveal anything to the family about Takeaki Aoyagi's visits to the shrines of the Seven Lucky Gods. He felt it would be a mistake to let that particular cat out of the bag prematurely.

Fumiko tilted her head to one side and sucked her teeth.

"No one in the family is expecting. Nor are any of our

friends' daughters . . . No, I don't know anything about any baby."

"Did you discuss the subject with your husband recently? A married couple that's about to have a baby; perhaps a couple that's having trouble conceiving?"

Fumiko looked as nonplussed as ever. She rummaged through her memory but came up empty-handed.

"I'm sorry," she replied. "I really can't think of anyone."

"Okay. That's not a problem. Frankly, we don't know whether this is even connected with the case. We just wanted to check, that's all."

"Sorry, but I thought the case was solved? Yashima is dead. What more is there to investigate?"

Rather than respond immediately, Kaga reached for his teacup. "This looks delicious," he said. He drank a mouthful appreciatively, then emitted a long sigh.

"Mrs. Aoyagi," he said. "I am sure there are still many things about this case that don't feel quite right to you. Are you happy for things to be brought to an end like this? Are you willing to accept that?"

"No . . . no, I'm not." Fumiko looked at the floor and wrung her hands.

At that moment, there was a noise out in the hall. There was the sound of approaching footsteps and the door swung open. Yuto barreled into the room, then came to an abrupt stop like a character in a cartoon when he noticed Matsumiya and Kaga. He must have missed the two pairs of unfamiliar shoes at the step by the front door.

"Afternoon," said Kaga. Matsumiya acknowledged him with a nod.

Yuto made a sour face, thrust his chin out, and disappeared into the kitchen. There was the sound of the refrigerator door opening and closing and he reemerged holding a plastic bottle of Coke. He unscrewed the cap, took a swig straight from the bottle, and gazed defiantly at the two detectives.

"You guys still investigating shit?"

"Yuto, mind your language!" Fumiko said reprovingly.

"It's okay," Kaga said in a conciliatory tone. He looked up at Yuto. "We detectives are the same as any other wage slave. We just have to do what our bosses tell us."

Yuto snorted. "You drew the short straw. Getting put on such a stupid case."

"Stupid?" Matsumiya couldn't help reacting to the word. "How exactly is it stupid?"

"Come on. We all know it's an insignificant case. What, some dumb workplace accident cover-up? My dad did something mean and sordid; the guy he did it to got pissed off and stabbed him. Under normal circumstances, no one would give a damn. But because Dad died in such a showy way—not his style at all—the media jumped all over the story, meaning that you guys can't get away with any half-assed investigation. That's what this is all about, right?"

"The manner of a person's death has no effect on how we conduct our investigations."

"Oh yeah? I bet things would have been different if Dad

had died in a less famous location. I mean, he was lying there, stone-dead, smack in the middle of the bridge! Why'd he have to go and die like that?" As he said this, Yuto started shaking the Coke bottle.

Matsumiya fought back the impulse to give the boy's pale face a good brisk smack.

"Let me clarify something. Your father died in the hospital. Not on the bridge. And he wasn't lying on the ground, he was leaning up against the base of the *kirin* statue."

"*Kirin?*" Yuto frowned distrustfully.

"Midway over Nihonbashi Bridge there are a couple of *kirin* statues. Winged *kirin*. Mr. Aoyagi was leaning up against one of the statues and he wasn't moving. A policeman nearby noticed him there. As I think you know, the place where he was actually stabbed is a certain distance away. We still don't know why Mr. Aoyagi made his way from one place to the other."

Yuto snorted and took a sullen swig of Coke.

"Seriously, who even cares? If he had to be murdered, he could at least have done it without screwing everything up for us."

"*Yuto!*" Fumiko's voice was sudden and shrill. Her intervention had an impact; Yuto's expression hardened and he stalked out of the living room. They heard him stomping up the stairs.

"I'm sorry about that," said Fumiko apologetically. "The kids at school are giving him a hard time about his father."

Matsumiya knew what Yuto was going through. When someone in the family dies an unusual death, other people feel free to comment for years afterward.

"By the way," said Kaga. "Did your husband have a home office?"

Fumiko shook her head. "No, we don't have one of those. My husband almost never brought work home with him. Any paperwork he needed to do, he did here in this room."

"I see. Where did he keep his pens and such?"

"Over there." Fumiko pointed to a cabinet up against the wall. "In one of the drawers."

"Could we take a look?"

"Be my guest."

Kaga got to his feet, pulling on a pair of gloves as he did so. Matsumiya took his notebook out of his pocket.

Together they examined the contents of the drawer. They were hoping to find the unused Traditional Paper in Ten Colors. Assuming the witness statement they had gotten at Suitengu Shrine was correct, Takeaki Aoyagi should still be in possession of six hundred sheets of unused origami paper. It had to be somewhere.

They didn't find any paper. They had been half expecting that. Takeaki Aoyagi must have made his origami cranes outside the home.

It was time to wind things up. They were taking their leave from Mrs. Aoyagi just inside the front door when they sensed the presence of someone else. A girl with strikingly large eyes was behind them on the doorstep. It had to be Haruka, the daughter.

"Oh, hello, dear. These two gentlemen are detectives."

Despite Fumiko's introduction, Haruka didn't even give them a glance. She shot up the stairs without a word.

"I'm sorry," said the mother, apologizing for a second time.

They said their goodbyes, left the house, and were a certain distance from it when Matsumiya turned around to look back at the place. "What's wrong?" Kaga asked.

Matsumiya shook his head. "Oh, nothing," he said and resumed walking.

This case isn't over. We've solved nothing, he was thinking once again.

20

At the investigation meeting the next morning, it was officially announced that a couple of investigators had managed to locate the place Fuyuki Yashima went for his job interview.

It was a company called Stock House that sold handmade furniture and other bric-a-brac. It was located in Kyobashi, a ten-minute walk from the movie theater where Yashima went with his girlfriend the night before.

"It's a small outfit: just three employees and a CEO. Their showroom, which doubles as an office, is up on the second floor of a building. The help-wanted flyer was stuck on the front door. I should mention that it had actually been taken down by the time we got there. A witness had told us about the flyer, so we questioned all the tenants in the building. That's how we found out about Yashima going to Stock House." Nagase, who was one of the older and more experienced detectives on the task force, spoke slowly. "Yashima first dropped in at around seven o'clock on the evening before the incident to inquire about the job vacancy. Only one member of staff was still on the premises. When he called the boss, the boss said, 'Tell him to come back tomorrow.' The staffer duly relayed the message to Yashima, who returned around six the next day, when he met the company boss."

The scenario was almost exactly what Kaga had imagined. The only difference was that it involved a furniture shop rather than a bar or restaurant. Still, given what Kaori Nakahara had told them about how ill-suited Yashima was to the hospitality business, it seemed a smart choice on his part.

In one section of the furniture showroom, you had to remove your shoes. That explained why Yashima had been hunting for socks with no holes in them; he was expecting to have to take his shoes off.

"The boss didn't offer Yashima the job because he had completely the wrong idea about what the job involved," Nagase went on with his report.

"Got the wrong idea? How come?" asked the deputy commissioner, looking peeved.

"The company was hiring temps for a trade show that's happening any day now. They'd managed to recruit a certain number of people by contacting friends and acquaintances, but finding themselves shorthanded, they posted the help-wanted flyer. It turned out that Yashima had been hoping for a job that involved actually *making* furniture."

"So that's what you were getting at. In that case, I really have trouble understanding why no one at the firm bothered to get in touch. They can hardly claim not to have heard about the incident, can they?"

"They just hadn't made the connection."

"Meaning?"

"It was the CEO who spoke to us. He had heard about the murder, but never in his wildest dreams had he imagined that the young man he'd met was the suspect. The job interview was brief to the point that he didn't even remember Yashima's name and he only read a short online article about the whole incident. He never saw a photograph of Yashima either."

"That happens a lot lately," Ishigaki said, sounding rather apologetic. "From what I hear, Yashima's picture is on the internet, but it's too small to see what he really looks like."

The deputy commissioner nodded. His expression was as sour as ever.

"There's one more thing," continued Nagase, referring to his notebook. "According to the Stock House CEO, Yashima looked so crestfallen at not getting the job that he took pity on him. He advised him that if he wanted a job making furniture, he should try his luck with another firm not too far away. The company he recommended is called Azuma Furniture; it's located near Edobashi Bridge."

A murmur rippled through the room. Matsumiya had been surprised at the news the night before.

"Edobashi Bridge?" The deputy commissioner's voice rose higher. "That's our crime scene."

"Indeed it is. When we went to speak to the second furniture company, it turned out Yashima hadn't actually been to see them. They closed their offices at six thirty on the day in question. That is everything I have to report," said the veteran detective as he sat down.

The deputy commissioner glumly scratched the back of his head.

"How are we meant to make sense of this? Wasn't Yashima supposed to have made an appointment to meet the victim?"

"When you consider the time frame, the likelihood of them having made an appointment is low," Ishigaki said. "Had Yashima's job interview gone well, he had no way of knowing how long he would have been there. But since there's no record of the victim's number on his phone, Yashima couldn't have called to change the time of their rendezvous."

"Then how did the two men meet?"

"Chance is a possibility."

"Chance?"

"Another investigator has already reported that the victim did the Seven Lucky Gods pilgrimage circuit repeatedly. It is possible that, on the day of the incident, he wandered into the vicinity of the Edobashi Bridge after visiting all the shrines and bumped into Yashima, who was on his way to the second furniture shop."

"You think that's when the two of them went to the café?"

"The timing works out. In that scenario, though, we can no longer explain how Yashima came to have the knife on him."

The deputy commissioner's face twisted into a scowl. "The knife? I'd forgotten that."

"If Yashima encountered the victim purely by chance, then he had no reason to bring a knife with him."

"Couldn't he have been carrying it for self-defense?" the deputy commissioner hazarded.

"Self-defense?" Ishigaki's voice was lukewarm.

The meeting came to an end without that particular point being resolved. Ishigaki and Kobayashi went and sat down on either side of the deputy commissioner and the three men launched into a discussion. Matsumiya assumed they were discussing the knife.

Suddenly, one of the younger detectives on the task force burst into the room. He went up to the table where the top brass were sitting and said something. Even at a distance, Matsumiya could see their expressions cloud over as they listened.

Ishigaki ran his eyes around the room. His gaze came to a stop on Matsumiya, who wasn't surprised to hear his name called.

Matsumiya went over. "Yes, sir, what is it?" he asked. Ishigaki said nothing and gestured for him to come closer. Matsumiya went and stood to one side of his three seated superiors.

"I need you and Kaga to get yourselves over to the victim's house ASAP."

"Has something happened?"

Ishigaki nodded curtly and scowled. "The daughter slit her wrists earlier this morning."

Instinctively, Matsumiya gasped.

"She was taken to the hospital in an ambulance and

got patched up. Her injuries weren't grave, but the hospital alerted the local police. She's back home, apparently. I'd like you to go and check in on her."

"Yes, sir."

Matsumiya went back to Kaga and explained the situation. He caught his breath. Clearly, the news was a shock for him too.

"I only saw the girl for a second or two yesterday, but there was something not quite right about her," Matsumiya said as they made their way to the subway station. "People have began giving her a hard time, despite her being part of the victim's family."

"Murder cases are like cancer cells. Once they get their hooks into you, the pain and misery just keep on spreading. Whether the killer gets caught or the investigation is brought to a successful conclusion doesn't make any difference; it's almost impossible to stop the advance of the disease."

Kaga's quiet words struck a chord with Matsumiya. *He's right about that,* he thought.

Everything was quiet in the vicinity of the Aoyagi house. But not that long ago, an ambulance had pulled up here. The neighbors must have heard the siren and opened their windows for a look. When they saw the daughter being brought out, their imaginations must have gone into overdrive. Matsumiya prayed that the incident didn't trigger a new bout of malicious gossip.

He pressed the intercom. He'd been expecting to hear Fumiko's voice, but a young man answered. It had to be Yuto.

Matsumiya gave their names and explained that they

were there to ask some questions about his sister. A brief pause was followed by a curt "Come in."

As Matsumiya and Kaga approached the house, the door opened and Fumiko peered out. Her eyes were red from weeping and her face looked taut and strained.

"Sorry to keep bothering you like this." Matsumiya bowed his head. "We heard the awful news about your daughter."

"They gave her something. She's asleep right now. She's in no fit state to talk to anyone."

"In that case, we'll just speak to you, Mrs. Aoyagi. Could you tell us what happened?"

"If I must. Come on in, then."

"Thank you." They went inside. Someone had dumped a sports bag in the entrance hall. It was probably Yuto's.

Yuto himself was in the living room. Or more precisely, he was in the Japanese-style room adjoining it. He was sitting cross-legged in front of the memorial photograph of Takeaki Aoyagi. He didn't turn to look at the two detectives as they came in.

"Time you got off to school, Yuto. We'll be fine here," Fumiko said.

"Not today. I already called the school and told them I'd probably not make it."

"Yes, but—"

"*I said it's okay.* Just get off my back." Yuto crossed his arms over his chest and gazed intently at his father's photograph.

Matsumiya and Kaga sat down on the sofa. Seeing Fumiko

about to make a beeline for the kitchen, Kaga spoke up. "Please, don't worry about us," he said. "We just want to hear what happened, then we'll be on our way."

Fumiko sat down, a miserable expression on her face.

"When Haruka didn't come down at the normal time, I got worried and went up to her room. The bed was all covered with blood . . . and she was just lying there."

"What did she use on her wrists? A razor?"

"A box cutter. It was on the floor. She'd sliced her wrists to shreds."

"Was she conscious?"

"Yes, but she didn't respond. She just kept crying and crying."

"What about after she'd been seen to at the hospital? Did you manage to talk to her then?"

Fumiko gave a weak shake of the head.

"Until you got here, I was up in her room. She didn't say a word."

"Have you any idea what triggered this?"

Fumiko sighed. "I don't know the details. All I know is that she's having a very hard time at school because of what happened to her father. She just shuts herself up in her room when she gets back home."

A loud thud came from the Japanese-style room. Yuto had smacked the tatami mats with both fists.

"Haruka's an idiot. Committing suicide is as good as admitting Dad's guilt."

Matsumiya frowned at Yuto.

"That's not a very nice thing to say. Think about what your sister's going through."

"I don't need you to tell me. I'm going through the same thing myself."

Yuto jumped up, walked past Matsumiya and Kaga, and ran up the stairs.

Kaga waited until the sound of his footsteps had faded, then asked Fumiko, "Did anything out of the ordinary happen between last night and this morning?"

"Not that I'm aware."

"Could Haruka have come across some new information about the case online or on TV?"

Fumiko shook her head. "We all try our best to see as little news as we can."

"A visitor to the house, perhaps?"

"No. Like I said, someone must have said something to her yesterday at school."

Kaga nodded in silence. As he listened to their exchange, Matsumiya wondered why Kaga was pressing the point so hard. Considering the daughter's general situation and the way she had looked last night, her cutting her wrists didn't strike him as anything unusual. Plus she was at an emotional age.

Matsumiya put the question to Kaga once they had left the Aoyagi house. "Oh, it's nothing important. I was just checking something," came the reply.

Matsumiya called Ishigaki to update him. The unit chief seemed relieved to hear that things weren't as bad as they might have been.

"That's good news for us. A member of the victim's family committing suicide would only have ignited another media feeding frenzy."

"The girl is recuperating. The family can handle things from here. We're heading back your way."

"No, don't do that. I need you to reconfirm the movements of the victim on the day of the incident. That's something we've got to clarify."

"His movements?"

"I want confirmation that Aoyagi did the Seven Lucky Gods circuit on the day of the crime. If Yashima and the victim didn't arrange to meet, as was suggested at this morning's meeting, they must have just bumped into one another randomly on the street. We now know why Yashima was in the Edobashi Bridge area. That just leaves us with the victim."

"I understand."

"You two guys have the best grasp of the victim's behavior. We're counting on you."

"Yes, sir."

Matsumiya ended the call and relayed Ishigaki's instructions to Kaga. Kaga cocked his head and looked skeptical.

"He thinks they just bumped into each other? . . . I suppose it's not completely out of the question."

"I wonder how he's planning to explain away the knife, though. It doesn't hang together."

"I guess he's planning to fudge the issue. Anyway, let's get on with it and verify Aoyagi's movements."

They took the train to Ningyocho and started walking.

They now knew the streets so well they didn't need a map. They walked the Seven Lucky Gods circuit. They tried all the shops and restaurants near the different shrines, including revisiting the establishments where they had already made inquiries. People sometimes remember things on a second visit that they forgot the first time around.

Despite pursuing their inquiries for hours, they couldn't find any evidence of Takeaki Aoyagi having done the Seven Lucky Gods circuit on the day he was killed.

"He could always have visited all the shrines without stopping off anywhere en route," said Matsumiya as they passed Takarada Ebisu Shrine. The street was already dark.

"Or he didn't do the shrine circuit at all," Kaga muttered.

"Seems unlikely to me. I mean, in that case, why would he even be here in Nihonbashi at all?"

"Your guess is as good as mine. I'm working from the assumption that whenever he did the Seven Lucky Gods circuit, he always brought a bunch of one hundred origami cranes along. And no one left any cranes in Suitengu Shrine on that day."

"Maybe he didn't bring cranes every time. Why not?"

Kaga lapsed into silence, a skeptical look on his face. Presently, they came to the corner with the traditional Japanese paper company. The store on the first floor was still open.

Kaga stopped. "Let's pop in for a look."

"What! We were only there yesterday."

Ignoring Matsumiya's outburst, Kaga went in. Matsumiya reluctantly trailed after him.

The young female store clerk they had dealt with the day

before approached them. She looked uncomfortable, despite her smile. "Shall I call the manager?"

"No, no need for that. Could we take another look at the Traditional Paper in Ten Colors again?" Kaga asked.

"This one?"

Kaga took the item she was holding out and examined it closely. It was the same product he had bought the day before.

"What's this all about?" Matsumiya asked.

"Could you tell me something?" Kaga asked the store clerk. "With this particular product, are the colors always arranged in the same order like this? Or do they sometimes vary?"

The store clerk looked flummoxed. "Wait a moment, please," she said and disappeared into the back of the store.

Matsumiya examined the shelf display. The colors were arranged in the same order in every pack: pink on top, then red, orange, brown, yellow, green, and so on.

The store clerk came back just as Matsumiya was about to ask Kaga why on earth he was worrying about something so trivial.

"Sorry about that. With this product, the colors are always in the same order."

"Really? Thank you very much." Kaga replaced the pack he was holding on the shelf.

"What's this all about?" Matsumiya asked after the store clerk had left. "Who cares about the order of the colors?"

Kaga slowly turned to face Matsumiya.

"Do you remember what the man at Suitengu Shrine told us? What color was the first set of cranes he found?"

"Of course I remember. They were yellow."

"That's right. To me, that suggests that Aoyagi bought ten complete packs of this brand, extracted ten sheets of the same color from each of the packs, and then made his one hundred cranes. Don't you think it's a bit odd, though? In his shoes, what would you do? If you were making cranes, wouldn't you normally use the paper in the order it came, from the top on down? The top ten sheets are pink. The yellow is somewhere around the middle of the pack. Why do you think he made a deliberate decision to use the color in the middle?"

Matsumiya took another look at the pack of Traditional Paper in Ten Colors. Kaga had a point about the order.

"He had a reason to start from yellow. Is that what you're thinking?"

"That's what I'm thinking. The question we have to answer is what that reason was."

21

The statue of the twelfth-century warrior monk Benkei was far smaller than she had expected. She had pictured something she would have to look up to, but in actuality, the thing was little more than life size. It wasn't on a high pedestal or protected by a fence, so you could reach out and touch it.

Kaori was in the Hamacho Green Road park. It was a little before ten at night and the air was cold and crisp. With the trees muffling the glow of the streetlights, it was dark underfoot.

From the TV reports, she learned that Fuyuki fled to this park on the night of the crime. She hadn't caught its name, but the Benkei statue had furnished a clue.

She was eating dinner in her apartment when she got a sudden urge to see the place: the place where Fuyuki had made his last ever phone call. It was cold, so she put on her coat and wound a muffler around her neck before setting off. She found a diner in the area that was still open, popped in, and asked where the park with the Benkei statue was. The lady in the diner was really nice.

She took a deep breath. She could feel the cold in her lungs. She suppressed a shudder. When she exhaled, she was surprised that her breath wasn't white.

The place was eerily quiet, but Kaori decided to walk down the wooded path nonetheless. She passed a bench nestled in a stand of dense trees. *Where did Fuyuki hide that night?* she wondered. *Did he crouch down behind some trees?*

"Kaori." She heard his voice; it was more like a groan. Her name: that was the first word Fuyuki had uttered when he called her that night.

"I've done something awful. Something terrible's happened. I don't know what to do."

What state of mind was he in when he called her? It was right after the call that he had tried to run away from the police officer and been hit by a truck.

Something had gone wrong—that was the only possible interpretation of events. Fuyuki would never kill another human being.

She noticed what looked like a large package on a bench. Curious, she walked toward it, before coming to a sudden, startled stop. A white wrist was protruding from beneath a gray blanket. It was a person, huddled up and asleep.

Suddenly, Kaori felt afraid. This section of the park was unusually dark.

She spun on her heel and walked back the way she'd

come. As she approached the Benkei statue, she saw that someone was standing beside it. It was a tall man. She couldn't make out his face, there was a streetlight behind him, but he was looking at her.

She turned and started to walk away.

"Ms. Nakahara."

Startled at the sound of her name, she almost tripped and fell.

The man dashed up to her. "Are you all right?"

It was that detective. The one called Kaga from the local Nihonbashi police.

"I'm sorry. I scared you," he said with a smile. The sight of his white teeth reassured her somehow.

"It's me who should be apologizing. I couldn't see your face."

"What are you doing here at this time of night? Are you . . . ?"

"Yes." She nodded. "I wanted to see where Fuyuki made his last phone call and the place where the accident happened."

"I thought as much. It's actually that way. The accident happened at that end of the park." Kaga pointed along the path in the opposite direction from which Kaori had come.

"Oh."

"Do you want to see the place? I can show you."

"Could you?"

"Of course."

She felt much safer with the detective around and agreed unhesitatingly.

"No Detective Matsumiya today?" she asked as they advanced along the tree-lined path.

"We went our separate ways a few minutes ago. We try to see as little of one another as possible outside of work. We'd only get sick of each other."

She could tell that he was trying to put her at ease. She smiled.

"Why are you here, Detective Kaga?"

"Oh, no special reason. When I get stuck on a case, I always revisit the place where it all started. That's my modus operandi."

"The place where it started . . ."

"That's what this place is. After all, that's why you're here too. Or am I wrong?"

Kaori shook her head wordlessly. She was starting to detect the same warmth and humanity in Kaga that she had already sensed in his partner Matsumiya. At some point, her initial distrust had evaporated. *Are all detectives like this, or are these two just special?*

The trees cast dark shadows on the ground. So frightening a moment ago, they now struck her as no more than fantastic patterns.

They were approaching the park exit. A large road, with a great deal of traffic, came into view.

"Shin-ohashi Boulevard," Kaga explained. "This is the road your boyfriend ran out into."

"Here . . ."

It was so ridiculously unfair. To one side, there was a

three-lane highway. To the other, an off-ramp for the elevated expressway.

She pictured the truck hitting Fuyuki. She closed her eyes. She could feel the emotion welling up and knew she was on the verge of breaking down. She was determined not to cry.

She took a number of deep breaths, then reopened her eyes.

"Thank you. Thank you for showing me where it happened."

Kaga nodded, appeared to hesitate for a moment, then said, "Could you come with me a bit farther? Just over there."

"Of course I can. What for?"

"Just a small thing," Kaga said vaguely as he set off down the street.

They went along Shin-ohashi Boulevard. Kaori had no idea where they were headed.

After a short distance, they got to a convenience store. "Could you wait here a moment?" Kaga asked. He ducked inside, before quickly reemerging with a plastic bottle of hot Japanese tea and a can of milk tea.

He held them out to Kaori. "Which one do you prefer?"

"I'll take the Japanese tea. Thanks."

"These were the only hot drinks they had. I'd have preferred cocoa."

"You like cocoa?"

"It's not that. I thought something caffeine-free would be better for you."

"Ah . . ." What a thoughtful man he was. More considerate than she was for sure.

Kaga started drinking his milk tea. Kaori unscrewed the cap of her plastic bottle.

"My boyfriend adored cocoa, you know," she said after drinking a mouthful of her hot Japanese tea. "Whenever we went to the diner, he would be up and down getting nonstop refills at the drinks bar."

"Had a sweet tooth, did he?"

"I guess. And he liked a drink too."

She would never get the chance to go to a diner with Fuyuki again. Nor to clink glasses at a pub.

"How are you, physically? I imagine you've been told not to move around too much?" Kaga asked as he walked along, can of tea in hand.

"It's not a problem. The doctor told me it's good to be active."

"Really? I'm pleased to hear it. Which reminds me, have you told people that you're pregnant?"

"Not yet. I plan to tell my friends back up north any day now."

"What about your boyfriend . . . Mr. Yashima? Did he mention having told anyone?"

She was pleasantly surprised when Kaga referred to her boyfriend as "mister" rather than as "the suspect."

"If he did, he didn't tell me. He hadn't really been seeing much of other people recently."

Neither she nor Fuyuki had anyone with whom they were especially close in Tokyo. Thinking back, it would have been good for them to have had someone they could turn to for advice.

Kaga came to a stop at a large intersection. There was a store with a large signboard advertising doll cakes, the local specialty.

"Is my being pregnant significant? Do you think it's connected to the case?"

"I don't know. By the way, are you familiar with Suitengu Shrine? It's a place people go to pray for safe childbirth. That's what it's famous for."

"The name's kind of familiar."

"Have you been?"

"No."

"And you didn't discuss it with your boyfriend?"

"No." Kaori's hand went automatically to her belly. Praying for safe childbirth. The thought had never even occurred to her. Any normal couple would have friends and family around to give them advice about stuff like that. "Why does that matter?"

In response, Kaga pointed to the far side of the intersection. "See the neighborhood police station over there?"

"Yes."

"It's a bit hard to make out, but Suitengu Shrine's just behind it. That's why this intersection is called . . ."

Kaori looked up at the traffic light Kaga was pointing at and understood. This was Suitengumae Intersection.

"Takeaki Aoyagi, the man who was killed, used to visit Suitengu Shrine. On a regular basis."

Kaori started and looked hard at Kaga.

"Well? Jog your memory?"

"What are you getting at? I never met Aoyagi."

Kaga nodded. The expression on his face was bland and devoid of surprise.

"As I thought. Good."

"What's this all about?"

Kaga grunted and tilted his head to one side. "Maybe someone else is pregnant."

"Who?"

Kaga gave a rueful grin and scratched his head. "Beats me. That's why I decided to come back to where the whole thing started."

Kaori scrutinized the detective's face. *Kaga didn't believe that Fuyuki was guilty.* That was why he was so preoccupied.

"It's gotten colder. You should probably be thinking about going home. I'll take you."

"Don't worry about me. I want to ask you a favor, Detective Kaga."

"What is it?"

"The crime scene is within walking distance, isn't it? Could you take me there?"

Kaga's eyes widened. "Right now?"

"Yes. Is it too much to ask?"

"I'm not saying that . . ." He furrowed his brow, thought for a few moments, then gave an emphatic nod. "It's fine. Let me just double-check: The doctor is okay with you moving around?"

"That's what he said."

"Fine, then. Come with me."

The traffic light changed as if on cue. Kaga set off and Kaori followed.

They took a left at the next intersection. Most of the shops and restaurants were closed. The only places that were still open were the bars.

"What sort of person was Fuyuki?" Kaga asked. "What did he do for fun? Did he like reading?"

"Let me see," said Kaori. "I never saw him read a book. He hardly even read comics. If you put me on the spot, I'd probably say watching sports. He watched plenty of baseball and soccer on TV. He wasn't a die-hard fan, though."

"The two of you went to a movie the day before the incident, didn't you? Did Fuyuki like movies?"

"Oh . . . well, we went to the movies from time to time. We don't have much money, so we only went when someone gave us tickets or we won tickets for a preview screening."

"Preview screening?"

"Yes, whenever we found out about a preview screening, we'd apply straightaway. We used to win quite a lot of tickets."

"You did? Is there a trick to it?"

"There certainly is."

Kaga turned to look at Kaori, startled at her emphatic tone.

"A postcard," she said. "You apply by postcard. With most of the offers, you have to apply via text or email. We don't try for those. Loads of people apply because it's so easy to do, and the competition is ferocious. Applying with a postcard is more hassle and costs money, so most people aren't interested. That increases your chances of winning."

"I can see that."

"There are some offers where you can apply online or by

mail. Even then, you stand a better chance of winning if you apply by postcard. I think they have separate draws for the two kinds of applications. We don't have a lot of money, but we always keep a stock of prepaid postcards."

"So that's the secret."

"Where you get your information from is another factor. If information about the offer is available on your phone, then the competition will be brutal. We always look for offers that are not online."

Kaga came to a stop. "Where, like in movie magazines?"

"Close." Kaori held up a finger. "Think about it. Who reads movie magazines? People who love movies, of course. So they're likely to apply for free movie tickets. No, what we do is to check the movie section in regular magazines, and not women's magazines either, but men's magazines."

"Why?"

"Can't you figure it out, Detective Kaga? Women love getting something for nothing and they don't think twice about the hassle involved. Men are different. If there's even the slightest bit of effort involved, they'd rather just pay the money and get it over with."

Kaga nodded briskly and resumed walking at a slow pace. "I've learned something new today."

"That whole thing was my idea, not Fuyuki's. If it were up to him, he'd just go out and buy tickets. You should give it a go yourself, Detective. With my system, you're sure to score some tickets."

"I'll give it a try."

Kaga was walking at a very leisurely pace, and keeping

up with him was easy. Eventually, she saw a bridge ahead. "That's Edobashi Bridge," Kaga said.

They crossed a wide road and walked across the bridge. They reached a set of stairs at the foot of which there was an underground passage. Kaori recoiled. She remembered that the crime had taken place in an underground passage.

"Was it in there?"

"Yes." Kaga nodded.

The passage was short and rather narrow. The white walls were brightly lit.

Just being there was enough to make Kaori start trembling all over. A man had been murdered here and everyone thought Fuyuki was responsible. It was like an invisible wall closing in on her. She had nowhere to run.

"Are you feeling okay?" Kaga asked her.

Kaori looked at the detective. "Detective Kaga, Fuyuki didn't kill anybody. He's just not capable of it. Believe me. I beg you."

She knew her protestations wouldn't accomplish anything, but she couldn't help raising her voice. It reverberated in the cramped underground passage.

Kaga looked at her. His gaze was cool, detached. *He's got the eyes of a detective,* Kaori thought. *That's the face of a man who trusts only the facts and never lets his emotions get the better of him. Appealing to a person like that is a waste of time.*

Kaga's next remark caught her completely off guard. "Yes, I know that," he said.

"What!" Kaori peered into the detective's face. "You know? You mean . . ."

Kaga nodded and headed for the exit. Kaori scuttled after him.

Once they were outside again, Kaga pointed at the street corner in front of them.

"After the victim was stabbed, he made his way along this street to Nihonbashi Bridge."

"Ah . . . yes, I saw that on the news," Kaori said, then sighed. "But why there of all places."

Kaga frowned briefly in puzzlement, then a look of comprehension dawned on his face.

"Of course. Matsumiya told me about it. How you two hitchhiked all the way down here to Tokyo."

"That's right."

"Nihonbashi Bridge must mean a lot to you. Anyway, have you seen what you wanted to see?"

"No, I want to go to the bridge," Kaori answered brusquely. "I want to see it again."

"Okay," Kaga said.

They set off, side by side. There was almost no one on the street, although they were in the middle of the capital city and it wasn't that late at night. And there were almost no cars. *Someone who'd been stabbed could be staggering along here and there isn't anybody to notice,* she thought.

"I'm going to ask you a question. I don't want you to take it the wrong way," Kaga said. "What are you planning to do about the baby? Raising a child will be difficult, the way things are now."

"Are you saying I shouldn't have it?"

"I'm not saying that. Just—"

"I'm going to have the baby," Kaori interjected, cutting Kaga off. She placed her right hand on her belly as she walked. "I'm going to have the baby," she said again. "If I don't have this baby, I really will be completely alone. I know it won't be easy. Not having a father will make life tougher for the child. But I'll make it work. I'll make a go of it somehow."

Without her intending, her voice had grown more forceful, partly because she was trying to reassure herself. *I mustn't give up. I've got to be strong for me and for my baby.*

Kaga said nothing. Kaori peered at his profile, wondering what he thought of her. He was looking resolutely in front of him.

"I suppose you think I'm just talking tough," Kaori ventured. "That I'm being naïve and sentimental."

Kaga turned and looked her full in the face. "If you're being sentimental, then that's good news as far as I'm concerned. I'd be a whole lot more worried if you had lost all hope and had nothing to look forward to in your life."

"Detective Kaga . . ."

"You'll be okay. I know plenty of women who've done a great job raising their kids on their own. Matsumiya's mother for one."

"Your partner? What, his mother was a single mom?"

"You'd never think so to look at him. He looks like he was born with a silver spoon in his mouth."

Kaori nodded. That was her impression of him too. She felt slightly reassured.

Nihonbashi Bridge with its magnificent monumental stone parapet came into view. Kaori recalled the first time

she'd seen the bridge. She was astonished to find such a splen-
did structure buried under an expressway.

They walked toward the foot of the bridge. They had
just begun to cross it, when Kaga came to an unexpected
stop. He was looking straight in front of him.

A figure was loitering halfway across. A young man of
high school age wearing a hooded parka. He was gazing up
at the ornate lamppost on the parapet.

He turned and started walking in their direction, then
came to a jerky and abrupt stop. Surprise was all over his
face.

Kaga went up to him and said a few words. Making
an impatient gesture with his hand, the young man turned
around and took off in the opposite direction.

Kaori went up to Kaga. "Who was that?" she asked.

"The son of the victim. I'd told him that we found his
father leaning against the base of the statue there. That's why
he came to have a look, I suppose." Kaga looked up at the
statue beside them. There were two dragon-like creatures
seated on either side of a lamppost.

"Are they dragons?"

Kaga smiled.

"They look like dragons, but they're actually *kirin*, creatures from Chinese mythology. You've probably seen them
on the beer labels."

"Of course." Kaori nodded. "I didn't know they had
wings."

The bronze statues they were looking at had wings on
their backs.

"Traditionally, *kirin* don't have wings. The architect opted to give his *kirin* statues wings after deciding to use them to adorn his bridge, or so the story goes."

"Why did he do that?"

Kaga pointed to the midpoint of the roadway. "Because this was once the point of origin for all the roads in Japan."

"Of course—I knew that. 'Kilometer zero' . . . Is that what they call it?"

"That's right. Kilometer zero for all the roads in Japan. This was people's jumping-off point for journeys all over the country. That's supposedly why he decided to put wings on his *kirins*' backs."

"I didn't know that." Kaori took another look at the statues.

They're like us with all our hopes and dreams back then, she thought. *We left the sticks and hitchhiked all the way down here. We thought that was only our first step. We thought we had the whole world at our feet. We had such big dreams. We felt as though we had wings and could fly off into a bright, shining future.*

In the end, they had never managed to get off the ground.

And Fuyuki was dead.

22

"On the day before the incident, the suspect, Fuyuki Yashima, and his live-in girlfriend, Kaori Nakahara, had arranged to see a movie. They agreed to meet at eight p.m. Yashima, who got there slightly early, went for a stroll around the neighborhood, in the course of which he came across a help-wanted advertisement at Stock House, a furniture and home goods store, in Kyobashi. He went in, but the boss had already left for the day, so an employee asked Yashima to come back again at six p.m. the day after."

Kobayashi's strong voice resounded in the hushed incident room. Nearly all the investigators were present, and the deputy commissioner and the rest of the top brass were seated at the dais at one end of the room.

"While Ms. Nakahara knew nothing about the help-wanted advert, we think this slipped Yashima's mind rather than being something he was intentionally keeping secret. The next day, Yashima left the house sometime after five p.m., when he texted Nakahara to say that he was going for a job interview. A little after six, Yashima arrived at Stock House, where he discovered that the job being advertised wasn't what he had been expecting. Feeling sorry for him, the Stock House boss gave him the name of a similar business based in Edobashi and encouraged him to try his luck there. Yashima then left Stock House and, we assume, made his way toward the offices of Azuma Furniture, the company he had just been told about. But it turned out that Azuma had already closed up shop for the day. We do not know whether Yashima went all the way to the Azuma office or not, but we conjecture that he ran into Takeaki Aoyagi somewhere near Edobashi Bridge. Yashima, who had previously been employed at Kaneseki Metals, accosted Aoyagi in the hope of getting his old job back. He could well have alluded to the business of the workplace accident cover-up at this point. It seems unlikely that the firm's head of production would recall someone who was only a contract worker. The fact that the two of them then proceeded to a café suggests that Aoyagi felt himself to be in a weak position. They spent a little under two hours at the café before they left. Whose idea it was we don't know, but they then set off in the direction of Edobashi Bridge. As they were going through an underpass just this side of the bridge, Yashima checked that there was no one else around, stabbed Aoyagi, stole his wallet and briefcase, crossed Edobashi Bridge, and ran away. While we don't know what route he took, he ended up hiding in the Hamacho Green

Road park. At some point after eleven p.m., he called Ms. Nakahara and told her that, I quote, he had done something awful and that something terrible had happened. Precisely then, he was discovered by an officer on patrol and once more took to his heels. That was when he was hit by a truck in the middle of Shin-ohashi Boulevard and taken to the hospital."

Kobayashi looked up from the sheaf of documents in his hand. "That's everything," he said and sat back down.

Ishigaki turned to the deputy commissioner. "What do you think, sir? This is what we get if we make a timeline using everything we know, assuming that Yashima was the perpetrator."

The deputy commissioner stuck out his lower lip. He didn't look happy.

"Where are we with the murder weapon? You didn't even mention the knife."

"Somebody else will provide a report on that. Sakagami."

Sakagami got to his feet when his name was called.

"We haven't yet managed to find any evidence that the knife used in the crime belonged to Yashima. Ever since his first job at a small building contractor, Yashima was in possession of electricians' knives and other knives he used for work, so he could either have purchased the knife in question himself or been given it by a third party. According to an expert I consulted, the knife used in the crime is an outdoor knife, suitable for whittling wood, and often used in woodworking. That's everything from me."

Sakagami sat back down. The deputy commissioner looked as grumpy as ever.

"That's not much use. You haven't explained why Yashima had a knife on him on that particular day."

"Apparently, Yashima was hoping to secure a practical job at Stock House, sir."

"A practical job?"

"A job as a woodworker, a craftsman. The job on offer turned out to be a temporary job at a trade fair. Which is why the boss of Stock House recommended him another firm to apply to."

"He was hoping to get a practical job as a woodworker and that's why he had a knife with him?"

"Since he was after a practical job, he was expecting to have to showcase his woodworking skills at the interview. In that case, there's nothing odd about him bringing his own tools with him."

"I see where you're coming from." The deputy commissioner's face suddenly brightened. Crossing his arms, he leaned back in his chair. "They always say craftsmen have a strong attachment to their own tools. Yeah, I like that idea. Nice."

"As an explanation, it irons out any contradictions."

"Good, let's go with it. We'll run with this."

"Yes, sir," Ishigaki replied. He looked rather less cheerful than his boss.

After the main meeting broke up, the investigators huddled in their individual groups. Kobayashi, who was Matsumiya and Kaga's supervisor, looked morose.

"Do you buy it?" Matsumiya asked Kobayashi, speaking softly.

"The whole knife thing?"

"Yeah."

Kobayashi grimaced and scratched the tip of one of his eyebrows.

"What do you expect? There's a lot of pressure from the higher-ups to cobble together a credible scenario and close up the case quickly. The unit chief doesn't like it any more than we do. Do you think we should just roll over and accept it?"

"No, I don't."

"I don't either. Look, if Yashima was planning to do any serious woodworking, it stands to reason he'd use a proper woodworking tool. But what can you do? We've got to do as we're told."

Kobayashi looked as if he had just bitten into a particularly sour lemon. Matsumiya realized he had pushed things as far as he could. *In the end, we're all nothing more than private soldiers*, he thought.

The three-man meeting concluded with Matsumiya and Kaga being detailed to go through Fuyuki Yashima's phone and question his contacts. Kobayashi wanted to get a sense of the victimhood Yashima felt about the workplace accident cover-up. Anything they discovered would be used to bolster the story that Ishigaki and Kobayashi had come up with.

"Making Yashima the villain of the piece certainly gives us a nice, neat sequence of events, but is it really okay?" said Matsumiya as he walked down the corridor alongside Kaga.

Kaga said nothing. His body language was clear enough: no, it wasn't okay.

"Oh, by the way, I got an email from Kanamori," Matsumiya said as they stepped out of the police station. "Says she wants to meet to discuss the memorial service with you. She texted you, but got no reply."

"It's not a priority for me right now."

"Surely you've got time to talk? She's busy too, you know. If you don't reply, then I'll go ahead and arrange it with her myself, Kyo."

"Be my guest. More importantly—" Kaga stopped and took a quick look around. "I've got a small favor to ask."

"About the memorial service?"

Kaga frowned and made a dismissive motion with his hand. "Absolutely not. About work. I need you to give me some time, starting right now. A half-day should do it."

Matsumiya looked his cousin full in the face. "What are you planning to do?"

"It's a grandstand play, frankly," said Kaga, surveying the road in front of the police station. "The chances are it won't work out. That's why I want to do it alone. If it succeeds, I'll let you know."

"At least tell me what you're looking into."

After thinking for a moment, Kaga fixed his eye on Matsumiya. "I heard that Fuyuki Yashima really loved his cocoa."

"Cocoa?"

"He only drank cocoa—and a lot of it—at the local diner."

"Where did you hear that?"

"Last night, after we split up. I bumped into Ms. Naka-hara."

"You did?"

"Remember what the server in the café said in his state-ment about Aoyagi? 'I don't recall his exact order, but it was definitely two of the same thing.' If Aoyagi was meeting with Yashima, then it's quite likely they ordered a couple of co-coas. They have cocoa on the menu at that café."

"What does that tell us?"

"I checked the autopsy report. There was no cocoa in the undigested stomach contents."

Matsumiya's eyes widened and his mouth gaped.

"I never thought Yashima was in the café in the first place."

"Meaning that someone else was there with Aoyagi."

"So it would seem." There was a faint smile on Kaga's lips, but his eyes were deadly earnest.

"And you think that person's the real culprit?"

Kaga grunted and tilted his head. "That I don't know. All I know is that the present scenario falls to pieces if it turns out Yashima was never in the café."

"The server at the café didn't even see Aoyagi's compan-ion. You'll have a struggle proving it."

"I'm not so sure. There are tried-and-tested tricks to prove that someone wasn't in a certain place; techniques we use all the time."

"Tried-and-tested tricks?" Matsumiya replied after think-ing for a moment. "Are you talking about alibis?"

"That's the one," Kaga said with a nod. "If Fuyuki

Yashima wasn't in the café, then where was he and what was he doing in the roughly two hours between him leaving Stock House and the murder? That's what I mean to ascertain."

"And how exactly are you going to do this 'ascertaining'?"

Kaga didn't answer his question.

"See you tonight," he said instead. He turned briskly on his heel and strode off before Matsumiya could get a word in.

23

When Yuto walked into the career guidance room, Sanada blinked as if dazzled, then motioned to a chair on the other side of the table. "Take a seat."

Yuto pulled out a chair and sat down.

"How's it going? Are things a bit better?" Sanada asked.

Yuto cocked his head to one side. "I don't know. The case hasn't been solved yet, so no, I wouldn't say things are much better."

"I can understand that." Sanada sighed and looked at the paper he was holding.

"There's too much going on right now for you to seriously review your options. I get that. As I'm talking to all the boys in your year, I asked you to come in too. I just want to get a rough idea of how you're thinking about things. Just answer as best you can."

"Okay," Yuto replied.

"Good. Let's start with the basics. In the interview we did after you moved into third year, you told me you were hoping to go to college. Can I take it that is still the case?" Sanada asked, looking up from Yuto's file.

Yuto didn't reply. He couldn't.

Sanada looked up. "What is it? Have you changed your mind?"

Yuto released the pent-up breath in his chest before speaking. "I feel a bit lost."

"Lost? How exactly?"

"It's . . . uh . . ." Yuto hunched forward and looked at the floor.

"Is it a financial issue?"

"That's one thing."

"There's something else, then?"

Yuto stayed silent. He wasn't ready. This was neither the time nor the place.

"Hey, Aoyagi," Sanada said. "At least look at me."

Yuto lifted his head but kept his eyes fixed on the floor.

"I understand how you feel. After what happened to your father, you're worried about your family. College costs money, a lot of money. You'd rather get a job and do your best to help your mother and sister. That's what you're thinking, right?"

Although Yuto's actual feelings were nothing like this, he replied, "Yeah, I guess that's it."

"Huh." Sanada nodded to himself. "I expected as much. I admire you for thinking like that and I'll do everything I can to support you if that's what you decide to do. But listen, Aoyagi, this is a serious decision. For starters, finding work is that much harder when you've only got a high school diploma. I help a number of kids like that find work every year, and it's getting tougher all the time. If you're worried about providing for your family, your best bet is to go to college or even vocational school."

Sanada's speech didn't register with Yuto. He wasn't thinking about looking for a job, and going on to university was the last thing on his mind. *Now* was what mattered. What was he going to do right *now*?

"Isn't there anyone who could provide you with financial assistance? A relative, for instance?" When Yuto said nothing, Sanada added, "Your father held quite a senior position in his company. He must have some savings."

"I've no idea."

"Have you spoken to your mother about this?"

"Not since my father's death, no."

"I see." Sanada intertwined his fingers on the desk. "You'll need to have a proper conversation with your mother about this. My guess—and that's all it is, a guess—is that she will be very keen for you to go on to college. On the money side, scholarships can always be found. I'm sure something can be worked out. Anyway, talking it through with her should be your first step."

"Yes, sir."

Yuto made his way back to the classroom. Although school had finished for the day, several of his classmates were still there, Sugino among them. When they spotted Yuto, they all picked up their bags and left the room, one after another. Only Sugino stayed behind.

"Sure you don't want to go with them?" Yuto asked. "You won't do yourself any favors, hanging out with me."

Sugino scowled. "I'm not like that," he said. His voice lacked conviction.

"It's no skin off my nose. I can't reach Kurosawa. Any idea why?"

"Kurosawa?"

"He doesn't reply when I text him and he doesn't pick up when I call. Think he's got a new phone?"

"Dunno. Anyway, why Kurosawa?"

"There's something I need to discuss with him. And with you. The three of us, in fact."

Sugino's eyes widened in shock and his expression stiffened.

"Something? You mean . . . ?"

"Uh-huh," Yuto said. "That's what I mean."

Sugino turned away. "It's too late. There's nothing to talk about."

"That's not good enough. It's not too late. That's why I want us to talk."

His eyes still fixed on the floor, Sugino asked, "Why? Has someone said something?"

"No, no one—" Yuto cut himself off mid-sentence. "Or perhaps someone did say something to me."

Sugino glanced up at him. "Who?"

"My dad."

"What!" Sugino started. "I mean, your father, he's . . ."

"Forget about it. I need you to contact Kurosawa. I'm counting on you." Saying this, Yuto grabbed his bag and walked out of the classroom.

After leaving the school grounds, Yuto headed for the subway station. Whenever he passed groups of his friends strolling along, he could feel his face flush. The chill of the air felt good on his skin. His mood darkened when he thought of what he was about to do. His burden was a heavy one, but he wasn't going to run away anymore. He wasn't going to avert his eyes.

He caught a train and disembarked at Nakameguro Station. He was nearly home when he recognized the person walking in front of him.

Yuto accelerated until he caught up with him. When they were neck and neck, the other person noticed him and stopped.

"Oh, it's you, Yuto." Kotake forced his square face into a smile. "Heading back home?"

"That's right. You too?"

"Yeah. Got a few official company communications I've got to deliver. I'm the liaison guy."

"What's happening with the accident cover-up?"

Kotake's mouth twisted with distaste at Yuto's question.

"We've handled that. It probably wasn't very nice for your family, but it's not something you need to worry about anymore. Try to put it behind you."

"You handled it? How'd you handle it? My dad . . . Takeaki Aoyagi is the mastermind behind the whole thing—that's meant to be the end of the story?"

"'Mastermind'? Now you're being melodramatic."

Turning, Yuto saw a cynical smirk on Kotake's face. His whole body grew hot.

"Yeah and what about you?" he yelled. "You get away with no blame at all?"

Kotake glowered at him. "Let me tell you, young man, I have been reported to the Public Prosecutor's Office. For complicity in the cover-up of a workplace accident."

"But no one's going to fire you! You aren't going to lose your factory manager job. Because you shunted all the blame onto my dad."

"I just did what I was told to do. By your father."

"You're lying."

"No, I'm not."

"My dad would never tell anyone to do anything mean and sordid like that. I bet you did it all on your own."

"What are you talking about? You're just a know-nothing kid," snarled Kotake.

Hot blood only surged more furiously through Yuto's veins. His body seemed to move independently. He brought his bunched fist down into Kotake's square face.

24

Matsumiya was on his way to see the fourth person on his list when Kaga called him. It was a little after five p.m. He hadn't managed to extract any genuinely useful information from any of the three people he'd interviewed so far. It was all very well to classify them as acquaintances of Fuyuki Yashima, but they'd often been work colleagues briefly or had a quick chat after a job interview. They'd exchanged contact details but nothing more.

Matsumiya was walking as he took the call. "Hi there. Did you find anything?"

"I don't know yet. Where are you now?"

"I'm in . . . Kameido, I think," said Matsumiya, looking around.

"Perfect. Ditch your inquiries and come give me a hand."

"What do you want me to do?"

"Bring me Ms. Nakahara. There's something I need to ask her."

"Hang on a second. Bring her to you? Where am I meant to go? Where are you?"

"I'm in a bookstore."

"A bookstore?" Matsumiya came to an abrupt stop.

Kaga gave him the name of the place. It was a well-known bookstore in Nihonbashi.

I can see the logic, Matsumiya thought. There weren't that many places where men with time to kill could go. A café was about the only other option, but Fuyuki Yashima was probably too broke to go to cafés by himself. Browsing books and magazines had the merit of being free. The notion that Yashima had been in a bookstore was a thoroughly credible one.

"What do you want to question her about?"

"You'll find out when you get here. See you later." Kaga ended the call.

Self-important ass—cursing under his breath, Matsumiya raised a hand to hail an approaching taxi.

Kaori Nakahara was at home. Possibly because she wasn't wearing makeup, she looked rather pale and sickly. When Matsumiya told her he needed her to come with him right away, she reacted with puzzlement.

"If you plan to question me about the incident, I'm afraid there's nothing more I can tell you."

"That's not what we want. We need you to verify something."

"Verify?" The expression on her face was as despondent as ever.

"There's a chance," said Matsumiya, who was getting increasingly desperate, "that it will clear your boyfriend of suspicion."

Her eyes opened wide. "Prove his innocence, you mean?"

"I can't go that far. It's no more than a possibility."

Kaori took a deep breath and looked hard at Matsumiya. "Can you wait ten minutes? I need to get ready."

"No problem," Matsumiya replied.

When Kaori was ready, Matsumiya hailed a cab and they headed to Nihonbashi. On the way, Kaori again asked what it was they wanted her to verify. Matsumiya could understand why she was so jittery.

"I don't know the details. Detective Kaga will meet us there."

"Detective Kaga . . ."

"He mentioned that you two bumped into one another last night. What did you talk about?"

"Nothing much. Tricks for winning tickets for advance movie screenings, stuff like that."

"Tricks?"

Kaori ran through her conversation with Kaga. As Matsumiya listened to her, the penny finally dropped. Having confirmed from the cocoa evidence that Fuyuki Yashima hadn't been in the café with Takeaki Aoyagi, he had inferred that he must have been in a bookstore instead.

They reached their destination and got out of the taxi. Matsumiya phoned Kaga and then led Kaori toward the entrance. The surprise on her face as she looked up at the building was clear.

Kaga appeared at the door. He nodded at Matsumiya and apologized to Kaori for dragging her there.

"You really think you can prove that my boyfriend is innocent?"

"I don't know yet. Anyway, come this way," Kaga said. He walked into the store with her and Matsumiya followed.

They passed through a door marked "Employees Only" into the back-of-house area. Threading their way along a passage piled high with cardboard boxes, they reached a small room. The walls were completely covered with monitors and a middle-aged security guard sat in a chair.

"Oh, CCTV." Matsumiya realized what Kaga was trying to do.

"If someone was in Nihonbashi and wanted to visit a bookstore, this place would be their first port of call. The security cameras don't have complete coverage, but if he was in here for two hours, we can reasonably expect him to show up in one of the feeds."

"I can see that. Still, it's quite a store. They must have a ton of cameras."

"They certainly do. I went through all the footage from six thirty to eight thirty p.m. on the day of the incident and my eyes are killing me." Kaga massaged his eyelids with his fingertips.

Matsumiya looked hard at his cousin, who was a few years his senior. In the Homicide Division, Kaga had a reputation as a shrewd operator. He was definitely that, but his greatest asset was his almost scary level of tenacity.

"What was it that you wanted Ms. Nakahara to look at?" Matsumiya asked.

"Yes—could you play that footage we found?" Kaga said.

The security guard pressed a few buttons on the machine. The image on the monitor closest to him changed to a still image. A number of customers were standing in front of a magazine rack reading the magazines. Since the majority were women, Matsumiya inferred that it was probably the women's magazine section.

"Ready, Ms. Nakahara? We're going to run the footage. Tell us if you notice anything."

Kaori edged closer to the monitor.

"Play it," Kaga said.

The image started to move. Nothing much was going on: one woman would drift away from the rack, and another would wander over and take her place.

After a few more moments, Kaori gasped.

"Pause it," Kaga said.

"There. I think that's Fuyuki."

Matsumiya peered at the part of the screen she was pointing at. There was a man about to pass behind the women standing at the magazine rack. He was captured from behind and at an angle, so his face was hard to make out, but the resemblance to Fuyuki Yashima was undeniable.

"Play it again," Kaga ordered the security guard.

The footage played again from the beginning. After watching it a second time, Kaori nodded her head emphatically. "That's definitely him."

Matsumiya felt a surge of warmth. There was a time stamp in one corner of the image. It read 19:45. That was when Takeaki Aoyagi had been in the café—meaning that whomever he had been with, it wasn't Fuyuki Yashima.

"Could you run the next set of footage?" Kaga said. His calm voice contrasted with Matsumiya's excitement.

A new sequence started. "That's Fuyuki," Kaori said after a moment or two. Matsumiya recognized him as well. He was plucking a magazine from a shelf. Unfortunately, his back was to the camera, but you could recognize him from the clothes he had on.

Although this supposed Fuyuki Yashima stayed where he was for over twenty minutes, he never once turned to face the camera before moving on.

"This is the final bit of footage."

The location in this footage was different from the other two, with very few people and bookshelves on both sides. Clearly, this wasn't one of the heavily trafficked floors with magazines on sale.

Matsumiya gasped. A man had walked into the frame. His back was to the camera, but it looked like Fuyuki Yashima again.

The man stopped, stood there, and picked several books off the shelves on the left side of the screen. From time to time, you could glimpse his face in profile. He looked like Fuyuki Yashima.

The man eventually wandered off without buying anything.

"That's Fuyuki. I've no doubt about it," Kaori declared categorically.

Kaga nodded. "You think so? If you're that sure, then you're probably right."

"Is this enough to prove his innocence?" Kaori looked at Kaga beseechingly.

Kaga didn't reply. He glanced at Matsumiya. "Take Ms. Nakahara home."

"Why?" Kaori's voice rose. "I'm here because you told me I could help prove my boyfriend's innocence."

Kaga looked at the floor, exhaled, then fixed his gaze on her. "Proving anything takes a great deal of hard work. I need you to understand that."

Kaori said nothing.

"Take her home," Kaga repeated.

Matsumiya led Kaori out of the room. She didn't say a word and Matsumiya couldn't think of anything to say. Kaga was right. The last thing they wanted to do was to raise the young woman's hopes.

"I'll take it from here," said Kaori as soon as they were outside the bookstore.

"Are you sure? I'm happy to see you home."

Kaori shook her head. "Seeing as I'm here, I think I'd like to walk around. This is the last part of town my boyfriend was in."

"Ah . . . yes, of course."

"Detective Matsumiya." She looked at him with avid eyes. "Do whatever it takes to sort this out. I'm relying on you." She bowed deeply as she said this.

"We'll do our best," he replied. Cliché or not, he was sincere.

He watched the young woman walk down the street before going back to the security guard's room in the store. Kaga was sitting in front of the bank of monitors.

"You didn't take her home, then?"

"No. She said she wanted to take a walk around. So, what do you plan to do with this footage?"

"Take it back to the task force, obviously. I don't think it's enough to change the higher-ups' minds, though."

"How so?"

Kaga looked at the monitor in front of him. "We have no proof that the man in this CCTV footage is Fuyuki Yashima. I thought he resembled him, which is why I got Ms. Nakahara over here for confirmation. Even if she's prepared to state that it definitely is him, that doesn't actually constitute proof. She's not a third party."

Matsumiya stared at the monitor. "There aren't any images where his face is clearer?"

"I've checked all the footage. The sequences I showed you are all we've got, I'm afraid."

Matsumiya bit his lip. There was a freeze-frame on the screen. It was the final scene and showed Yashima replacing a book on the shelf prior to walking off.

Matsumiya had a sudden idea. He jabbed a finger at the monitor. "Fingerprints! If we dust all the books in that shelf, maybe we'll find Yashima's prints!"

"That's certainly conceivable."

"Which floor is this? We need to collect all the books.

God, I hope no one's gone and handled them or bought the darn things. Come on, what's the floor number?"

"Keep your hat on. The evidence isn't going anywhere."

"Yes, but—" Matsumiya was protesting when the words stuck in his throat. Kaga had pulled a paper carrier bag out from beneath the table. It was full of books. One of them was a volume called *The Best 100 Japanese Sci-Fi Movies*.

25

The expression on Ishigaki's face was grim as he looked up from the CCTV footage on the laptop. He groaned softly.

Matsumiya and Kaga stood facing him across the table. They were in one of the smaller meeting rooms at Nihonbashi Police Station. The two detectives had got Ishigaki to meet them there to avoid anyone else seeing the footage.

"You're up to your old tricks, I see." Ishigaki fixed his eyes on Kaga. "Anyway, that's neither here nor there," snorted Ishigaki, curling his lip. "This footage is the important thing. He certainly looks like Yashima. Looks like—and nothing more."

"That's why the fingerprints—"

Ishigaki lifted a hand to cut Matsumiya off. He crossed his thick arms, shut his eyes, and sighed.

Matsumiya knew what his boss was thinking: that finding Yashima's fingerprints would completely overturn their current reading of the crime. How could he explain that to his superiors? How could the investigation be reconfigured on a new vector? There were no easy answers.

Ishigaki reopened his eyes. He glowered first at Matsumiya, then at Kaga. "Let's take this to Forensics. They won't be thrilled about it coming out of nowhere."

Matsumiya exhaled with relief. "Thank you, sir." He bobbed his head gratefully.

"But there is one thing." Ishigaki spread his hands on the table and leaned toward them. "If Forensics doesn't find any fingerprints, then we'll just forget all about this footage. Are you okay with that?"

Matsumiya darted a glance at Kaga.

"That's fine," replied Kaga. From his face, you could see that he had been expecting Ishigaki's response.

"You did a good job," said Ishigaki. "Oh, I meant to tell you." He had clearly just remembered something. "The son was taken into Meguro Police Station yesterday evening."

"The son . . . what, you mean Yuto?" Matsumiya said. "Taken in? Why? What did he do?"

"Bodily harm. He beat up an employee of Kaneseki Metals in the street. A local resident reported them before the fight got underway. They were already in a shouting match."

"Who was the Kaneseki Metals guy?"

"The factory manager, I think."

"Ah." Matsumiya remembered him. Kotake. They had met once at the factory. "I wonder why Yuto went for him."

"According to the eyewitnesses, the boy was insisting

that his father was innocent. He was yelling that his father would never do anything mean or sordid."

Matsumiya and Kaga exchanged a surprised look.

"The family's having a dreadful time of it, what with the sister's suicide attempt. The other party didn't want to make things any worse, so the boy was quickly sent home. Just thought I should let you know."

"Thank you, sir," said Matsumiya. He and Kaga left the room.

"I can hardly bear to think how the mother must be feeling," Matsumiya said. "Murder really is like a cancer cell—pain and misery spreading unstoppably."

"I agree. But there's something not quite right here."

"What?"

"Why was Yuto so angry on his father's behalf? Didn't he tell us last time we saw him that his father got what he deserved?"

"I'd hazard that, in his heart of hearts, he believed in his father all along. That aside, have we done all we can with the CCTV?"

"The footage by itself doesn't have a great deal of evidentiary value, so let's hope we find some prints." Kaga glanced at his watch. "Seven fifty? I should make it by the skin of my teeth."

"Got plans?"

"I'm meeting someone. You want to come?" As Kaga said this, he marched off at high speed.

"Do you want me to come? Who are you seeing?"

"You're the one who told me to get a move on and contact her."

"What? Is it—?"

"Ms. Kanamori," Kaga replied breezily. "We're meeting at eight regarding the memorial service for my father."

"So you did get in touch with her, Kyo?"

"Yes, at the bookstore, while I was waiting for you to show up. I thought eight would give me enough wiggle room, but we're cutting it pretty close."

Being pressed for time, they jumped into a taxi outside the police station. They got out in Ningyocho and soon found the restaurant. It was in an old two-story house.

They went in and were escorted upstairs to a large room with rows of low rectangular dining tables. They spotted Tokiko Kanamori right away. She was at a table at the far end of the room with an open notebook in front of her. She smiled when she caught sight of Matsumiya and Kaga.

"It's been a while," Matsumiya greeted her with a small bow before he took his place. They sat cross-legged on flat cushions.

"It's been too long. I'm glad to see you looking so well." Tokiko Kanamori grinned at Matsumiya. She was a little thinner than two years ago, but her smiling face radiated good health. "Are you working this case with Kaga too?"

"That's how it turned out," Matsumiya replied.

Kaga opened the menu. "The beef stew is what this place is famous for. And the croquettes. I'm sure everything else is good too, though."

"Why don't you order for all of us, Kaga?"

After a minute or two's reflection, Kaga summoned the waitress and ordered a number of dishes. His familiarity with the menu suggested that he'd been here several times before.

"So, how are things looking? Can you make time for the service?" Kanamori asked Kaga after they had clinked their beer glasses.

Kaga took a swig of beer, then tilted his head to one side. "I can't say. At least, not until we've cleared up our current case."

"I heard the Nihonbashi Bridge murder case was pretty much wrapped up."

"That's just the media jumping to conclusions. We don't have a single piece of evidence proving that the young man who died in the hospital actually did it."

"Surprised to hear that. Still, hardly my area of expertise . . . Anyway, what I'd like is for us to proceed according to the schedule we agreed on earlier. Everyone's okay with that, aren't they?" Her voice was gentle but firm.

"Yes, I suppose so," Kaga concurred in the vaguest possible terms.

Matsumiya was rather enjoying the sight of his cousin's discomfiture at the hands of Kanamori.

Their food was brought to the table. The croquettes were fragrant and went down easily with the beer. The deep-fried shrimp was crisp and smelled delicious. The chunks of meat in the beef stew melted in the mouth.

Even while singing the praises of the food, Tokiko Kana-mori never lost sight of her goal for the evening. From time to time, she would put down her chopsticks, open the notebook by her plate, and solicit Kaga's opinion on the program for the memorial service. There seemed to be a great number of things that needed to be decided: how to contact relatives and friends; what gifts to give to attendees; where to have the meal after the service, and so on. Kaga's responses, however, all took one of two forms: either "Do the standard thing" or "You decide."

"Listen, Kaga," Kanamori said with a stern look on her face. "This memorial service is for your father. Can't you muster a bit more enthusiasm and help me sort this stuff out?"

Kaga sipped his after-dinner coffee appreciatively and tilted his head to one side. "As I've already told you, I personally don't see any need for this service. You were the one who said I should provide the opportunity to memorialize my father to the people who wanted to do so—"

"You need it too, Kaga," Kanamori said. "Why not remember your father just once a year?"

"I'm not saying I don't think about him. Just that for me, it's all over and done with."

"'Over and done with'? What's that supposed to mean?"

"That I've worked through all the problems I had with my dad. I don't need to keep looking back."

"You're wrong. You still have absolutely no idea."

She spoke with such firmness that even Matsumiya, who wasn't directly involved in the conversation, started.

"What do I have no idea about?"

"How your father felt at the end. Have you given even a moment's thought to how he was feeling when he took his leave of this world?"

Kaga coolly put his coffee cup down on the table. "I daresay he felt all sorts of things. But why do I need to think about it?"

"You need to think about it: about how desperate he was to see his son, his only blood relative."

Matsumiya started and looked at his cousin. Kaga just smiled sardonically. "We've already discussed this. It was something Dad and I agreed on a long time ago."

"His ex-wife . . . your mother, she was alone when she died. She didn't get to see the face of her only child. So did your father also tell you, 'I don't need you hanging around the place when it's time for me to die'?"

"Yes, he did," Kaga agreed. "We promised. One man to another."

There was a mocking smile on Tokiko Kanamori's lips. "Pathetic."

"What did you just say?" Kaga's voice dropped suddenly.

"I'm saying that promises you and your father made when he was alive mean nothing. Have you ever watched someone die, Kaga?"

"Many times. Too often to count. It's part of my job."

Kanamori slowly shook her head. "No, what you've seen are corpses, not people. I have watched people die. God only knows how many times. People rediscover their real feelings when death is coming up on them. They jettison their pride and stubbornness and finally open up to their true hopes and desires. The living have a duty to listen to what they say then, to their final message. You abandoned that duty, Kaga."

To Matsumiya, her words felt like boulders that were

sinking down into and piling up in his heart. Wondering how Kaga would respond, he stole a sideways glance at his cousin, but Kaga just sat there in brooding silence. The pained look on his face wasn't something Matsumiya had seen many times before.

"I'm sorry," Kanamori said gently. "I've no business getting on my high horse like that. I'm sure there wasn't anything wrong with the way you and your father parted. All I'm asking you to do is . . . to try to imagine how your father must have felt."

Kaga frowned and ran his tongue over his lips. "Thank you," he murmured.

When they had finished their dinner, the three of them left the restaurant. With perfect timing, an empty taxi was coming along the street. Kaga raised his hand and stopped it.

"Thank you for dinner. Good night," Kanamori said as she climbed in.

They watched the taxi as it drove away, then Kaga started walking. He obviously wasn't interested in finding a cab for himself. Matsumiya fell in step beside him.

"It's not like you to be out-argued like that," Matsumiya ventured.

Kaga said nothing and continued striding straight ahead. From his expression, it was impossible to tell what he was thinking about so intently.

They were approaching Edobashi Bridge. Matsumiya wasn't surprised. Something in Kaga's pace had suggested that the crime scene rather than the police precinct was his destination.

Kaga crossed Edobashi Bridge and went through the underpass. He stopped for a moment just outside it, then set off again in the direction of Nihonbashi Bridge. He didn't say a word the whole time.

They passed in front of the Nihonbashi Bridge local police station and began to make their way across the bridge. Kaga stopped when they reached the middle of the bridge. He was close to the two *kirin* statues sitting back-to-back on their haunches. He stared up at them.

"The living have a duty to listen to the last message of the dying . . . was that what she said?" Kaga's eyes suddenly widened as he whispered the words to himself. To Matsumiya, they seemed to glow with a brighter luster.

Kaga strode off again. He was walking even faster than before.

Matsumiya scrambled to catch up. "Where to now?"

"Back to the station. I think I may have been seriously wrong about something."

26

Shubunkan Junior High School was in the middle of a peaceful residential neighborhood. The gentle glow of the carved school crest on the pillars of the gate exuded history.

Kaga sauntered through the gate as if he owned the place. Matsumiya just followed in his wake.

Matsumiya had requested Kobayashi for complete freedom of action for the day. Kobayashi had gone and consulted with Ishigaki for a few minutes before coming back to Matsumiya. He looked at him probingly.

"I got you your permission. No idea what you're planning to do, but make sure and report back to me."

"Yes, sir."

He bowed his thanks and was about to move off when he felt a hand grab his arm. Kobayashi pressed his face to Matsumiya's ear.

"You can tell me. You think Yashima didn't do it."

"I can't yet."

His arm was yanked violently.

"What are you after? What's your line of inquiry?"

Kobayashi was clearly not willing to let him go without getting an answer. "It's the son," Matsumiya replied reluctantly.

"*The son?*" There was an incredulous expression on Kobayashi's face. "The victim's son?"

"We don't know yet," he said and shook off Kobayashi's hand.

That was the truth: they didn't yet know. They could be completely off the mark. But Matsumiya sensed that they were onto something. The truth was out there. Kaga was pushing forward and it was somewhere in his path.

A PE lesson was in progress in the schoolyard. One group of boys was playing basketball and another was playing volleyball. The older man with them had to be the instructor. He seemed to be keeping a rather distracted eye on the games rather than doing any active coaching.

The administration office was on the first floor of the main building. Kaga had a word with the person at the reception desk. After a short wait, a woman emerged from the office.

She led them to a room labeled "Visitor Reception." It contained a low table with old-fashioned but expensive-looking sofas around it. The woman invited them to take a seat on a three-person sofa, then brought them some tea.

"I've not been inside a school for ages. I can't think how

many years it's been," Matsumiya said. They could hear the sound of children singing. The music room was probably nearby.

Kaga got up and walked over to a showcase in which various trophies and shields were displayed.

"The school seems to take its sports very seriously," he snorted.

"How about the swim team?"

Kaga pointed to one of the trophies. "They came in second in the relay at the national championships."

"Impressive."

"It is ten years old, though."

At that moment, there was a knock on the door. "Come in," Kaga said.

A broad-shouldered man entered the room. His head was large and his eyebrows thick. Matsumiya wondered if he came from the far south of Japan.

The teacher's name was Itokawa. He was the man Takeaki Aoyagi had contacted by phone three days before he was killed. Kaga had already questioned Itokawa about that. He'd explained that Aoyagi had concerns about his troubled relationship with his son.

Matsumiya introduced himself. Itokawa responded with a nod and a disinterested look.

"Sorry to disturb you. I know you're a busy man," said Kaga apologetically. "Were you teaching?"

"No, this is a free period for me. Anyway, what are you here for today? If it's the same thing as last time, there's nothing more I can tell you. You even asked me for an alibi."

"I'm sorry about that, sir. As I explained to you, that's something we do with everyone who has any kind of link to the case. I apologize if I made you uncomfortable."

"Don't worry. I'm comfortable enough. So, what's today about?"

"We don't want to talk about the current case but about something that happened quite a while ago."

At Kaga's words, a mistrustful crease appeared on Itokawa's brow. "A while ago?"

"Three years ago, in fact. An accident that took place during the summer vacation three years ago. I think you know what I'm talking about."

"Oh, that business?" A guarded look came over Itokawa's face. "What about it?"

"In the course of investigating the current case, we've realized that we need to take a second look at that accident. We'd like you to tell us what happened."

Itokawa forced his face into a tense and unnatural smile. He looked first at Kaga, then at Matsumiya.

"Not much I can tell you. Why do you think that the accident and your current case are connected? They're two completely separate things. Besides, you already know who's guilty. The man who died was the killer, right? Why's the investigation still ongoing?"

"Because the case isn't closed yet," Matsumiya chimed in. "We don't know for sure that he really was the killer."

"Oh. Still, I don't quite get why you need to dredge up an accident that happened years ago." Itokawa tilted his head to an exaggerated angle.

"Not an episode that you want to revisit, then?"

"I guess not."

"What? Is it uncomfortable for you if we dredge it up?"

Itokawa's eyes goggled. "What's that supposed to mean?"

"As detectives, that's the interpretation we put on it. If someone is reluctant to cooperate under questioning, we naturally assume that the matter must be awkward and uncomfortable for them."

Itokawa's mouth twitched. "What do you want to know about the darn accident?"

"Details. I believe you were first on the scene, Mr. Itokawa?"

"Yeah. Yes, I was."

"If you can, I'd like you to talk us through the events leading up to the accident. I believe there'd been a swim tournament at a sports center that day?"

Itokawa ran his tongue over his lips and drew himself upright in his chair. "Okay, I can do that," he said, looking Kaga in the eye. Matsumiya scrutinized the teacher's face for any evidence of lying.

After they had parted with Tokiko Kanamori the night before, Kaga had announced his intention to return to the police station. Since his partner gave every sign of being onto something, Matsumiya had tagged along. Back at the station, Kaga went online and, after doing some web searches related to shrines, began trawling through old news stories. Matsumiya was surprised to see the three keywords Kaga had typed in: "Shubunkan Junior High School," "swim team," and "accident." Why those particular search terms? he asked.

"We know for a fact that Suitengu Shrine was the main focus of Aoyagi's shrine visits because that's where he got his origami cranes burned in the ritual bonfire. All the assumptions we made up to that point were valid, but that is when we veered off course. We got too hung up on Suitengu's association with safe childbirth. Suitengu offers another benefit: protection from drowning."

"Drowning . . ." Matsumiya hadn't known. Now that Kaga mentioned it, though, he vaguely recalled having seen a water-sprite mask in the shrine shop.

"Tokyo is full of shrines that protect people from accidents and disasters. The majority offer protection from fire; shrines that protect against water-related accidents are much rarer. Apart from Suitengu, the only other one is Sogenji, a temple in Taito Ward. I came up with a theory that some sort of water-related accident could be driving Aoyagi's regular visits to Suitengu. That's when I remembered that his son had been on the swim team in junior high school."

What Kaga said jogged Matsumiya's memory. "And Aoyagi contacted Yuto's old swim team coach three days before the murder."

"Now do you see why I'm searching with these keywords?"

Kaga's interpretation of events was soon proved to be correct. This was one of the three-year-old newspaper stories he found.

At about seven o'clock on the night of the eighteenth, a second-year student was found drowning in the swimming pool of Shubunkan Junior High School. He was rushed by ambulance to the hospital where he remains in a coma. The student is said to be a member of the swim team who had slipped into the school without permission and was swimming alone when he had an accident, the cause of which is unknown. There had been an interschool swim meet at a sports center in the afternoon of the same day and the student was supposedly depressed after having performed poorly. It was the coach of the swim team who found the student. He had gone to the pool for a routine check when he discovered the student lying at the bottom of the pool.

Unfortunately, they couldn't find any follow-up stories. All they knew for sure was that this was the only drowning-type accident to have happened at Shubunkan Junior High.

Itokawa spoke in a flat voice, frowning in an effort of memory. The swim meet had ended around four. The post-competition team meeting at the sports center lasted about an hour, after which he had dismissed everyone. He assumed that the boys then went home; he himself had gone back to the school in order to input the results of the meet into his computer.

"I was busy inputting the data when I realized that I needed a particular document. I went to the coach's room to retrieve it. It's right beside the pool. Glancing down at the paved area by the side of the pool, I noticed a pile of clothes as if someone had gotten changed. That alarmed me. When I went down for a look, I found someone lying at the bottom of the swimming pool. I pulled him out straightaway. He turned out to be a member of the second-year swim team. I called 911 and performed mouth-to-mouth and CPR while waiting for the ambulance. All the other teachers had gone home by then, so it was the security guard who came to alert me when the ambulance arrived. Only then could I get in touch with the boy's family and the headmaster. I was on my own, so I couldn't do anything until the ambulance got there."

Itokawa exhaled heavily. "That's everything I can tell you about the accident." He glared at Kaga, as if challenging him to pick holes in his account.

"What was the name of the student who had the accident?" Kaga asked. Itokawa frowned and pursed his lips. "We can easily find out, if we have to," Kaga added.

Itokawa sullenly provided them with the name. The boy was called Tomoyuki Yoshinaga.

"I heard the family's moved out of Tokyo to Nagano Prefecture. I don't know the address."

"Did he make a full recovery?"

"No, you see . . ." Itokawa looked uncomfortable. "The accident had long-term effects. It's really too sad."

The boy had barely managed to escape with his life.

"Did anyone bring up the school's liability?" Kaga asked.

"The issue was raised. Should the school be so easy to break into? And it's a valid point. The school buildings can be locked, but on a practical level, it's simply not possible to stop people getting into an outdoor pool. Yoshinaga's parents accepted that, so the case never went to court."

"Is it something that happens a lot? Kids sneaking in and swimming without authorization?"

"I can't say it never happens. From what the students tell me, it's still going on from time to time. Not just current students, apparently, but former students who live nearby as well."

"The newspaper story claimed that Yoshinaga was upset because of his performance in that day's swim meet."

"I blame myself for that," Itokawa said gravely. "I had very high hopes for the lad and probably gave him too harsh a dressing-down. I had no idea he was so down. He must have got a leg cramp or suffered some sort of heart attack while swimming laps by himself."

Kaga, who was jotting down his replies, abruptly looked up from his notebook.

"Was he really by himself?"

"I'm sorry? What do you mean?"

"Oh, just that perhaps someone was with him. I mean, doing laps with your teammates is more fun than doing them alone."

"He was in no mood for fun. Anyway, daily distance training is something they always do by themselves. Besides, if anyone else had been there, the accident wouldn't have happened in the first place."

Kaga nodded. "I see," he said, despite looking mildly dissatisfied. "Could you show us the pool?"

"I can, though there's no water in it at this time of year."

"Not a problem." Kaga got to his feet. "After you."

They left the main school building and skirted the sports ground as they made for the pool, which was located on the far side of the school gymnasium. It was far enough from the main school building to make it possible to swim without being seen. In addition, the fence around the pool was so low that a junior high school student could easily climb over it.

They followed Itokawa up the side of the twenty-five-meter-long pool. The pool was empty and carpeted in dead, windblown leaves.

"I see there isn't any lighting here," Kaga said.

"There are emergency lights. We don't normally use them."

"You found Yoshinaga at seven at night. I know it was summertime, but I'm assuming it was already quite dark."

"Yes, it was pretty dark."

"You did well to spot him."

"Sorry?"

"You managed to spot Yoshinaga, who was lying at the bottom of the pool, in the dark. That's impressive. You mentioned that his clothes were in a pile at the side of the pool. Still, there was no reason for his body to be near them."

Itokawa took a deep breath. "I had a flashlight," he said.

"Ah." Kaga nodded. "Incidentally, what was Yoshinaga's best stroke?"

"Freestyle. He was particularly good at sprints. The fifty meters."

"Was that the race he competed in at the meet that day?"

"Yes, it must have been—look, I know it's my civic duty to cooperate and I'm trying my best to be helpful, but what's the point of all this, Detective? Personally, I can't see any link to the incident in Nihonbashi." Itokawa's voice had an edge to it; he could no longer conceal his irritation.

"You've got every reason to feel annoyed. I understand

that," Kaga rejoined blandly. "Whenever I question people, I always end up getting on their nerves—asking a million questions without telling them anything at all. There is a reason for my taking this approach, though."

"Yeah, yeah, I know. You have to keep the details of ongoing investigations secret from the general public. I get it, but still—"

"That's not all. If I tell the person I'm questioning why I'm questioning them, they can start developing preconceptions. I need answers untainted by anything like that."

Itokawa sighed and ran a hand over his face. "I can see that."

"By the way, have you got a directory of former swim team members who've graduated? If you have, I'd like to borrow it."

Itokawa responded to Kaga's request with a shake of the head. "I can't do that. That's personal information. If you want it, you'll need to get a warrant."

"Really? Okay, then." Kaga didn't insist. "Thank you very much for everything."

"Are we done?"

"Yes, that's everything. I'll be in touch if I have any further questions." Kaga bowed his thanks. "Let's go," he said to Matsumiya.

27

"We may be onto something here," Kaga murmured as soon as they were outside the school gates. "My sixth sense is telling me that there's a link between the accident from three years ago and our current case. I also get the feeling that the teacher is hiding something."

"I agree. When Aoyagi contacted Itokawa three days before his murder, do you think it was the accident he wanted to talk about?"

"Almost certainly. Though there's still a lot that doesn't add up."

Kaga stopped after they had reached the end of the block.

"I know a guy in the local precinct. I called him this morning and asked him to dig up all the files on the pool accident for me. I'm going to go and collect them. Let's meet up later."

"I'm heading to Aoyagi's house."

There was a slight look of surprise on Kaga's face as he turned to Matsumiya.

"If it's Yuto you want, he'll be at school."

"Yeah, I know. I'm going to ask the mother to give me his junior high school directory."

Kaga nodded approvingly. "Good idea."

They went their separate ways after arranging to meet at Nakameguro Station later.

Fumiko Aoyagi was home. Haruka was taking the day off school and was up in her room, she explained.

Fumiko invited Matsumiya into the living room, but he kept his shoes firmly on and made a deprecatory gesture.

"I'm fine here. I just want to borrow something."

Fumiko looked puzzled when he mentioned the school register from Yuto's swim team days. "Is it relevant to the case?"

"I can't yet be sure. All I can say is that it might be."

"I thought that guy was the killer?"

"If you mean Fuyuki Yashima, that's a conclusion that the media have jumped to all by themselves. As far as the police is concerned, we haven't yet made an official announcement."

Fumiko looked at him, wide-eyed. "Are you saying that he didn't do it? Then why? Why was my husband killed? Who really did it?" Her voice was shrill.

Things were getting awkward. Matsumiya was worried. What would Kaga do at a time like this?

"Just calm down, please. At this stage, I'm not at liberty to share any details with you. For now, could you just fetch me the directory and leave it at that?"

279

Fumiko looked at Matsumiya with an expression of mixed chagrin and perplexity before shifting her gaze to the top of the staircase. "The directory's in my son's room, I think. He'll get mad at me if I just go in and help myself to it."

"I'll photocopy it and give it straight back to you. No one outside the force will see it. I promise you that."

Fumiko capitulated and grudgingly agreed. "All right, wait here a minute."

"Thank you," said Matsumiya, bowing deeply.

A few minutes later, Fumiko handed him a pamphlet with the title *Shubunkan Junior High School Swim Team 60th Anniversary Commemorative Issue* on the cover. The back pages contained a list of the names and contact details of all the school's present and former swim team members. The pamphlet was probably published every ten years or so, Matsumiya guessed.

"I'll get this right back to you," said Matsumiya with a nod of thanks. He had opened the door and was about to head out when something came into his head and he spun around.

"Three years ago, there was an accident at the swimming pool of Shubunkan Junior High School. Do you remember it?"

Fumiko's eyes widened in surprise. "Yes, I do . . . A boy in the year below Yuto's drowned, I think."

"Have you discussed the accident recently, as a family?"

"No, not that I'm aware."

"I see. Thank you. I'll be right back."

Matsumiya went to the local convenience store, where

he photocopied the necessary pages of the pamphlet. There was a foreword written by Itokawa on the first page, so he copied that too.

After going back to the Aoyagis' house to return the pamphlet, Matsumiya called Kaga as he headed to the train station. Kaga was already ensconced in a café nearby.

"According to the records, the accident seems to have happened as Itokawa described it to us." Kaga pushed his coffee cup to one side and placed a bundle of files on the table. "The accident was deemed to have been caused by Tomoyuki Yoshinaga's own negligence, so no one else was held liable. I wanted to find out more, so I tried calling the Yoshinagas. I got no answer. As Itokawa said, they must have moved."

"What does it all mean? What on earth prompted Aoyagi to start visiting shrines that offer protection from drowning at this stage of the game? It would make a little bit more sense if Yuto was the one doing it." As he said this, Matsumiya placed the photocopied pages of names and addresses on top of Kaga's pile of documents.

"Another mystery is why Aoyagi kept his shrine visits secret from his family, Yuto included."

"Maybe there's some sort of connection between Aoyagi and Tomoyuki Yoshinaga."

"Like what?"

"Like . . ." Matsumiya lowered his voice. "Like Yoshinaga being Aoyagi's secret love child."

Kaga broke into a broad grin. "I don't think so."

"Why not? We won't know until we check it out."

"Let's check it out, then." Kaga picked up the photocopied

pages. "Look, here's a new address for Tomoyuki Yoshinaga, despite that teacher fellow claiming not to know what it was. Karuizawa, eh? The perfect distance for a day trip."

"I'll have a word with Chief Ishigaki when we get back to the task force room. As we're busy doing our own thing, he's guaranteed to make some sarcastic crack."

"Great. You do that. Look at what Itokawa wrote here. 'Water never lies. Lies have no affinity with water. Try to cheat the water and your deception will rebound on you.' Quite the poet, isn't he? If Itokawa really believes what he wrote here, then our current line of inquiry is doomed."

Matsumiya sipped his coffee and looked intently at Kaga. "Isn't it time you told me?"

"Told you what?"

"How you worked out that the motive for Aoyagi's visits to Suitengu Shrine was protection from drowning and not safe childbirth. I'm prepared to accept that intuition had something to do with it, but there must have been a more tangible trigger."

Kaga put down the photocopies and reached for his coffee cup. "Yeah, I don't know."

"So, what was the trigger?"

"It wasn't so clear-cut. I just couldn't get my head around the one-hundred-and-eighty-degree change in Yuto's attitude. One minute, he's saying all these things that suggest he has nothing but contempt for his father, then the next, everything changes. The news about him beating up Kotake, the factory manager, only reinforced my impression."

"I noticed that too. Personally, I thought his sister slitting her wrists was what prompted his change of heart."

"I don't think so. Don't you remember what Yuto said? He said that doing that is tantamount to an admission of Dad's guilt. That suggested to me that he had decided to believe the best of his father even before the drama of his sister's attempted suicide."

Matsumiya reran the episode in his head. Kaga was right.

"So what do you think prompted his change of mind?"

"I think he was given some new information about his father. But we know that no one in the family had any contact with anyone else overnight. Mrs. Aoyagi also said they deliberately hadn't watched TV or checked the news online."

Kaga had raised those very points with the mother at the time, Matsumiya recalled. Meaning he had already noticed the change in Yuto and was trying to find what was behind it.

"The question then became: Who gave Yuto the information? I had no way of knowing, but then the answer came to me in the most unexpected way."

Matsumiya searched his memory, but couldn't come up with anything like an answer himself. He scowled and glared at Kaga. "All right, you win. Without being too condescending about it, tell me who it was."

Kaga grinned merrily. "None other than your own good self."

"Me? What did I say?"

"When we were at the Aoyagi house the day before the

sister cut her wrists, you mentioned the *kirins*. The statues on Nihonbashi Bridge, I mean."

"The statues? Come to think of it, I did. But mention them was all I did. Yuto just went straight back up to his room after that."

"In fact, though, your words had a powerful impact. You remember me telling you how I bumped into Ms. Nakahara in Hamacho Green Road park? Later on, we saw Yuto half-way across Nihonbashi Bridge."

"Yuto? On the bridge?" It was the first Matsumiya had heard of it.

"I didn't think much of it at the time, but on reflection, I realized that he'd been gazing up at the *kirin* statues. I began to think that perhaps he'd figured out why Takeaki dragged himself all the way to Nihonbashi Bridge after being stabbed. Whatever the reason was, it had some sort of connection to the *kirin* statues and was enough to completely transform the way he thought about his father. Voilà, an explanation for his change of heart."

"What's the significance of the *kirins*?"

"I don't know. What I can say is this: the *kirin* statue was a final message from Takeaki to Yuto, from a dying father to his son."

"From Takeaki to Yuto, a dying father to his son . . . ," repeated Matsumiya, before he worked it out. "Kyo, you got that idea from something Kanamori said."

"I believe in leaving the process of deduction to my imagination. Anyway, that's not important; it's Yuto we need to be thinking about. He understood the message his father sent him. That means that he must also have understood the motivation behind his father's otherwise inexplicable behavior. Why was Takeaki Aoyagi making repeated visits to Nihonbashi? I tried taking a new angle. What if Takeaki wasn't praying for himself? What if he was praying on behalf of his son, Yuto? What if Yuto had a girlfriend and he had gotten her pregnant? But we saw no evidence of anything like that."

"Which is how you made the leap to the whole protection-from-drowning angle." Matsumiya nodded and sighed. "Now I get it."

"What about your theory of Tomoyuki Yoshinaga being Takeaki's love child?"

"Scrub that. Takeaki Aoyagi was making his shrine visits on his son's behalf: I'm sure you're right there. In which case, we need to speak to the kid himself."

"I know." Kaga glanced at his watch. "School's out soon."

They finished their coffee, left the café, and set off for the Aoyagi house. They went as far as a truck that was parked at the side of the road not far from the house. They decided to watch the house from there.

"What do you think really happened at the pool?" Kaga asked Matsumiya.

Matsumiya thought for a moment, then shook his head. "I'm not sure. I've a hunch that Yoshinaga wasn't alone."

"If his teammates were there, they'd have realized soon enough that something was wrong. But to need an ambulance, he must have been at the bottom of the pool for a while. It doesn't make any sense."

In what sort of circumstances could something that

made no sense have happened? Despite racking his brains, Matsumiya came up empty.

"Hey." Kaga jerked his chin and Matsumiya looked in the direction he indicated. Yuto Aoyagi was approaching from the far end of the street, dragging his feet as he walked.

The two detectives set off in his direction. Yuto had his eyes on the ground, but he must have sensed something. He looked up, saw the two men, and stopped in his tracks.

"We want to ask you a few questions," Matsumiya said. "All right?"

"What's with the ambush tactics?" Yuto glared at them defiantly.

"We just want to talk to you," Kaga said. "We think there's a better chance of getting honest answers if your mother and your sister aren't around."

"What do you want to know?"

"I don't want to do this out here on the street. Let's start by finding a place we can sit down and relax."

Kaga stalked off. Matsumiya indicated with his eyes for Yuto to follow him.

They ended up back at the same café they had just left. Kaga ordered a coffee and Matsumiya an English tea, while Yuto opted for an iced coffee.

"I gather you don't do any extracurricular activities at your present school," Kaga began. "How come?"

"No special reason . . . Not interested."

"How about swimming? We know you were a keen swimmer back at junior high."

Yuto blinked. "Is this the official interview?"

"I guess it must be. What's wrong? You look slightly uncomfortable. You don't like talking about your time on the swim team?"

"No, I don't mind . . . ," Yuto replied, his eyes fixed on the floor.

"Let's talk about something else. Your father was a frequent visitor to the Nihonbashi area and we know why. He was doing the Seven Lucky Gods pilgrimage circuit, with Suitengu Shrine as his main destination. Taking his hundred origami cranes along with him. But I think you already know that."

Yuto half looked up, then ducked his head back down and shook it from side to side. "No idea. First I've heard of it."

"Sure about that? You don't seem very surprised."

"What do you want me to do? What is this Suitengu business, anyway?"

"We came up with a theory that your father was visiting Suitengu to pray for protection from drowning. The logical next step for us was to see if your father had been involved in any accidents involving water recently. That led us to the accident that occurred at Shubunkan Junior High three years ago. I'm referring to the accident that resulted in the hospitalization of Tomoyuki Yoshinaga. I assume you've not forgotten it."

Yuto passed his tongue over his lips. "Naah," he croaked hoarsely.

"We want you to tell us about the accident. In detail. Whatever you know."

Yuto said nothing for a while, then he picked up his glass, sucked some iced coffee through his straw, and sighed feebly.

"Yuto," said Kaga.

"I don't know anything," Yuto replied. His voice was strained. "I really don't. Yoshinaga snuck into the pool by himself and drowned. That's all I can tell you."

"Then why was Mr. Aoyagi—why was your father—doing what he did? What do you think he was praying for at Suitengu Shrine?"

"I don't know."

"Listen, Yuto, this is a serious matter. There could well be a link to your father's murder. In fact, we're convinced that the two things are connected. Come on. Why not just tell us the truth?"

Yuto's cheeks were twitching. He breathed out heavily, then raised his head. "I don't know." He looked Kaga in the eye. "Can I go now, Detective? I can't answer any of your questions."

"Listen, Yuto—" Matsumiya began. Kaga gestured him to be quiet.

"You can go if you want to. It's a pity, though, a real pity. We could solve this case a whole lot faster if you were willing to help us."

Yuto grabbed his bag and got to his feet. "Right, I'm off, then. Thanks for the iced coffee." With a brusque nod of the head, he made for the door. His retreating figure seemed to radiate intransigence.

Matsumiya sipped his tea and cocked his head to one side. "I wonder what that was all about. There must be something very uncomfortable for him involved."

"I don't think that's quite it. If he was only thinking about himself, he wouldn't have had that look in his eyes."

"His eyes?"

"He's covering for someone. I can tell from his eyes. When a youngster has that look, nothing an adult says can make a jot of difference."

Matsumiya was wondering what Kaga meant when his phone started vibrating. It was Kobayashi.

"Matsumiya here."

"Kobayashi. Something urgent's come up. Can you talk?"

"Sure. What is it?"

There was a brief pause. "We found some prints," Kobayashi said.

"Prints. You mean . . . ?" Matsumiya felt the sweat forming in his armpits.

"They found Yashima's prints on the books you guys brought in. We've managed to confirm that the man in the CCTV footage is Fuyuki Yashima. Meaning that whoever was in the café with the victim, it wasn't Yashima."

28

When evening came, the temperature dropped suddenly. People's breaths formed into faint white clouds in front of their faces. Winter was around the corner.

Yuto was walking along, carrying his schoolbag. He was nowhere near his house. He had originally intended to go straight home but had changed his mind after being waylaid by the detectives.

"Listen, Yuto, this is a serious matter. There could well be a link to your father's murder." Was what Detective Kaga told him true? What exactly did he mean by "link"? Was he just talking about Dad's reasons for being in Nihonbashi, or was it something beyond that?

Yuto felt confused and conflicted. For a brief moment, he'd considered telling the detective everything. In the end, though, he couldn't bring himself to do so. It wasn't a decision he could make alone.

The familiar row of houses came into view. He walked toward one of them. It was a large house in the European style. The name *Kurosawa* was engraved on a plaque on the gatepost.

Yuto pressed the bell on the intercom. There was a short interval. "Hello," came a woman's voice.

"Good afternoon," Yuto said. "My name's Aoyagi. I was in the same class as Shota at junior high school. Is he there?"

"Oh . . . Could you wait a moment?" The woman seemed to have recognized him straightaway.

A little while later, the front door opened and Kurosawa peered out. "What's up?" he asked, a startled look on his face.

"Got a moment?"

"Sure. A moment."

Yuto pushed the garden gate open and walked up to the front door. "Why don't you pick up when I call? And you're not replying to my texts either."

"Ah." Kurosawa's mouth hung half-open. "Just a second." He drew his head back inside and shut the door.

There was the sound of someone scrabbling around, then the door reopened. Kurosawa was holding a phone.

"Got myself a new one. Sorry. Didn't get around to giving you the new number."

Yuto snorted.

I bet that's not true, he was thinking. *Kurosawa must know how my dad's being demonized because of the workplace accident cover-up thing. He probably thought he'd be better off giving me a wide berth.*

After Kurosawa had given him his new number and email address, Yuto looked at his friend.

"We three need to get together and have a talk. I said the same thing to Sugino."

Kurosawa's eyes clouded over. "Talk about what?"

"When I say 'the three of us,' I think you know exactly what I mean."

Kurosawa looked at the ground. "Why now?"

"What does that matter? *Because I say so.*"

"All right. All right."

"You got time today?"

Kurosawa looked up, frowned, and shook his head. "Today's no good for me. My private tutor will be here any minute now. I've got to stay home."

"Okay. Tomorrow, then?"

"Tomorrow . . . What time?"

"Got to be after school. How about five o'clock near Nakameguro Station somewhere."

After a little hemming and hawing, Kurosawa agreed. "Fine," he said.

"See you tomorrow, then. I'll tell Sugino."

Yuto was already walking off when Kurosawa called him back. "Ao!" Yuto turned around. "What on earth's happened?" Kurosawa asked.

"You know what's happened," Yuto replied. "My dad was murdered."

Turning his back on a dazed-looking Kurosawa, Yuto pushed the garden gate open and went back out into the street.

29

Matsumiya and Kaga caught the bullet train. It left Tokyo Station at nine twenty and was due to reach Karuizawa at ten thirty-two.

"It'll probably be freezing up there. Are you ready?" Kaga put his rolled-up coat on the luggage rack and took his seat. Matsumiya had a bag with him, but Kaga, as usual, was traveling light.

"I think of Karuizawa as a place people go to escape the summer heat. When you come to think of it, some people must live there year-round," Matsumiya said. "She told me that they're living in what used to be their old holiday home."

The "she" Matsumiya was referring to was the mother of Tomoyuki Yoshinaga. Matsumiya had phoned her the night before to tell her that they would be coming today. He kept the real reason for their visit under wraps, simply saying that they wanted to ask her a few questions about her son.

They got permission to make the trip to Karuizawa much more easily than expected. The theory of Yashima being the culprit had been shaken to its foundations.

The discovery of Yashima's fingerprints on the books in the bookstore proved that the person Takeaki Aoyagi met in the café wasn't Yashima but someone else, completely subverting the original scenario.

But it didn't completely eliminate the possibility of Yashima being guilty. The case could still be made that Yashima had bumped into Aoyagi after leaving the bookstore and made a spur-of-the-moment decision to rob him. That interpretation begged the question why whoever had actually been in the café with Aoyagi wasn't coming forward. Were they staying quiet just because they didn't want to get involved?

"The line you two are pursuing may well be the right one," Ishigaki had said. There was the subtlest hint of menace in his eyes. *I've let you march to the beat of your own drum. Now I need you to show me some results*, they seemed to say.

In fact, neither of them had any idea of what kind of secret lay concealed behind the accident at the swimming pool three years ago. After questioning Yuto Aoyagi the day before, Matsumiya and Kaga had talked to a couple of other swim team members from the same year. Neither of them gave the impression that they were hiding anything or entertained any suspicions of their own about the accident.

"I thought Yoshinaga was crazy, sneaking into the pool by himself like that. He had a very high opinion of himself.

The volunteer assistant coach, an alumnus of the swim team, always praised his swimming to the skies—so the outcome of the meet must have come as a big shock to him," one of the young men said with emotion in his voice.

The idea that the accident had occurred during a swim team training session simply wasn't credible. It would be too hard for everybody to get their stories to match, and someone was sure to have let the cat out of the bag in the end.

As Matsumiya was fuzzily rehashing the case in his head, the train pulled into Karuizawa Station. The two detectives had hardly said a word to one another during the journey. Kaga stood up, stretched his arms, and rolled his head on his shoulders. *He must have been asleep.*

They found a cab waiting outside the station and gave the driver their destination.

The taxi rolled through the leafy landscape. Although the ground wasn't yet covered in snow, you could feel the chill of the winter air inside the vehicle. Everyone in the street was dressed for seriously cold weather.

The taxi stopped at a cluster of holiday homes. "Should be somewhere around here," the taxi driver said. Matsumiya got out and inspected the gatepost of the nearest house. There was a wooden plaque on which the name *Yoshinaga* was engraved.

"This is the place," he said to Kaga, who was still in the backseat.

Kaga paid the driver and slid out. "God, it's cold." He began to do up the buttons of his coat.

As there was no intercom, they pushed the gate open

and went in. The garden was a decent size and a longish path led up to the house.

The house itself was a mostly brown structure that exuded tranquility. There were shutters on the windows and the front door was a little above ground level, presumably to stop it getting blocked by snow.

There was an intercom on one side of the front door. Matsumiya pressed the bell. "Yes, hello," came the swift response. It was a woman's voice.

"I am from the Tokyo Metropolitan Police. We spoke yesterday."

"Of course."

A few seconds later, they heard the lock turning and the door opened. A small woman with a small head was standing there. She was wearing jeans and a sweater and must have been around fifty. Her hair, which was flecked with gray, was tied at the back of her head. Matsumiya knew that her first name was Mieko from their phone conversation.

The two detectives introduced themselves and she invited them inside. The house was warm with a faint scent of flowers.

"Where's Tomoyuki?" Kaga asked after taking off his shoes and putting on the slippers she offered them.

Mieko Yoshinaga clasped her hands lightly and looked at the two detectives one after the other. "He's in the living room."

She led them along a passage. There was a door at the far end. "In here," she said, and they went inside. It was an expansive two-story living room with a kitchen and dining area. There were some solid-looking sofas and tables dotted about and a rocking chair near the window. In that rocking chair—

A young man was seated. His upper body was wrapped in a blanket and he had sneakers on his feet. He was facing them, but his eyes were shut tight. He was emaciated and his skin was as white as porcelain. His fringe was cut in a neat line just above his eyebrows.

Matsumiya slowly walked over and examined the boy. The boy didn't move a muscle. He was as inert as a corpse.

"He can breathe for himself," Mieko Yoshinaga said with evident pride. "On a good day, his expression even changes."

"Does he ever open his eyes?"

Kaga was taken aback at the bright smile Mieko gave him. "He's sleeping, so, no, he doesn't open his eyes. He's just asleep. That's all."

She seemed keen to emphasize that her boy was fine and that there was absolutely nothing wrong with him. She was probably saying it more for her own benefit than for theirs.

"Please, sit down," she said. The two of them went over to one of the sofas.

Mieko made some tea, which she served in bone china cups.

"When did you move here?" Kaga asked.

"It must have been the year after the accident. My husband retired, so we took the opportunity to sell our house in Tokyo and move out here, all three of us. We wanted to look after Tomoyuki in a place with good, clean air."

"Where is your husband today?"

"He's in Tokyo. Even though he's officially retired, he works as an adviser to a number of companies, so he has to go into the city from time to time," she replied with a cheerful smile.

It's lucky they're so well-off, Matsumiya thought. *The cost of Tomoyuki's care would probably be too much for an ordinary family.*

"What do you want to talk to me about?"

Kaga leaned forward slightly. "It's about your son. Our records show that you didn't initiate legal proceedings of any kind. Does that mean you didn't have any questions or doubts about the accident?"

Mieko gave a small shake of the head. "To be quite honest, I have nothing *but* questions. I simply don't believe that Tomoyuki snuck into the pool all by himself. The same with him drowning. He'd been going to swimming lessons since he was a little boy; he was completely at home in the water, but he also knew that you have to treat it with respect."

"You nonetheless accepted the explanation the school gave you?"

"We had no choice. The police told us they hadn't found anything suspicious. Besides, our top priority was always taking care of our son. The question of responsibility was far less important." Mieko glanced over at the rocking chair. "I was prepared to believe that yes, maybe things did happen that way. He was always a serious and responsible kid . . ."

"What are you getting at?"

"Tomoyuki was really anxious in the days leading up to the swim meet. He said over and over, 'What if I let my teammates down?'"

"Let them down?"

"He was selected for the relay team. The other boys in it were all third years; he was the only second year. He didn't want to disappoint his older teammates."

"So he was in the relay, was he?"

"Excuse me," said Mieko. "But exactly what sort of investigation is this? Why are you making inquiries about his accident now?"

It was a perfectly legitimate question.

"There was recently a murder in Tokyo," Kaga said. "That's what we're investigating."

"A murder?" Mieko's expression darkened uneasily.

"Don't worry. There's no question of anyone in your family being involved. However, we believe that there may be a link between your son's accident and certain behaviors of the murder victim. That's why we are here to see you."

"Who was the victim?"

"A man by the name of Aoyagi. Takeaki Aoyagi. Do you recognize the name?"

"Aoyagi . . . It sounds familiar, but no, sorry, I don't think I know him."

If she had heard the name, it would have to be through Tomoyuki, thought Matsumiya. *Tomoyuki must have talked about the older boys on the swim team at home.*

Kaga, however, was adamant that they should not volunteer the information that Takeaki Aoyagi was the father of a boy in the year above Tomoyuki.

"Do you know Suitengu, the shrine in the Nihonbashi area? It's famous as a place people go to pray for safe childbirth; it's also known for protecting people from drowning."

Mieko blinked at Kaga's question. "Yes, I know the place."

"We have reason to believe that Mr. Aoyagi was a regular visitor to Suitengu Shrine. Offering up origami cranes, one hundred at a time. Does that ring any bells with—"

Kaga broke off in the middle of his sentence. Matsumiya could see why. The expression on Mieko's face had undergone a visible change. Her eyes had opened wide and she was gasping for air.

"Obviously, it does," Kaga answered his own question.

Mieko Yoshinaga was nodding her head frantically. "It certainly does. He must be 'Tokyo Hanako.'"

"*Hanako?*"

"Bear with me a minute." Mieko left the room as she said this.

Matsumiya caught Kaga's eye. Brilliant detective though his cousin was, Kaga seemed to have no idea what was going on either, but the sense that they were about to get their hands on an important clue had brought a gleam to his eye.

Mieko came back into the room. She was holding a laptop.

"I actually have my own blog. When I started, it was a journal about me taking care of my son, but over time, people started sending me all sorts of supportive messages." Mieko switched on her computer while she was talking.

"And Tokyo Hanako is one of those people?"

Mieko nodded in response to Kaga's question. "At some point, Hanako and I started exchanging emails. The thought occurred to me she might be a man. Gosh. Are you saying that's who was murdered?"

"You know about the hundred origami cranes?"

"Yes. Tokyo Hanako broke up the traditional one thousand cranes into ten sets of a hundred to offer at the shrines. You can read all about it on my blog." Mieko swiveled her computer around so that the two detectives could see the screen. "This is a bit embarrassing."

On the screen there was the top page of a blog. It was dotted with colorful illustrations.

"Look!" Kaga jabbed a finger at the top of the page. Matsumiya squinted at the screen and gave a start.

The name of the blog was *The Wings of the Kirin*.

30

It was after two p.m. by the time they got back to Tokyo Station. At Kaga's suggestion, they decided to go directly to Shubunkan Junior High School.

When they got there, they went to the office. The woman who had escorted them to the visitors' room the previous day was taken aback to see them again.

"I'm sorry," Kaga said, "but we need to have another word with Mr. Itokawa."

The woman made a few keystrokes on her computer. "He's teaching right now. Is it urgent?"

"No. If he's busy, we're happy to wait until the class is over. Can we use the same room as yesterday?"

"You're welcome to. Can you find your own way?"

"No problem."

They went to the visitors' reception room and sat on the

sofa side by side, just like the day before. Neither of them said a word. They had said all that needed saying on the bullet train back. (Though it was primarily Matsumiya listening as Kaga expounded his theory.)

A number of things had come to light over the last twenty-four hours. Both men were confident they would uncover the truth any minute now.

The bell rang for the end of the lesson. This was accompanied by a roar that got louder and closer until they could hear a mass of boys surging back and forth along the passage outside.

A few minutes passed and the door opened. It was Itokawa. He came across as even more leery than the previous day.

Matsumiya and Kaga both got up and greeted him with a bow.

"What do you want now? I really don't think there's anything more I can tell you." Itokawa spoke gruffly, making no attempt to conceal his annoyance.

"I do apologize. Actually, we would like you to show us something," Kaga said.

"What?"

Kaga paused a moment. "The swim meet results," he said. "As you know, there was a swim meet on the same day the accident occurred three years ago. We would be grateful if you could show us the official record of the event."

Itokawa's face twitched.

"Why on earth do you want to see that?" His tone was defensive.

"Everyone says that Tomoyuki Yoshinaga did what he did because he was so upset at how poorly he had performed at the meet. Given that, we think it makes sense for us to see just how bad his results were."

Itokawa frowned. "What's the point of that? Everyone knows Yoshinaga performed badly. I can tell you that myself."

"What we want to do"—Kaga took a step forward—"is to get the details. We would appreciate your cooperation."

Itokawa looked uncomfortable as the tall detective loomed over him.

"Fine. If you'd just wait here."

"No, we'll come with you. The staff room's just across the way, isn't it?"

"The records aren't kept in the staff room, they're in the coach's room."

"That's not a problem. We'll come with you."

Matsumiya got to his feet and stood shoulder to shoulder with Kaga. "Let's go."

Ever so grudgingly, Itokawa turned around and left the room. Matsumiya and Kaga went after him.

Students stood chatting to one another in clusters outside the main school building. They looked inquisitively at Matsumiya and Kaga as they went by. Any grown-up other than a teacher was a person of interest in their little world.

The coach's room was on the second floor of a small building immediately beside the swimming pool. The changing rooms were on the first floor.

Itokawa unlocked the door. The room was small and

contained a desk, some lockers, and a cabinet. On the shelves, there were rows of thick binders. The titles on the spines showed that they contained the results of the meets.

"Exactly what we're after." Kaga pulled out a pair of white gloves. "You're okay with us taking a look?"

"Knock yourself out," Itokawa replied gruffly.

As Matsumiya pulled his gloves, he watched Kaga rapidly leafing through one of the files.

His hand stopped when he reached a certain page. The date of the meet was August 18, three years ago. The day the accident had happened.

Matsumiya skimmed through the different events and the swimmers' names until he found the name Tomoyuki Yoshinaga in the fifty-meter freestyle. Yuto Aoyagi had swum in the same race, he noticed.

With his gloved hand, Kaga was pointing at another part of the page. It was the entry for the two-hundred-meter relay. Matsumiya gulped as he read the names of the team members.

First leg	Yuto Aoyagi (3rd year)
Second leg	Tatsuya Sugino (3rd year)
Third leg	Tomoyuki Yoshinaga (2nd year)
Fourth leg	Shota Kurosawa (3rd year)

"Take a note of this," Kaga whispered. Matsumiya didn't need to be told; he had already pulled out his pen. The race results were of no interest to them; all they cared about was who had been on the relay team.

Neither Yuto Aoyagi nor Tomoyuki Yoshinaga had taken part in any other events.

Kaga closed the file and put it back on the shelf. The two detectives turned around at the same time and were confronted by Itokawa standing there. His face was gloomy and there was a cunning glint in his eye.

"Happy now?" Itokawa asked.

"Very happy. Could I ask another question?"

"What now? I've things to do, you know."

"What subject do you teach?"

Itokawa frowned suspiciously. "Math."

"Really? Well, there are all sorts of formulas in junior high school math: Pythagoras's theorem, the quadratic equation, that sort of thing."

"And what's that got to do with anything?"

"Memorizing formulas enables you to solve a whole variety of problems. If, however, you memorize a formula wrongly to start with, you'll end up getting things wrong over and over again. That can happen, can't it?"

"Indeed, it can." From the expression on Itokawa's face, he was clearly wondering what on earth Kaga was getting at.

"Make sure to get your students to memorize all the formulas correctly."

"Thank you, but I really don't need you to tell me that."

"I don't suppose you do. Yes, sorry. Thanks for your help," said Kaga, speaking quickly and signaling to Matsumiya that they should be on their way.

After leaving the school, they went to a local diner and had a late lunch.

Once they finished their meal, Matsumiya extracted a few sheets of paper from his bag. It was the photocopy of the registry of swim team members.

"Tatsuya Sugino and Shota Kurosawa? These two were involved in the accident three years ago along with Yuto Aoyagi. We can be one hundred percent sure of that."

Kaga nodded as he drank his after-lunch coffee.

"Very probably. Or at least, they have important information about the accident. Something that they can't reveal to anyone. Yesterday, it seemed clear that Yuto was protecting someone. That's got to be the other two boys. I'm guessing he feels he can't tell us the truth without getting their permission first."

"We need to get the three of them together to get them to talk to us."

Kaga slid the photocopy to his side of the table. "I'll go for Tatsuya Sugino. You handle Shota Kurosawa."

"Got it."

The addresses showed that they lived quite a way from one another.

"It's four thirty now. School will be over soon," said Kaga, glancing at his watch.

"Shall I bring Shota Kurosawa to you?"

Kaga pondered a moment. "How about we use the Aoyagi house as a base?" he replied. "Yuto will probably be there now. And if he's not, he soon will be."

"Yeah, fine. I'll call you when I've found Shota Kurosawa."

"Got it."

Matsumiya parted from Kaga outside the diner and caught a cab. The driver had GPS, so Matsumiya got the driver to input Shota Kurosawa's address.

The taxi stopped in the middle of a residential district. Matsumiya paid the fare and slid out. In front of him there stood a row of substantial houses. He walked along inspecting the nameplates and soon found the Kurosawa house. It was a rather grand residence in the European style.

Matsumiya pressed the intercom and gave his name. As soon as the woman who answered heard the words "Tokyo Metropolitan Police," her voice became one degree shriller.

The woman who appeared at the front door was elegantly dressed in a lilac cardigan. This had to be Shota Kurosawa's mother. She squirmed uncomfortably when Matsumiya told her that he wanted to speak to her son.

"Has he done something wrong?"

"No, no." Matsumiya smiled and made a deprecatory gesture with his hand. "I just want to ask him a couple of questions. Isn't he back yet?"

"He did come back, but then he went straight back out. He said something about meeting a friend."

"A friend? What, from his current school?"

"No. A friend from his club in junior high."

"Club? You mean the swim team?"

The mother seemed disconcerted to find the detective so well informed about her son. "That's right." She looked anxious and tucked her chin defensively into her neck.

"Which friend?"

"It's . . . Aoyagi."

Matsumiya caught his breath. Was this just a coincidence?

"Do you know where they're meeting?"

"I'm not sure." She tilted her head to one side. "He said something about meeting at the station."

Matsumiya's heart started pounding. The situation was becoming critical.

"I need you to call your son right now and ask him where he is. Don't say a word about me."

"Wha—! . . . How do I phrase the question?"

"That's up to you."

Shota Kurosawa's mother went back into the house, a shell-shocked look on her face. Matsumiya called Kaga and explained the situation while he waited on the doorstep.

"That's certainly worrying. I'll head for the station too. We've got to find them."

"What about Tatsuya Sugino?"

"He's not yet back from school. Who knows, perhaps he's going to rendezvous with Yuto and Shota."

"All three of them at this specific moment . . . Do you think it's a coincidence?"

"No way. The murder of Yuto's father provoked a change of mind in Yuto. On top of that, I reckon the questions we put to him about the accident yesterday got him thinking about links between the accident and the murder."

"I'm on edge."

"Good. Relaxing is the last thing we want to do right now. We've got to locate the boys."

"Got it," Matsumiya said. The front door opened just

as he ended the call. Shota Kurosawa's mother looked crest-fallen.

"He's somewhere near the station, but he wouldn't tell me exactly where."

Nothing doing, then. Matsumiya got the woman to give him Shota Kurosawa's cell phone number and took off.

When he got to the Nakameguro Station area, he started looking into all the cafés and fast-food restaurants, keeping in touch with Kaga by phone as he did so. The fact that there were so many youngsters of the same age around only complicated things.

He was walking past a burger joint when a school uniform he recognized caught his eye. He stopped and looked in. Yuto Aoyagi was sitting at the counter by the window. Was the long-haired youth sitting next to him Shota Kurosawa?

Matsumiya called Kaga to let him know.

Kaga soon showed up and the two of them made their way into the restaurant. They went straight over to Yuto and Shota. The long-haired youth, who was the first to notice them, swiveled around on his stool. A look of surprise came over Yuto's face when he followed suit.

"You're Kurosawa, right?" Kaga said to the long-haired youth.

"What if I am?" Kurosawa said defensively.

Kaga looked down at Yuto. "Expecting Sugino any minute now?"

Yuto said nothing. From the sideways view of the boy's face, Matsumiya could see that he was trying to tough it out, the way kids do.

"Guess I'm right."

"Piss off," Yuto said, his eyes averted. "Who we see is none of your business. We're not breaking any laws."

"Isn't it *because* you broke the law that you arranged this little get-together?"

The blood drained from the two young men's faces at Kaga's remark.

Shota Kurosawa's eyes visibly reddened.

"What time is Sugino coming?" Kaga asked.

"He's not coming," Yuto replied sulkily. "I told him five o'clock, but he hasn't shown up yet. He doesn't pick up when I call or reply to my texts."

Matsumiya looked at his watch. It was already after half past.

"When did you arrange this meeting?" Kaga asked.

"Lunchtime. I sent him a text. We're at the same school, but he'd be a marked man if the other kids saw him talking to me. I wanted to spare him that."

"Did he reply to that text?"

"Yeah. He was like, 'I'll do my best to be there,' so I followed up with, 'You've got to come.' Fat lot of good that was." Yuto clucked his tongue.

Kaga held out his hand. "Show me that text."

Yuto gasped and his eyes widened. "What?"

"Just show me the damn thing. *Now.*"

Intimidated by Kaga's forcefulness, Yuto pulled out his cell phone.

Matsumiya looked over at the phone in Kaga's hand. Yuto had indeed sent two texts to Tatsuya Sugino today. The first one read: "Need to talk to you. Also contacted Kurosawa. We're meeting at the Nakameguro burger joint at 5." Sugino's response was: "Got stuff to do at home. Not sure I can make it. I'll be there if I can." That was when Yuto had sent his follow-up text. "This is SUPER important. You MUST come. May be linked with my dad's case. Yesterday the cops questioned me about Yoshinaga's accident," it said.

Kaga gave Yuto back his cell phone and turned to Matsumiya. Matsumiya flinched at the sight of his cousin's face. The eyes had a piercing look that he had never seen in them before.

"Call the incident room. Tell them to track down Tatsuya Sugino urgently. Worst-case scenario, we could already be too late."

31

Although the temperature in the room wasn't that low, he felt as cold as if he were trapped in a refrigerator. Was it the blinding whiteness of the walls? The long, narrow table and the pipe chairs only served to increase his anxiety. He had been in the same room before. It was right after his father's death, when the whole family had been brought into Nihonbashi Police Station to identify his possessions.

Yuto was on his own. Kurosawa had been brought into the station with him, but he must have been put in another room. He wondered what was happening to his friend. Although they had managed to meet in the burger joint, Yuto hadn't gotten around to saying what he wanted to say; he had been waiting for Sugino to show.

He had no idea what was going on. What got that Kaga fellow so worked up that he started shouting about locating

Sugino? And what were they planning to do, bringing him and Kurosawa to a place like this?

He looked at his cell phone. No reply from Sugino yet. Should he call? No. He'd already called him countless times and not gotten through once.

Yuto had just put his phone back in his pocket when there was a knock on the door. He pulled himself upright in his chair.

Kaga and Matsumiya came in and sat down, facing him across the table.

"We haven't managed to track down Sugino yet," Kaga said. "We've got the police all over Tokyo looking for him. Under normal circumstances, we'd be part of the search, but we've got a job of our own: our job is to get you to talk."

Yuto tried to swallow, but his throat was too dry.

Kaga looked him in the eye. "I need you to tell me everything you know. Starting with the accident three years ago."

Yuto looked down and began inspecting a small crack on the surface of the meeting room table.

"I know you feel guilty," Kaga said. "That's got to be the reason you made those paper cranes. Why you went to Suitengu Shrine. And the reason why, when that still wasn't enough for you, you started visiting all the Seven Lucky Gods shrines in Nihonbashi. That's right, isn't it?"

Shocked, Yuto lifted his head. He couldn't believe that the detective already knew so much.

Kaga's gaze was deep and piercing. This wasn't a man who could be fobbed off with cheap lies. Even so, he was no longer the frightening person he had been in the burger joint.

He exuded bigheartedness. Yuto felt that he would hear his confession, no matter what it was, with an open mind.

"You're the original Tokyo Hanako, aren't you? And the person who took over the handle from you was Takeaki Aoyagi, your father?"

Hearing Kaga's words, Yuto realized that he had reached the end of the road. The time had come for him to tell them everything.

"You're right," Yuto replied.

Kaga exhaled sharply. "You're ready to talk?"

"Yes," he said.

"Where shall we start? The accident at the pool?"

"Fine. I'll start there. Could I get a glass of water first?"

Matsumiya stood up. "You're okay with water? There's tea or coffee, if you want."

"Water's fine," Yuto responded. In his mind, he had already jumped three years into the past.

Tomoyuki Yoshinaga was an uppity second-year student.

More precisely, he was a second-year student whom Yuto and his mates—who were all third years—*regarded* as uppity. It wasn't Yoshinaga's fault that the other boys thought of him like that. He trained hard and always did what he was told. He was a serious and cooperative member of the team.

It was a casual remark from an alumnus who came by to help with the coaching that first brought Yoshinaga to the attention of the third-year boys. After watching them all swimming for a while, the alumnus got them all together and made a little speech.

"Yoshinaga here has the best stroke of the lot of you. You should all study his form. And I don't just mean the first and second years; I mean the third years too."

Yuto was there and the alumnus's comments came as something of a shock to him. The comments crystallized something that he'd been doing his best to ignore.

There was no doubt that Yoshinaga had beautiful form. He still lagged in terms of his physical strength, so Yuto's times were faster, but he knew that would probably change before long. And he wasn't alone in feeling that way.

After practice ended, the third-year boys all got together. They quickly started bad-mouthing Yoshinaga and the alumnus coach.

"That alumnus fellow doesn't know the first thing about swimming. Yoshinaga wallows around in the water like a hippo."

"You don't need to tell me that. Conceited little jerk. Grinning like a monkey."

From that day, the attitude of the third-year students to Yoshinaga underwent a complete transformation. None of them would speak to him, and if he ever approached them for advice on technique, they would respond with sarcastic put-downs like, "How should I know? What could I possibly hope to teach a great master like you, Yoshinaga?" When Yoshinaga's times were bad, they would all exchange high fives behind his back.

It may not have been hardcore bullying, but it was right on the borderline.

That was what was going on when a major swim meet

took place. Everyone on the Shubunkan Junior High School team participated in a race of some sort, but their results were very far from stellar. Their performance was a major letdown for the team coach, Itokawa, who had been expecting much more of them. The times they achieved in the two-hundred-meter and medley relays were far inferior to the sort of times they regularly managed in practice. Reproducing their normal times would have been quite enough for them to win.

"You disappointed me today, boys," said Itokawa, addressing the team after the meet. "I want you to think good and hard about what you did wrong today. Once you've figured that out, take corrective action. Keep going the way you are now and you're just going to keep right on failing."

Yuto was one of the members of the two-hundred-meter relay team, with Sugino, Kurosawa, and Yoshinaga being the others. All four of them got together for a chat after the post-race meeting.

"I suppose Itokawa means we should train harder," Sugino said.

"We're already doing more than enough training. We can't train any harder."

"It's my fault," Yoshinaga murmured just then. "It's because of me that we lost ground."

What Yoshinaga was saying was true, but the other three were all aware that his performance wasn't the only reason for their disastrous showing. Nonetheless, in their eagerness to find a scapegoat, the three older boys jumped at the opportunity he offered them.

"Those nice things the alumnus coach said about you

went to your head. You started thinking you're something special," Kurosawa said.

Yoshinaga shook his head. "No, I didn't."

"What was today all about, then?"

"I'm sorry . . . I'll train harder, starting tomorrow."

"Tomorrow's not good enough. You'll start *today*. Yes, let's get to it right now. Intensive training." Kurosawa's eyes gleamed. He clearly felt that he had come up with a brilliant idea.

"Now?" Yuto looked at Kurosawa in surprise. "Where?"

"The school pool. We can get in easily enough."

"At this time?" It was already after five and they would probably only make it back to the school sometime after six.

"Yeah, I've snuck in before. There's this one place where it's easy to climb the fence." Sugino was up for it.

Yuto knew what Kurosawa and Sugino really had in mind. They were going to use the intensive training as a means to punish Yoshinaga. It wasn't that they were angry with him or disliked him. They were just going to use him as an outlet for their pique at being reprimanded.

"It's a stupid idea. Don't do it."—that was all he needed to say. But he hadn't been able to. It was because he didn't want the other two to see him as a spoilsport. For all Yuto knew, Sugino and even Kurosawa, who had come up with the idea, secretly felt the same way.

Yoshinaga couldn't very well say no, so the four of them snuck into the school. It was summer vacation and the place was deserted. It was just starting to get dark.

318

They got changed on the pool surround and jumped into the water. At first, they just swam about a bit to warm up, then Kurosawa ordered Yoshinaga to swim as fast as he could.

"No kicking allowed. Swim only with your arms. We'll be holding on to your legs and you've got to pull us along."

What they did was this. One of them (it was Kurosawa) dived down and grabbed hold of Yoshinaga's ankles. As Yoshinaga swam, the first boy was pulled to the middle of the pool, where a second boy was waiting to take his place. When he reached the end of the pool, a third boy would grab hold of Yoshinaga's ankles. Yoshinaga had to keep on swimming with someone hanging on to him all the time.

He had completed two laps of the twenty-five-meter pool and was in the middle of his third when the accident happened. Kurosawa, who was holding on to Yoshinaga's ankles, was about to make way for Sugino. Yuto, meanwhile, was running along the side of the pool.

He made out two heads bobbing in the water. It was too dark to recognize who they belonged to.

"What's wrong?" Yuto asked.

"He's gone." It was Kurosawa speaking. "Yoshinaga's gone."

"How can he be? Weren't you holding on to him?"

"I was about to hand over to Sugino. I let go, then he just disappeared."

"Has he bolted?" Yuto looked around the pool. There was no sign of anyone surfacing. It was too dark to see the pool bottom.

"Oh God!" Sugino shouted. "He's here. He's down here."

Yuto convulsed in shock, then dived in and swam over to the other two.

Together, they pulled Yoshinaga up to the surface and dragged him onto the edge of the pool. He was limp and motionless. He didn't respond to his own name. He didn't appear to be breathing.

Sugino started pumping his chest. Yoshinaga remained unresponsive.

Yuto was wondering what on earth they were going to do when it happened.

"Hey, you lot, what are you doing?"

The sudden sound of another voice sent Yuto's heart into his mouth. When he looked up, he saw Itokawa running toward them holding a flashlight.

"What the hell are you doing?"

None of them said a word. Yuto looked at the inert Yoshinaga.

"What's going on? What have you done to Yoshinaga?" Itokawa grabbed Kurosawa by the shoulders.

"We were doing intensive training."

"Intensive training?"

"Yes. Then he just sank like a stone . . ."

"You damn fools," Itokawa spat. He pulled out his cell phone and glared at the three boys. "Why are you just standing there? Keep massaging his heart. And give him mouth-to-mouth. Like I taught you."

Sugino went back to massaging Yoshinaga's chest. Yuto

performed artificial respiration as best as he could remember how.

When Itokawa had finished his 911 call, he took over massage duties from Sugino. "All of you, get dressed and get out of here," he told the three boys. "The ambulance will be here any minute. Best you're not around for that."

"Where should we go?" Sugino asked.

"Get out of here and make sure no one sees you. Go home and stay there. Don't tell anybody about what happened here. Not even your parents. After the meet, you all went home separately; you didn't travel with Yoshinaga. Let's make that the official story. Got it?"

None of the three boys said a word. "*Got it?*" Itokawa repeated.

"Yes," they replied listlessly.

"Good. Now get going. Make sure no one sees you."

Yuto and his friends hastily pulled on their clothes and went back the same way they had snuck in. They had climbed over the fence and were outside the school grounds when they heard the ambulance approaching.

The three boys had no clear idea what happened after that. Yuto, however, got a phone call from Sugino much later that night.

"Itokawa called me. Yoshinaga made it."

Yuto felt an overwhelming sense of relief at the news. He had been tormenting himself, worried that Yoshinaga had died on them. Unable to eat his dinner, he'd shut himself up in his bedroom.

"Thank God. Seriously, what a relief," Yuto said. His sincerity was unfeigned.

"There's not much to be relieved about." Sugino's gloomy tone contrasted with Yuto's elation. "He's still unconscious."

"No!"

"He started breathing again, but he's still in a coma and he's still in the hospital."

After a brief moment of relief, Yuto's emotions were once again a crushing weight on his chest.

"The whole swim team will be assembled tomorrow morning. They'll ask us all loads of questions, but Itokawa wants us to keep our mouths shut."

"Is that okay?"

"Itokawa says it's the best option. The swim club could be shut down otherwise."

That was quite possible. Yuto once again had an acute sense of the enormity of what they had done.

The next morning, a policeman came to the school. He got all the swimmers to assemble in one place and questioned them about the events of the previous day. Naturally enough, the three members of the relay team Yoshinaga had been in were questioned in the greatest detail, but they all answered as Itokawa had told them to do. The policeman appeared to suspect nothing.

Yuto eventually figured out what had happened.

Itokawa's story was that he had returned to the school after parting from the team outside the sports center where the swim meet was held. He was busy recording the team's results when he suddenly realized that he needed a document and set out for the coach's room. On his way there, he spotted a heap of clothes on the side of the pool and checked the pool area using a flashlight. It was then that he found someone lying on the bottom of the pool. After getting the boy out of the water as fast as he could, he discovered it was Tomoyuki Yoshinaga, a second-year student. He immediately called 911 and started performing CPR. The ambulance arrived soon afterward and whisked Yoshinaga off to the hospital.

"After the meet, I gave him quite a dressing-down. He must have blamed himself for us losing the relay and made up his mind to sneak in and do some solo training," is what Itokawa told the police.

Nobody questioned his story. Yoshinaga took things seriously and he'd told some of his fellow second years that it was his fault they'd performed so badly in the relay.

But Yuto still felt uneasy. Perhaps no one suspected anything now, but the truth was bound to come out when Yoshinaga emerged from his coma.

"That's a conversation we'll have to have when the time comes," Itokawa said after calling the three boys in to see him. "We'll apologize to Yoshinaga and his parents and explain that we only lied in order to save the swim club. I'll be there, bowing in apology, shoulder to shoulder with you. Until then, you need to keep your damn mouths shut. No blabbing." His manner brooked no dissent.

Despite their reservations, Yuto and his friends did what Itokawa told them to do. They prayed for Yoshinaga's rapid recovery, while a part of them wanted him to stay in a coma.

When he looked back on it later, Yuto realized that Ito-kawa knew all along that Yoshinaga would never regain consciousness. He never did come back to school. The months passed. Eventually, Yuto and his two friends graduated from junior high school, their psychological wounds very much unhealed.

32

It was Sugino who first alerted Yuto to the existence of the blog. "Have you heard of *The Wings of the Kirin*?" Sugino asked him. His face was intensely serious.

"*Kirin*? What's that?"

"I thought you wouldn't recognize it. It's the title of a blog. It's written in katakana: *Kirin* no Tsubasa."

"A blog, eh? What about it?"

Sugino wouldn't answer.

"See for yourself. Just google the thing," was all he would say.

Yuto had no trouble finding the blog. Its full title was *The Wings of the Kirin—Dreaming of the Day It Will Take Wing*. The writer seemed to be a woman. This was the first passage that caught Yuto's eye.

The *kirin* in our house is sleeping again today. I cut his nails, which had grown quite long.

His hair and nails keep growing even though he's asleep all the time. Soon I'll need to give him a haircut. Perhaps this time I'll go for a slightly more grown-up look.

Next week is the official start of spring. Let's hope this year will bring us good luck.

What the hell is this? Yuto thought. *Just a load of rambling nonsense. And who is this* kirin *anyway? A pet? A baby? It's just twaddle either way.* He really couldn't figure out why Sugino mentioned the blog to him at all. Or was this the wrong one?

The blog included the occasional photograph: knick-knacks and outdoor shots, mainly. The pictures weren't particularly eye-catching or well taken.

When one particular picture appeared on the screen, Yuto immediately stopped scrolling.

It was part of the entry for January 1, New Year's Day. The photograph showed a young man in a wheelchair. He was dressed in a suit and even had a necktie on. His hair was closely shaved.

His eyes, however, were tightly shut, so although his horribly emaciated face was pointed toward the camera, he wasn't actually looking into it. A thick towel was rolled up behind his neck, presumably to keep his head in position.

"Our *kirin* celebrating the New Year. A commemorative snap of him in his brand-new suit," the caption read.

Yuto was aghast. Now he understood what Sugino had been trying to tell him.

The boy was Yoshinaga. And it was Yoshinaga's mother who was writing the blog.

Yuto went back and read the blog from the beginning. It had been started more than a year earlier and the early entries made clear what it was about.

The woman's son was in a coma as the result of an accident he'd had during summer vacation of his second year at junior high school. The doctors had given up any hope of him regaining consciousness. The parents, who were still hoping that he would wake up one day, had moved out to Karuizawa, where they were looking after him. The mother's goal in setting up a blog was to create a record of her son's condition and of their life together.

Yuto froze at his computer.

Yoshinaga was alive—

Yuto had persuaded himself that Yoshinaga was long since dead. About the time Yuto graduated from junior high, he'd heard rumors about Yoshinaga still being in a coma, but he'd assumed that he couldn't last long. For him, Yoshinaga had died when the accident occurred. He imagined that Sugino and Kurosawa probably felt the same way.

In fact, though, Yoshinaga was alive. He was asleep, just like back then. Now he had someone looking after him, someone who believed that at some point he would open his eyes.

Yuto was reminded of the wickedness of what they had done.

The episode was far from over and done. The whole Yoshinaga family were still suffering because of it.

Yuto ran into Sugino a few days later and told him that he had visited the blog. "Oh yeah?" Sugino said. "But . . . there's nothing we can do about it, is there?"

Yuto got the impression his friend was trying to persuade himself as much as him.

There's nothing we can do about it. That's just the way it is. That was certainly true. The time for them to take action had passed. They could confess and say they were sorry, but that wouldn't help Yoshinaga regain consciousness. If anything, they would probably only make the parents' lives even more unbearable.

But was continuing to do nothing really good enough?

Yuto started to check the blog on a daily basis. It wasn't updated all that often, so when there was no new entry, he would reread the old ones instead.

One day, he came across this passage.

There was something I had to do, so for the first time in ages I went back to Tokyo. I took advantage of my trip to visit the Suitengu Shrine. While everyone knows Suitengu as the place to go to pray for safe childbirth, another of the benefits it offers is protection from drowning and water-related accidents. I often went there after my *kirin* had his accident. Because Suitengu is one of the Nihonbashi Seven Lucky Gods shrine group, I ended up visiting the other seven shrines too. (They're called the Seven Lucky Gods shrines, but there are actually eight of them!!!) I'm digressing a bit, but it was when I was doing the circuit and saw the statues on Nihonbashi Bridge that I came up with the title of this blog. One thing I regret about moving out here is that it's pretty much impossible for me to visit the shrines anymore.

This was the moment when the words *Suitengu* and *Nihonbashi Seven Lucky Gods* were seared into Yuto's consciousness. The idea of doing something didn't come to him immediately. The shift from thought into action happened almost by chance.

A relative was getting married. The wedding was held at a hotel close to Suitengu Shrine.

Finding himself with time to kill, Yuto strolled out of the hotel and went to take a look at the shrine. As it was a weekend, the shrine precincts were packed. Most of the people there must have come to pray for safe childbirth, as they were all busy patting the celebrated statue of the mother dog and her puppy.

After tossing a few coins into the offertory box, Yuto offered a heartfelt prayer for Tomoyuki Yoshinaga's recovery. He then took a photograph of the shrine from a certain distance. When he rejoined his parents at the hotel, they asked him where he had been. Rather than tell them, he fobbed them off with some plausible lie.

After three days of dithering, he finally made up his mind to post a comment to the blog.

Hello. I'm a loyal reader of your blog and someone who sincerely hopes that your *kirin* will wake up soon. A couple of days ago, I got the chance to visit Suitengu Shrine, so I offered up a prayer for him. In fact, I took a photograph too. Best wishes. I am thinking of you.

He made the sender's name "Tokyo Hanako."
His comment elicited a rapid reply.

Thank you for your message. It means a lot to me. What sort of picture did you take? Can you share it with me?

Her post made Yuto slightly uneasy. He certainly could email her the photo. Provided he set up a fake account, he could keep his identity secret. Would it stay that way, though? If she started asking questions, how could he keep her at arm's length?

In the end, he emailed the photograph. He didn't want to upset her by not replying.

Once again, he got a swift reply. Yoshinaga's mother thanked him and asked permission to upload the photo to her blog. He wrote back that she was very welcome to do so.

The blog entry she uploaded the next day featured Yuto's photograph of Suitengu Shrine. She had added a brief caption: "Thanks to Tokyo Hanako for sending in this picture."

The moment Yuto saw the blog post, something inside him changed. He felt as though something that had been sealed up deep inside him had been cracked wide open. He knew it would never be enough to atone for his actions, but he still felt it was better to do it than not to. If nothing else, it beat simply trying to put the whole thing out of his mind.

Keen to see if he could take things a stage further, he made the circuit of the Seven Lucky Gods shrines, photographing all the different shrines en route. But that still wasn't enough.

One day he wandered into a store that sold traditional Japanese *washi* paper and found some origami paper. Inspiration struck. *This is it!*

Yuto secretly started making origami cranes. Although his original plan was to make one thousand of the things, that turned out to be far from easy. Instead, he began by making one hundred cranes using only pink paper. He then took them to Suitengu Shrine, placed them on top of the offertory box, and took a photograph of them. He emailed the picture to Yoshinaga's mother, who replied to him in no time. From her message, it was clear how delighted she was. And she uploaded Yuto's photo to her blog the next day.

The next month, he made another one hundred cranes, this time using only red origami paper. He took them not only to Suitengu Shrine but to several other shrines in the Seven Lucky Gods group and photographed them there. The following month, he made his cranes using the orange paper.

It was brown the month after. His plan was to keep changing the color to show that he wasn't just reusing the same cranes over and over again. He intended to keep at it until he had made at least one thousand cranes in total.

However, something unexpected happened. Yuto was sitting at his computer writing an email when his mother, Fumiko, called him downstairs. It wasn't for anything important, but right after, a friend called him. He ended up staying down in the living room for quite a while and when he went back up to his room, he bumped into Takeaki, who was just coming out.

Naturally enough, Yuto kicked up a stink. "You can't just barge into my room like that."

His father paid no attention. "What's that?" he asked.

Yuto was horrified. The email interface was on the screen of his computer.

"Did you read my email?" Yuto glared at Takeaki. "You may be my father, but there are still things you just can't do. You're violating my privacy."

Takeaki waved his hand dismissively. "That doesn't bother me. What's going on? Tell me! Who are you emailing under a girl's name?"

"Screw you. I'm not doing anything wrong." Yuto thumped Takeaki on the chest and barged past him into his room.

He went and examined his computer. He had carefully saved all the emails he had sent Yoshinaga's mother. Not knowing how many of them his father had read, he deleted them all on the spot.

Chagrin and disgust spread like a physical sensation through his chest. He felt as though something he cherished had been soiled, as though someone had blundered into a sacred space without even bothering to take off their shoes.

He went to check the cardboard box he kept hidden in his closet. It contained all the origami cranes he had made so far. As far as he could tell, no one had touched them. Nonetheless, he crammed them all into plastic bags, which he threw into the trash on his way to school the next morning.

Since that day, Yuto hadn't emailed Yoshinaga's mother. He deleted his fake email account so that her emails would no longer reach him. And he stopped making origami cranes or visiting the Seven Lucky Gods shrines in Nihonbashi.

He also did his utmost to avoid his father. About six months later, his father was killed.

Although Yuto often thought about the *Wings of the Kirin* blog, he never went back to it. Yoshinaga's mother must have been disappointed at Tokyo Hanako suddenly breaking off all contact. He was too afraid to try to find out how she was getting on. With time, the whole episode started to fade from his memory.

That was why, when he heard that Takeaki had died in the Nihonbashi district, he didn't associate it with the blog. Besides, the location of the actual stabbing was quite a way away from any of the shrines.

It was as if someone had emptied a bucket of cold water on his head when Detective Matsumiya asked him about the *kirins* on Nihonbashi Bridge. The statues of winged *kirins*—

Until then, Yuto had believed *kirins* to be real animals. When he had done an internet search for "*kirin*," "Nihonbashi," and "statue," he had quickly come across a statue of a *kirin*. That particular statue, which was quite famous, was of a different kind of *kirin*, a giraffe, which adorned a modern building in Nihonbashi. He didn't know that *kirin* was also the name of a mythical beast. Yuto just assumed that Tomoyuki Yoshinaga must have liked giraffes when he was a child.

Yuto's assumption was wrong. What really happened was that, after completing the Seven Lucky Gods shrine circuit one time, Yoshinaga's mother had looked up at the *kirin* statues when crossing Nihonbashi Bridge and decided to name her blog after them. For her, the *kirins* spreading their wings and gazing up into the sky were a symbol of her son waking up from his coma and recovering.

When Yuto realized that, he couldn't stop thinking about how Takeaki had dragged himself all the way to Nihonbashi Bridge to lean up against the base of the *kirin* statues after being stabbed. Was it really nothing more than coincidence?

For the first time in months, Yuto decided to visit the *Wings of the Kirin* blog. He found that it was still being updated. And it was then that he discovered something shocking.

Tokyo Hanako was still sending in photographs on a regular basis. The most recent photograph was of one hundred paper cranes made of lilac-colored paper. There were eight of the pictures in total. Whoever took the photos had been to all the Seven Lucky Gods sites in Nihonbashi.

Yuto went back and started reading the older blog posts. He found this entry.

Tokyo Hanako, who has not been in touch for a while, just emailed me a new set of photos. Apparently, her computer's been playing up! This time, she did the Seven Lucky Gods circuit with some yellow paper cranes she'd made. She got herself a new digital camera, so the pictures are gorgeous.

Frozen, Yuto stared at the screen for a while.

What the heck's going on? he thought. Not only had someone taken over the Tokyo Hanako moniker and started emailing Yoshinaga's mother with it, they had also appropriated his idea of the one thousand cranes.

He didn't need to think too hard to figure out who it was. There was only one possible candidate.

Yuto pictured Takeaki making the paper cranes. He saw him tying them together with string and carrying them between Suitengu and Koami Shrines. Startling though it was to picture such scenes in his imagination, they were simple matters of fact.

Why did Takeaki do it?

He must have found out about the *Wings of the Kirin* blog when he read Yuto's old emails. The emails must have raised his suspicions. Why was his son corresponding with this particular blogger? Why was he making cranes? There was no shortage of unlucky people in the world, so why was Yuto concerned about this woman in particular?

At some point, Takeaki must have worked it out. Worked out that the *"kirin"* who appeared in the blog was the kid from Shubunkan Junior High who had had the accident at the pool. Worked out that he was in the year below his son.

That must have only provoked new doubts. There wasn't anything wrong with praying for the recovery of a classmate who had been involved in an accident. So why use a false name? Why send emails in which you hid your connection to the event?

The simplest way to get those questions answered was to ask Yuto directly. Takeaki, however, hadn't done so. Was it because he sensed that a dreadful secret was lurking just beneath the surface?

What Takeaki did was to start making paper cranes. He decided to take over Tokyo Hanako's duties from Yuto. One of the older blog entries mentioned that Tokyo Hanako was using the Traditional Paper in Ten Colors brand for her paper cranes. Takeaki must have gone to considerable trouble to procure the same brand.

Yuto had no way of knowing what was motivating his father. Perhaps it was his way of saying he was sorry. Whatever the circumstances, maybe Takeaki felt guilty for having stymied his son's prayers and had decided to continue with them on his behalf, at least until the truth came to light.

There was a set of lilac cranes on the blog. Lilac was the last color from the Traditional Paper in Ten Colors pack. That meant that his father had completed all one thousand origami cranes.

Yuto now understood why his father had forced himself to go all the way to Nihonbashi Bridge when he was on the verge of death. Takeaki wanted to send him a message. "Be brave! Don't turn your back on the truth! Do what you know to be right!"

Yuto seemed to hear his father's voice. The tears welled up in his eyes and a flame of hope ignited deep inside his chest. At the same time, he felt a sense of deep remorse and self-loathing. Why hadn't he made more of an effort to understand what his father was feeling and thinking?

I should be proud of my dad. My father would never do anything sordid like covering up a workplace accident. No one else may want to believe in him, but I will, he thought.

He had a handkerchief clutched tight in his hand. He needed it to wipe away the tears that came streaming from his eyes. He couldn't understand. Why should he be crying so hard now, when he hadn't cried at all when his father had actually died? He felt no shame.

"Thank you for being so honest with us," Kaga said, speaking tenderly. "The origami cranes your father offered at Suitengu Shrine were yellow. For a long time, I couldn't figure out why your father used a color from the middle of the pack, but reading the blog cleared that up. Your father was taking over from somebody else."

"I couldn't believe that Dad did it. I didn't feel in the least embarrassed about it, though. I was more like, what the hell were we thinking? We'd completely wrecked another person's life and we were just going about our own lives as if nothing had happened. It was inhuman."

"Which is why you tried to get together with the others for a talk."

Yuto nodded.

"It's not too late for the three of us to tell the truth and to take our punishment. That's the only way we can become halfway decent human beings. That's what I was going to tell them."

Kaga abruptly pulled in his chin and looked at Yuto intently.

"You're a smart kid to realize that. We all make mistakes; what really matters is how you deal with them. Run away from them or ignore them and you'll just go on to make the same mistake again."

"But, Detective, tell me something. What's the link between the pool accident and the murder of my father? That's something I just can't understand."

Kaga's eyes darted briefly off to the side. He seemed to be hesitating. Yuto was taken aback. He had never seen the detective behave like that before.

At that moment, there was a knock on the door. Matsumiya got to his feet, walked across the room, and exchanged a few words with someone outside, then whispered something into Kaga's ear. Something big must be kicking off.

Kaga shifted in his chair.

"We've located Tatsuya Sugino. A local policeman who was out on patrol found him. Sugino was on a station platform at Shinagawa Station, getting ready to throw himself in front of a Keihin-Tohoku train."

Yuto was dumbfounded.

"Throw himself in front of a train? Sugino? Why? What does it mean?"

"I'm told that Tatsuya Sugino," Kaga said, then he paused to catch his breath, "has admitted to murdering Takeaki Aoyagi, your father."

33

Tatsuya Sugino was in no state to talk rationally. Since he was a minor, the police thought about sending him home, before finally deciding to hold him at the Nihonbashi Precinct station. They couldn't overlook the fact that he had already attempted suicide once.

The next day, Ishigaki ordered Matsumiya and Kaga to handle the boy's questioning, as they were best equipped to do so. That was how they had ended up in the interrogation room with Tatsuya Sugino. Since he was no more psychologically stable than the day before, getting him to talk coherently was all but impossible. Nonetheless, by dint of patient and persistent questioning, the two detectives managed to get an idea of the overall shape of the case.

What follows is a summary of the confession they

coaxed, prodded, and pieced together out of Tatsuya Sugino. His actual statement was a great deal less tidy.

It was on the day of the incident that Tatsuya Sugino had gotten the phone call. School was over for the day and he was about to head home.

He didn't recognize the number.

He picked up and the person at the other end gave their name. When he said he was Tomoyuki Yoshinaga's father, Tatsuya was incredulous.

"I want to talk to you about the accident at the swimming pool that happened three years ago. Could we meet?"

Sugino tensed. What could Yoshinaga's father want with him so long after the event? Had he worked out what had really happened?

"Will anyone else be there?" he asked.

"No, just you and me. I'll probably get around to talking to the others eventually, but I thought I'd start with you. So, can we meet?"

His tone was mild enough, but there was a steeliness in his voice that made it clear that *no* wasn't an acceptable answer. Unable to come up with an excuse on the spur of the moment, Sugino agreed. They arranged to meet at the turnstiles in Nihonbashi Station.

"There's a place I want to show you," Yoshinaga's father said.

The meeting was set for seven o'clock the same day. Sugino went home first. His mind was a swirl of fear and anxiety. What was Yoshinaga's father going to say to him? What was this place he wanted to take him to?

Sugino wondered if the police were involved. What they'd done to Tomoyuki Yoshinaga must be considered attempted murder. If Yoshinaga died, it could qualify as murder, plain and simple. Was Yoshinaga's father hoping to send all three of them to jail?

The life of the man's only child had been totally destroyed. Handing them over to the police probably wouldn't be enough for him. He would want revenge, of course.

That was it. Having finally discovered the truth, Yoshinaga's father was plotting his revenge on the three of them. And Sugino was first.

If that's what was going on, he would have to do something. Sugino knew that what he'd done was unforgivable, but he wasn't ready to pay for it with his life.

Would brute force be enough? Just because the guy was middle-aged was no reason to get complacent. Some men that age were as strong as any high schooler and hard to beat in a fight. And if the guy was set on revenge, he might bring a weapon with him.

Sugino extracted something from the drawer of his desk. It was a knife that one of his cousins had given him a long time ago. He slipped it into the pocket of his parka just in case.

At seven o'clock, he was at Nihonbashi Station when he felt a tap on his shoulder. He turned to see a suntanned man standing there. His head was big and his shoulders broad. If it came to a fight, Sugino could never beat the guy.

There was no sign of animosity on the man's face. "Shall we grab a coffee?" he said with a good-natured smile.

They went into a nearby café. When asked what he wanted to drink, Sugino said anything would be fine. Yoshinaga's father ordered two cafés au lait, which he brought to the table.

Once they were settled down across from one another, the next thing the older man said came completely out of left field. "I need to start by apologizing. The fact is, I'm not Tomoyuki Yoshinaga's father. I'm actually the father of your friend Yuto Aoyagi."

Sugino was astounded. Come to mention it, though, the man opposite him did look a bit like Yuto. Although Sugino had been to the Aoyagis' house on numerous occasions, he'd never run into Yuto's father.

"I said I was Yoshinaga's father because I wanted to gauge your reaction. If you had nothing to be ashamed of, then your response would have been straightforward and frank. Unfortunately, you sounded very jumpy on the phone. Frightened, even."

Sugino had no comeback. He felt conflicted: angry at having been tricked and curious as to why Aoyagi's father should be behaving like this.

"Look, Sugino," Aoyagi's father said. "Why don't you just tell me the truth about the events of three years ago? All I want is to know how the accident really happened. I'm pretty sure that my son, Yuto, was involved. I'm right, aren't I? You're his closest friend. You, if anyone, should know."

While Aoyagi's father clearly had his suspicions, he

343

obviously had no idea of what actually happened that day. Having convinced himself that Yuto was somehow involved, he wanted to get the truth from his son's friends.

"I don't know anything about it," Sugino replied. "Really, I don't." There was a quaver in his voice. Even he had to admit his performance wasn't convincing. In fact, his acting was a disaster.

"So you're involved too. I thought as much," Aoyagi's father said, seeing through him right away. "Listen, Sugino, I've made up my mind about something. If push comes to shove, I'm willing to make my son hand himself in. Try to pull a fast one on me, and you'll only make even more of a mess of your life. Just tell me the truth. You and my son—you both had a hand in the accident, didn't you?"

Sugino wanted to make a run for it. He wanted to yell, "No!" and get the heck out of there. But his legs refused to move. Besides, running away wouldn't solve anything. This guy was ready to hand his own son into the police, for God's sake!

"Well, are you ready to talk?" That was the question that pushed Sugino over the limit. He nodded his head.

Now there was no stopping him. He answered all Aoyagi's father's questions and confessed everything that had happened. As he spoke, he could feel his heart growing lighter. He had a renewed sense of what a monstrous lie he'd been living.

"Thank you for your honesty," Aoyagi's father said when Sugino was finished. "It all makes sense to me. Including the things my son has been doing."

Sugino was just wondering what that last remark meant

when Aoyagi's father announced, "There's a place I want you to see. It's already too late and we won't be able to get in, but we can still have a look at it. That will have to do. Come on, let's go together to the place of atonement."

He didn't get any more specific than that.

They left the café. "It's this way," Aoyagi's father said and started walking.

"What you boys did is quite unforgivable. You'd be demonized if word got out. It could well impact your chances of getting into college. But none of that matters. Your whole lives are still ahead of you. You can start over, but if you want that second chance, you've got to stop lying to yourselves."

As they walked along the street, Aoyagi's father spoke fervently about how making a clean breast of it was the best thing to do. His argument was compelling enough. At the same time, it gave Sugino a glimpse of all the difficulties that would lie ahead of him.

His future, his education—

Thanks to an official recommendation from his school, Sugino had managed to secure a place at his first-choice university. It had taken him three years of hard work to earn that place. Was it all going to be wasted?

He stopped. *I can't go along with this any further,* he thought.

"What's wrong?" Aoyagi's father asked.

"I can't do this. Just pretend you didn't hear any of what I told you back there. I'm begging you."

"That isn't possible. I'm going to tell everyone the truth. I believe that's the best thing for you and the best thing for my son. Come on."

Aoyagi's father resumed walking. To Sugino, there was something about his back that seemed to exude stubbornness.

Not even Sugino himself could explain his emotional state at that moment. He just knew that he had to do something, that he had to stop this man. His fingers closed around the handle of the knife before he even knew what he was doing.

Aoyagi's father must have sensed something, because he stopped and turned around. Sugino flung himself at him, holding the knife out in front of him.

He smashed the older man up against the wall so that their bodies were pressed tight together. It was only then that he realized they were in some kind of underpass.

Aoyagi's father barely uttered a sound. Backed up against the wall, he crumpled and then fell to his knees. The knife was lodged deep in his chest. Sugino made an effort to pull it out, but it wouldn't move. In desperation, he used his school tie to wipe the handle clean. Agitated though he was, he was still thinking about fingerprints.

He started to retrace his steps. That was when he spotted someone lurking in the shadow of an office block. Anxious not to be seen, Tatsuya Sugino took off. He ran as fast as his legs would carry him.

Back at home, he spent the night shut up in his room, trembling and fearful. Terrified that the police might show up, he didn't get a moment's sleep. When morning came, he anxiously checked the internet for news. What he discovered was completely unexpected.

A man suspected of killing Aoyagi's father had been hit by a car and was in critical condition.

Mystified, Sugino started rooting around. He discovered his extraordinary good luck. Not only was someone completely different suspected of the crime, the guy was also in a coma—

This is a miracle, Sugino thought. *Provided the guy doesn't recover, I'm out of danger. Who knows, perhaps I'll get away with it even if he does come around.*

That was when he got an email from Yuto Aoyagi. He felt a searing pain in his chest when he saw the subject line: "My Dad's Dead." Still, he'd already made up his mind to tell no one what he had done. Suppressing his agitation, he forced himself to compose a sympathetic-sounding message, which he sent off.

He was in a quandary when everyone at school started giving Aoyagi the cold shoulder after the workplace accident cover-up business came to light. Sugino didn't know how to interact with his friend. Not having much choice in the matter, he decided to keep his distance. His doing so didn't seem suspicious to Aoyagi.

When Fuyuki Yashima, the murder suspect, died without coming out of his coma, Sugino thought he was home and dry. That turned out to be premature. Yuto Aoyagi came out and said that he wanted to have a three-way discussion with him and Kurosawa. His refusal to say what he wanted to talk about only made Sugino more uneasy.

Then he had got the fateful text from Aoyagi. Aoyagi wanted to meet ASAP to discuss the accident at the school pool. The police knew that the accident and his dad's murder were linked and were taking steps accordingly.

Suddenly, everything went black.

He'd been found out. They knew he'd murdered Aoyagi's father. If the police were on the case, he would never get away with it. It was over. Over.

Sugino blundered through the streets in the grip of despair. *What should I do? What should I do?*

When the police asked him why he was in Shinagawa Station, he couldn't come up with an answer. He had no idea how he had gotten there.

He had a vague memory of having intended to throw himself in front of a train. *Dying seemed like the best thing I can do. And I still think it is—*

34

Although Itokawa was as defiant as ever, there was now a faint glint of panic in his eyes. The clammy marks his hands left on the tabletop were further proof. His palms were sweating.

Today's face-off was taking place in one of the interview rooms at the police station rather than at the school.

"That's everything I can tell you about the accident at the pool. The three boys will confirm it all."

Itokawa's statement matched the testimony of Yuto and his friends. Nonetheless, the two detectives had their doubts about his motivation for orchestrating the cover-up. Itokawa claimed to be "concerned about the boys' future," but was that actually true?

"If word got out that the accident took place when all four members of the relay team were training, it might have been seen as part of the swim club's official activities. You were worried that the school authorities might come after you as the coach. Is that why you decided to sweep it all under the carpet?"

Itokawa glowered at Kaga. "Spare me the insults. I'm not that sordid a character."

"Your actions were sordid enough."

"What do you—?" Despite the look of loathing on Itokawa's face, he was reduced to silence.

"Someone told us that it was your brilliant idea to get the boys to train by swimming with just their arms while someone held on to their legs. You didn't want anyone finding out about that, did you?"

Itokawa smacked the tabletop with the flats of his hands.

"Let's move on to the next question," Matsumiya said. "Takeaki Aoyagi called you three days before he was killed. Previously, you told us that he wanted to discuss his problematic relationship with his son with you. Would you like to modify that statement? This will be used as evidence, so think carefully before you reply."

Itokawa's breathing became labored. His chest rose and fell several times, then he muttered, "Yeah, I'd like to change my statement."

"Good. Give us an accurate account of your conversation."

Itokawa ran the back of his hand over his mouth.

"Aoyagi asked me to tell him more about the accident at the pool. I got the impression he suspected his son of being involved."

"What did you say?"

"I simply said there wasn't anything more to know. It had all been in the papers."

"Did Aoyagi buy that?"

Itokawa shook his head feebly. "Course not. He went for me. I had an obligation to tell the truth, he said. It would be the best thing for his son."

"What did you do?"

"I told him he couldn't talk to me like that and hung up. I didn't actually have the time to talk when he called."

"And that's everything," Itokawa added in a quiet voice.

"Why didn't you tell us this straight after Aoyagi's murder?" Kaga broke in. "If we'd known, we'd probably have handled the investigation differently."

"I don't know what to say . . . I didn't see any connection between the accident and Aoyagi's murder. And I thought I was doing what was best for the boys."

"'Best for the boys'? How is lying meant to do them any good?"

"I couldn't see the point of raking up an old story and causing the boys any more emotional distress. Especially now that the three of them are back to normal—"

Kaga sprang to his feet, reached out with his long arms, and grabbed Itokawa by the collar.

"Don't make me laugh! What's this bullshit about not wanting to cause emotional distress? You've no idea of all the harm you've caused, have you? Why didn't Sugino give himself up after he stabbed Aoyagi? Because you'd taught him the worst possible lesson. *If you do something wrong, just cover it up and things will sort themselves out*—that's the lesson you taught the three boys three years ago. That's why Sugino went and did the same thing all over again. All Aoyagi wanted to do was teach his son—whom you misled so badly—what was right. If you can't even understand that, you shouldn't be a teacher at all. You've no business teaching anyone anything."

Kaga pushed the other man away as if discarding a soiled article. Itokawa's face was pale.

35

Nearly everything in the apartment had been removed by the time Matsumiya and Kaga arrived. When they climbed up the stairs, they found Kaori Nakahara standing by the door with a large bag at her feet. She waved hello.

"We were hoping to give you a hand, but it looks like you've finished already," Matsumiya said.

Kaori shrugged.

"There wasn't a lot left by the time I'd gotten rid of all the stuff I don't need. I'm kind of amazed we managed to live off so little."

"What have you done with your boyfriend's things?"

At Matsumiya's question, Kaori looked sadly at the floor for a moment before lifting her head.

"There were plenty of things I couldn't bring myself to throw away. Too many, in fact. Still, I got rid of quite a lot,

Socks with holes in them, things like that." She forced a smile despite being on the verge of tears.

Kaga held out a paper carrier bag. "I'd like to return these things to you. Could you sign this receipt?"

The bag contained Fuyuki Yashima's cell phone, wallet, driver's license, and other personal effects. Tenderly cupping the cell phone, Kaori pressed it to her belly. "Here's something to remember Daddy by."

Kaga handed her the receipt and a pen.

"He was such an idiot, wasn't he?" Kaori said as she gave him back the receipt, which she had signed neatly. "Why did he do what he did? He could easily have earned the money some other way."

"He must have felt under pressure to do something," Kaga said. "That he was a father with a duty to support his family."

Kaori pressed her lips together to keep her emotions in check. "What an idiot," she murmured.

There was no way of knowing exactly what Fuyuki Yashima had done, but Tatsuya Sugino's testimony at least made it possible to speculate.

Yashima had spotted Takeaki Aoyagi when he was on his way to Nihonbashi Station after leaving the bookstore. It was unclear whether Aoyagi was still inside the café or out in the street at that point. Either way, Yashima had followed Aoyagi and Sugino. He was probably hoping to ask Takeaki Aoyagi for his old job back, but didn't accost him immediately because he wasn't alone.

Fuyuki Yashima was up the street when Tatsuya Sugino

stabbed Takeaki Aoyagi in the underpass next to Edobashi Bridge. He swiftly ducked into a nearby building when he saw Sugino emerge. He waited for Sugino to run off before going into the underpass, where he found Takeaki Aoyagi lying on the ground.

In her testimony, Kaori Nakahara had described Fuyuki Yashima as a thoroughly good person; on this one occasion, however, he had given in to temptation. He helped himself to Takeaki Aoyagi's briefcase and wallet and fled the scene.

His subsequent actions were known to them. He had hidden in the Hamacho Green Road park, made a call to Kaori, and been hit by a truck immediately afterward.

What an idiot!—Kaori was right there. As Kaga said, the knowledge that he was about to become a father must have put him under pressure.

Kaori Nakahara was heading back to Fukushima, her birthplace. She was going to help out at a restaurant run by a friend of hers from the orphanage.

The two detectives offered to take Kaori to the train station by taxi. The Tohoku bullet train leaves from Ueno Station, but Kaori said there was a place near Tokyo Station that she wanted to see before leaving the city for good.

"How come you two are looking so sharp today?" Kaori asked as they rode in the taxi. She was referring to their clothes, apparently.

"We're going to a memorial service," Matsumiya said. "A relative of ours."

"Oh," she said, looking from one to the other in astonishment. Kaga just sat in silence on the front passenger seat.

The taxi turned onto Chuo Boulevard. The Mitsukoshi department store slid past on their right. It wasn't long before the place Kaori wanted to see came into view.

Nihonbashi Bridge was looking as magnificent as ever beneath the brutish expressway above it. The *kirin* statues gazed resolutely into the future.

"I don't regret coming to Tokyo," Kaori said. She was speaking to both men. "Fuyuki and I made all sorts of happy memories here, memories that can never be lost or broken."

Matsumiya nodded in silence. There was no need to say anything.

They accompanied Kaori as far as the central ticket barrier of Tokyo Station. She took her bag from Matsumiya and bowed at them both.

"Thank you very much for your help today. I'll never forget how you cleared Fuyuki's name."

"You're welcome to forget that," Kaga said. "What we don't want you forgetting is your promise to do your best for the baby."

Kaori looked grave. "I know," she replied.

"Good luck, then," Matsumiya said.

"Thanks," she said, breaking back into a smile.

Kaori went through the ticket barrier and waved at them as she walked along the passageway farther into the station. Once she was out of sight, Matsumiya consulted his watch.

"We're in trouble. We've only got thirty minutes."

"Seriously? Kanamori will give us hell if we're late. Better get going." Kaga suddenly dashed off.

36

As he stepped down onto the station platform, the chilly air stung his ears. Resisting the urge to shrink from the cold, Yuto took a deep breath and drew himself up to his full height. *I can deal with this cold, just like I can deal with this situation,* he thought. *It may be uncomfortable, but we must take it on its own terms.*

Standing beside him, Kurosawa was looking up at the sky. It was ashen. The scudding clouds suggested that rain was imminent. *No, with this cold, it's more likely to be snow,* he thought.

"Let's go," Yuto said. Kurosawa grunted in assent. He was holding a paper carrier bag. It contained one thousand cranes, which they had both made.

It was Yuto who had suggested coming to see Yoshinaga.

"We've got to tell his parents the truth. And we've got

to say we're sorry. Both to the parents and to Yoshinaga himself. I don't expect them to forgive us, but we should apologize nonetheless. It's about the only thing we can do at this point."

Kurosawa agreed. He had proposed that they make the one thousand cranes.

Yuto doggedly set about making them up in his room. He bought another six packs of Traditional Paper in Ten Colors for the task. (Sometime after the case was solved, he had found several open packs in his father's car. All the colors from the yellow on down were gone. Yuto now knew where his father had done his crane-making. He must have parked the car somewhere on his way home and done it there.)

A multitude of thoughts ran through his mind as he folded the individual birds. In the end, though, all he was left with were regrets. *Why hadn't he come out and told the truth earlier? Why hadn't he apologized to Yoshinaga? Why hadn't he had a man-to-man talk with his father?*

Any one of those things would have been enough to keep things from ending as disastrously as they had. His father wouldn't have been killed. Sugino wouldn't have committed murder. Yuto had never met Fuyuki Yashima, but he was just another victim of Yuto and his friends.

The two boys had finished all the cranes on the previous day. They'd immediately called the Yoshinaga house. "There's something we want to tell you about your son's accident. May we come and see you?" they asked.

It was Yoshinaga's mother who answered the phone. If the detectives had visited her to verify certain facts as part of their investigation into Takeaki's murder, she must have some idea of the situation. On the phone, however, she didn't ask any questions; she simply said she was looking forward to seeing them. They took that to mean that she wanted to wait until they were face-to-face before getting serious with them.

"Itokawa quit his job at the school," Kurosawa said as the taxi drove them to the Yoshinaga house.

Yuto merely grunted. He had nothing to say.

"I'm sorry, Ao. Things wouldn't have turned out like this if I'd not suggested sneaking into the school. This whole thing is my fault." Kurosawa was on the verge of tears.

"Don't be stupid." Yuto flicked Kurosawa in the chest with the back of his hand. "If you go down that route, then everything is *my* fault, because I didn't stop you. We're equally guilty. Which is why we're both going to apologize, right?"

"Yeah," Kurosawa grunted.

After a while, the taxi came to a stop and the two boys got out. They were in front of a large house. A wooden plaque with the name Yoshinaga hung from the gatepost.

Yuto looked over the gate. The garden was blanketed in snow. At the end of it was the door of the house. Tomoyuki Yoshinaga was asleep inside at this moment.

Saying sorry isn't good enough. We need to pray, Yuto thought. *Pray that he'll wake up one day. Yes, we're really here in order to pray. When we see Yoshinaga, we'll try talking to him. We'll say we're sorry for what we did. Come on now, wake up! Wake up and then beat the crap out of us. Come on, don't keep us all waiting.*

Yuto exhaled. His breath formed a little white cloud of vapor. He slowly walked toward the house.